The Spiritual Hierarchies
and the Physical World

The Spiritual Hierarchies
and the Physical World

Reality and Illusion

RUDOLF STEINER

TEN LECTURES
DÜSSELDORF, APRIL 12–18, 1909

Translated by R.M. Querido
Revised and edited by Jann Gates

FIVE LECTURES
BERLIN, OCTOBER 31–DECEMBER 5, 1911

Translated by Jann Gates

℮ Anthroposophic Press

With grateful acknowledgment to Rudolf Steiner Press, London, for the use of the quotations from *The Fifth Gospel, The Occult Movement in the Nineteenth Century,* and *Rosicrucianism and Modern Initiation*; to Garber Communications, Blauvelt, NY, for the quotation from *Cosmic Memory;* and to Dr. Georg Unger for permission to reprint from his articles concerning the interchange of Mercury and Venus.

Part One, *The Spiritual Hierarchies and the Physical World,* was translated by R.M. Querido, revised and edited by Jann Gates, from the German edition, *Geistige Hierarchien und ihre Widerspiegelung in der physischen Welt: Tierkreis, Planeten, Kosmos* (GA110), published by Rudolf Steiner Verlag, Dornach, Switzerland, 1960. Part Two, *Reality and Illusion: The Inner Realities of Evolution,* was translated by Jann Gates from the German edition, *Die Evolution vom Gesichtspunkte des Wahrhaftigen* (GA 132), published by Rudolf Steiner Verlag, Dornach, Switzerland, 1987.

Published by Anthroposophic Press
RR 4 Box 94 A1, Hudson, NY 12534

LIBRARY OF CONGRESS CATALOGING-IN-PUBLICATION DATA

Steiner, Rudolf, 1861–1925.
[Geistige Hierarchien und ihre Widerspiegelung in der physischen Welt. English]
The spiritual hierarchies and the physical world; Reality and illusion / Rudolf Steiner.
   p.   cm.
   Subtitle of 1st title: Ten lectures, Düsseldorf, April 12–18, 1909 / translated by R.M. Querido, revised and edited by Jann Gates. Subtitle of 2nd title: Five lectures, Berlin, October 31–December 5, 1911 / translated by Jann Gates.
   ISBN 0-88010-440-6 (pbk.)
   1. Anthroposophy.   I. Steiner, Rudolf. 1861–1925. Evolution vom Gesichtspunkte des Wahrhaftigen. English.   II. Title.   III. Title: Reality and illusion.
BP595. S894G47313 1996   96-12061
299'.935—dc20   CIP

10 9 8 7 6 5 4 3 2 1

Printed in the United States of America

Contents

PART ONE

The Spiritual Hierarchies and the Physical World

Introduction

Christopher Bamford

IT IS GENERALLY ACKNOWLEDGED that the scientific revolution in astronomy caused by the adoption of the Copernican hypothesis presupposed a previous revolution, or series of revolutions, in theology, cosmology, and epistemology—in how we know the world and in the world itself that we know.

In other words, long before Copernicus proposed his abstract, purely mathematical model of a heliocentric system, the process of reducing the cosmos from a living, integrated organismic whole—in which humanity was a holographic microcosm-in-a-macrocosm—to an extended, more or less alien "otherness"—in which the Earth became a speck of dust amid the infinite spaces so terrifying to Pascal—must already have been well underway.

How this occurred is complex and necessarily ambiguous, because, in all evolution-of-consciousness phenomena, what is "lost" is always counterbalanced by the possibilities that are gained. Nevertheless, certain things are clear: the emergence of individualized observer consciousness, based on sense perception and brain thinking, demanded both the *diminution* of consciousness—finally, to the brain itself—and its *separation* from nature and the cosmos. Theologically, this meant the end of understanding creation as the work of the gods; cosmologically, it meant the end of angelology and the desacralization of nature, despoiled of its spiritual origins.

All emanation—any prolonging of the creative act through angelic "extensions" or Intelligences—became suspect. Religion grew deistic; God became the sole creator; and humanity's relation to meaning was reduced to what reason could manufacture on the basis of inferences from the senses alone. Previously, the human being was known to be a spiritual being, potentially a member of the tenth hierarchy, an angelic being born of an angelic world, and so able to communicate with the other angelic beings whose traces—presences—could be read in nature, in the stars, and even in the very constitution of matter (as the alchemists knew). But, in the centuries preceding Copernicus—really since the Council of Constantinople in 869 and the reduction of the threefold human being of body, soul, and spirit to a twofold being of body and soul—this whole understanding was progressively eroded. Once united, angelology, cosmology, and the cosmic nature of humanity fell apart. Human nature became isolated from the rest of creation. Human beings became "cosmic hermits" and finally, with the ascendance of heliocentrism and the ensuing loss of the truths of geocentrism, became alienated even from themselves. For the loss of geocentrism was not simply the loss of a "theory"; it was the loss of reality itself. In reality, space—physical, psychological, and spiritual space—is oriented by the Earth.

The space we inhabit today, as a result of these changes, is abstract, material, mechanical, and empty. It is what Rudolf Steiner called *maya*, the great illusion. We have the illusion that round about us different things are scattered in an otherwise empty space—some are nearer to hand, some further away, some larger, some smaller, but all exist in a continuum, an infinitely extended material sameness. How much richer—and not just richer, but also truer, and more *real*—earlier visions of the universe were! Geocentrism and heliocentrism coexisted. The Earth then rested, spiritually surrounded and permeated by the *seven* spheres, or states of consciousness or being, through which human beings descended to, and ascended from, earthly birth and whose influence and qualities ran through all earthly and temporal phenomena. Around, in, and interpenetrating these, the *nine* hierarchies of spiritual beings moved, and the fixed stars, the *twelve* houses of life, creators of space, reigned. Permeating these, the *four* elements—Earth, Water, Air, and Fire—and the *three* essential principles—call them Sulphur, Mercury, and Salt (or Father, Son, and Holy Spirit)—wove the dynamic lattice of creation. It was this kind of richness and reality (only suggested here) that Rudolf Steiner sought, again and again, to renew through anthroposophy.

Not that Steiner sought simply to revive earlier views. What he presents is new and his own—the fruit of his own experience and extensive spiritual research. This, indeed, is Steiner's great gift. On the basis of innate faculties, deep study, a rigorous scientific training, true, brain-free, living thinking, and—above all—long years of conscious meditative work, Steiner was able to open a way for modern consciousness to begin once again to live in the profound realities of the physical-spiritual worlds. Yet, at the same time, all that he presents has its roots in esoteric tradition.

Born in 1861, Rudolf Steiner spent his first forty years preparing the spiritual mission of marrying initiation wisdom and modern scientific consciousness. This preparation was thorough and manifold. Reading his autobiography, we note the following: a training in science and scientific thinking; a profound and experimental, phenomenological study of philosophy and epistemology; a deep immersion in the writings of Johann Wolfgang von Goethe (who besides being a great poet, dramatist, and novelist, was also a scientist in the Hermetic tradition of Paracelsus, Basil Valentine, and the Rosicrucians of the seventeenth and eighteenth centuries); an acquaintance with neo-scholasticism and the philosophy of Franz Brentano. Against this background, we may note that Steiner was an active participant in the cultural life of his day: a student of Nietzsche and Stirner on the one hand, and on the other a follower of Haeckel's evolutionary biology. More esoterically, we may observe that during these years Steiner encountered two figures who overlit his mission: the herb gatherer, Felix Kogutsky, and an otherwise unknown master, M.

Finally, mention should be made of an initiatory spiritual experience of the reality of Christ in cosmic evolution: "a conscious knowledge of true Christianity began to dawn within me. Around the turn of the century this knowledge grew deeper.... This experience culminated in my standing in the spiritual presence of the Mystery of

Golgotha in a most profound and solemn festival of knowledge."[1] Around 1900, then, Rudolf Steiner was ready to assume the mantle of teacher.

He did so initially under the auspices of the Theosophical Society. What he taught, of course, was always his own and in his own words. Working as a Theosophist, however, meant, in the first place, the transformation of theosophical teaching into "anthroposophy"—the path of modern western inner development. More particularly, it meant meditatively testing, confirming, and, where necessary, correcting the fundamental teachings of Theosophy as contained in such primary works as A.P. Sinnett's *Esoteric Buddhism*, H.P. Blavatsky's *Isis Unveiled*, *The Voice of the Silence*, and *The Secret Doctrine*—especially the sections dealing with the "Stanzas of Dzyan." Mention should be made, too, in this context, of the teachings contained in the lessons of the Esoteric Section of the Theosophical Society, as well as of what might be called works of "secondary literature," such as the works of Mabel Collins (above all, *Light on the Path*),C.G. Harrison's *The Transcendental Universe*, the works of Eliphas Lévi, and various Rosicrucian works such as the eighteenth century compilation *The Secret Symbols of the Rosicrucians*.

What all this meant, in detail, cannot be gone into here. Some indications may however be given. Steiner certainly meditated and realized, for instance, the reality of the following:

1. The truth of Number as Universal Cosmic Law (Unity; Duality or Polarity; Threeness; Fourness; Fiveness; Sixness; Sevenness; Nineness; Tenness; Twelveness, and so forth)

2. E.g., the mystery of Seven, the number of genesis, including:

a) the seven states or stages of consciousness, each associated with a planetary embodiment i. trance or universal consciousness; ii. deep sleep or dreamless con-sciousness; iii. dream or picture consciousness; iv. waking or object consciousness; v. psychic or conscious picture-consciousness;

---

1. *Rudolf Steiner: An Autobiography* (Blauvelt, NY: Steinerbooks, 1980), chapter XVI.

vi. suprapsychic or conscious sleep-consciousness; vii. spiritual or conscious universal-consciousness)

b) the seven life conditions (the three elementary kingdoms and the mineral, plant, animal, and human kingdoms)

c) the seven evolutionary conditions of form (the "globes" of Theosophical literature): i. arupa (formless); ii. rupa (form); iii. astral; iv. physical; v. plastic astral; vi. intellectual; and vii. archetypal—transformed into a sophisticated and enChristed evolutionary reality through the seven stages of Saturn, Sun, Moon, (Mars) Earth, (Mercury), Jupiter, Venus, Vulcan

d) the Seven Life Secrets or Mysteries (each associated with a state of consciousness and planetary embodiment): i. The Mystery of the Abyss; ii. the Mystery of Number; iii. the Mystery of Alchemy; iv. the Mystery of Birth and Death; v. the Mystery of Evil; vi. the Mystery of the Word or Logos; vii. the Mystery of Divinity

e) the Mysteries of the Seven Alchemical and the Seven Life Processes

3. The Mystery of the Three Creative Functions, the Four Elements, and the Twelve Zodiacal Realities

4. The Mysteries of the Rose Cross

5. The Mysteries of the Ten (or Twelve) Aristotelian categories and the ten Sephiroth of the Kabbalah

6. The Mysteries of the Nine Hierarchical (or Angelical) Orders

This list is by no means definitive or complete, but it provides some indication of the inner, esoteric work that Rudolf Steiner was performing during the first decade of the twentieth century. Traces of this work are apparent in the lectures he gave and the books he published during this time. In these, however, he presents the "results" of his research, in his own words, and in concrete, logically developed form. As a result, the meditative sources underlying his themes are often obscure or hidden. This is as it should be. For what Steiner is presenting represents the living reality—fresh food.

However, as we read his lectures (and books) today we should be aware that his original auditors knew much more of his sources, and worked with them as he did. Thus, in a sense, and, above all, in his lectures, Rudolf Steiner is always addressing "fellow researchers"— students and spiritual friends of the same path. Such, likewise, should be the attitude of present readers who wish to penetrate deeply into the spiritual gift before them. That is, Steiner's lectures must be read meditatively, not for information.

The two lecture cycles included in the present volume are among the most moving and exciting that Steiner ever gave. In them, Steiner goes a long way toward fulfilling the mission of anthroposophy—that is, to provide a unifying path between the spiritual in the human being and the spiritual in the cosmos.

At one level, these lectures provide essential background and corollary reading to the basic works of anthroposophical cosmology and psychology: namely, *An Outline of Occult Science* and *Theosophy*. At another level, they constitute the real beginnings of a modern understanding of the inherence of spiritual beings in the unfolding of the universe: angelology *as* cosmology. From this point of view, they form the work of preparation for Steiner's great 1912 lecture cycle, *Spiritual Beings in the Heavenly Bodies and in the Kingdoms of Nature*. Certainly, in these, as in other works—such as *Man as Symphony of the Creative Word* and *Man as Hieroglyph of the Universe*—Steiner single-handedly renewed the understanding of the work of spiritual beings for our times.

These lectures are equally important from other points of view as well. Here, for instance, we find the reality of the Christ and what Steiner calls "the Mystery of Golgotha" articulated with enormous passion and sincerity, together with the real sense that we are listening to words spoken out of *present experience*. Indeed, we should not forget that Rudolf Steiner often spoke in such lectures directly out of a meditative state. Thus, translating these texts, one often finds that a given referent is uncertain. Close examination reveals that Steiner is invoking something that occurred two or three pages before *as if he had just mentioned it*. In other words, it becomes clear that, for Steiner, all that he describes is present *all at once*. In the last lectures especially, we feel that we too stand "in the spiritual presence of the Mystery of Golgotha in a most profound and solemn festival of knowledge."

At quite another level, these lectures call for a transformation of our (scientific) understanding of humanity and the Earth within cosmic existence. This is a theme to which Rudolf Steiner returned repeatedly. In January, 1921, for instance, in the third of the "science courses" given to the teachers of the first Waldorf school in Stuttgart, Germany, he spoke as follows:

Astronomy as we know it today, including the domain of astrophysics, is fundamentally a quite modern creation. Before the time of Copernicus or Galileo, people thought essentially differently about astronomical phenomena than we do today. In fact, it is extraordinarily difficult to indicate how people of, say, the thirteenth or fourteenth centuries thought about astronomy because their way of thinking has become completely foreign to us. Nowadays, we live solely in ideas formed since the time of Galileo, Kepler, and Copernicus. From a certain perspective, it is right and just that we do so. However, these ideas essentially treat of the distant phenomena of universal space—insofar as these concern astronomy—*only in a mathematical and mechanical way.* We think of astronomical phenomena only mathematically and mechanically. When we observe astronomical phenomena, we base our ideas upon what we have acquired from abstract mathematical science or the equally abstract science of mechanics. We calculate distances, movements, forces. The *qualitative* outlook, which still existed in the thirteenth and fourteenth centuries and which distinguished individualities in the stars—an individuality of Jupiter, or of Saturn, for instance—has been completely lost to modern humanity. I will make no criticism of these things at the moment, but wish only to point out that the mechanical and mathematical way of treating what we call the domain of astronomy has become the only one. Even when we acquaint ourselves with the stars in a popular way, without understanding mathematics or mechanics, we still find it presented to us, even though in a manner suited to the lay mind, entirely in terms of space and time, i.e., in mathematical and mechanical concepts. And no doubt at all exists in the minds of our contemporaries, who believe their point of view is authoritative, that this is the only way in which to regard the starry heavens and that any other way would be amateurish....[2]

Certainly, these lectures are in no way "amateurish."

---

2. From *The Relation of the Diverse Branches of Natural Science to Astronomy*, lecture 1. This lecture course exists at present only in typescript, available from the Rudolf Steiner Library. An edition is planned. The first two "science courses," are the so-called Light and Warmth Courses.

Prologue

ALL THAT ARISES IN TIME ORIGINATES IN THE ETERNAL. But the eternal is inaccessible to sensory perception. Nevertheless, ways to the perception of the eternal are open to us....

At a certain level of cognitive power a person can penetrate to the eternal origin of the things that vanish with time. Indeed, once we broaden our powers of cognition in this way, we are no longer limited to external evidence where cognition of the past is concerned. Then we can *see* in events what is not perceptible to the senses; we can see the part that time cannot destroy. Thus, we advance from transitory to non-transitory history, which is written in characters other than our ordinary history. In gnosis and theosophy, this history is called the "Akasha Chronicle."

Only a faint conception of this Chronicle can be given in language. For language is based upon the world of the senses. Whatever we indicate with language immediately contains the character of the sense world. To the uninitiated, then, who are not yet convinced by their own experience of the reality of a specifically spiritual world, the initiate easily appears to be a dreamer, if not something worse.

Those who have acquired the ability to perceive in the spiritual world come to know past events in their eternal character. They do not stand before them like the dead witnesses of history, but in full *life*. In a certain sense, what has happened takes place before them. Those initiated into the reading of such a living script can look back into a much more remote past than external history presents and can also describe it—out of unmediated spiritual perception—in a much more dependable way than history can.

Here, in order to avoid possible misunderstanding, it should be said that such spiritual perception is not infallible. Such perception also can be deceived, can see in an inexact, oblique, wrong manner. No one is free from error in this field, no matter how high that person stands.

Therefore one should not object when communications emanating from such spiritual sources do not always entirely correspond. But the dependability of observation is much greater here than in the external world of the senses. What various initiates can relate about history and prehistory will essentially agree.

—from *Cosmic Memory*

. . . .

OUTWARDLY, AS YOU KNOW, WE BEGAN our movement by linking ourselves—but only outwardly—with the Theosophical Society, and we founded the so-called German Section of that Society in fall 1902, in Berlin. Now, in the course of the year 1904 we were visited in various towns in Germany by prominent members of the Theosophical Society[1].... The first edition of my *Theosophy* had just been published in the spring of 1904 and the periodical *Lucifer Gnosis* was appearing. In it, I had published articles that dealt with the problem of Atlantis and the character of the Atlantean epoch.... These articles contained a number of communications about the Atlantean world and the earlier, so-called Lemurian epoch.[2] Several articles of this kind had already appeared and, just at the time when the members of the Theosophical Society were visiting, an issue of the periodical containing important communications was ready. One of the visiting members, highly respected in the Theosophical Society, had read these articles dealing with Atlantis and asked me a question.... "How, then, were these communications about the world of Atlantis actually obtained?"[3] The question was full of important implications because, until then, this member knew only the methods by which such information was usually obtained in the Theosophical Society— namely, by means of a certain kind of mediumistic investigation. Information already published by the Theosophical Society at that

---

1. Rudolf Steiner accompanied Annie Besant on a lecture tour through Germany in September 1904, visiting Hamburg, Berlin, Weimar, Munich, Stuttgart, and Cologne between September 15 and September 24.
2. See *Cosmic Memory* (Blauvelt, NY: Steinerbooks, 1990).
3. Bertram Keightley. Steiner had stayed in Keightley's house in 1902 during his visit to the Theosophical Congress—so they knew each other. Indeed, they stayed in contact, for Keightley visited Steiner as late as June 1923.

time was based upon investigations connected in a certain way with mediumship.[4] That is: someone was brought into a mediumistic state—one cannot say a trance but into a kind of a mediumistic state—and conditions were established that made it possible for the person, although not in the ordinary state of consciousness, to communicate certain information about matters beyond the reach of ordinary consciousness. This is how communications were obtained at that time, and this Theosophical Society member, who thought that information about prehistorical events could be gathered only in this way, inquired who we had among us whom we could use as a medium for such investigations.

As I had naturally refused to adapt this method of research and had insisted from the outset upon strictly individual investigation, and as what I had discovered at that time was the result entirely of my own, personal research, the questioner did not understand me at all. He did not understand that it was quite a different matter from anything that had been done before in the Theosophical Society. The path I had appointed for myself, however was this: to reject all earlier ways of investigation and—admittedly by means of supersensible perception—to investigate by making use only of what can be revealed to the one who is him- or herself the investigator.

—from *The Occult Movement in the Nineteenth Century*, lecture 2

. . . .

IT IS WELL NEVER TO LOSE SIGHT OF THE FACT that, fundamentally, there is nothing in the universe but consciousness—consciousnesses. Everything outside the consciousness of beings—of whatever order— belongs to the realm of *maya*, the Great Illusion. This fact can be gathered from two particular places in my writings. There are other passages as well, but I am thinking of two in particular. The first is to be found in *Occult Science* (Chapter IV), where the evolution of the Earth from Saturn to Vulcan, the progression from Saturn to Sun,

---

4. Steiner goes on to discuss Scott Elliot's book, *The Story of Atlantis* (1896).

Sun to Moon, Moon to Earth, is described primarily in terms of states of consciousness.[5] If we are to reach the heights of these mighty cosmic facts, we must rise to a level where we have to do with states of consciousness only. When attempting to describe the realities, therefore, we can describe only states of consciousness.

The same can be gathered from a passage in a book that appeared this summer, *The Threshold of the Spiritual World*.[6] There it is shown how, in gradual ascent, the eye of seership rises above the objects and processes of the world around us, to a level where all these things pass away and melt into nothingness, until finally the region is attained where beings alone exist—beings in certain states of consciousness.

The only true realities in the universe are therefore beings in different states of consciousness. It is because we who live in the state of human consciousness have no complete survey of the realities that what is not reality appears to us as if it were.

In this connection, I have often used an analogy. Ask yourselves the following: Is a human hair a reality in itself, even in the most limited sense? Has it any independent existence? It would be nonsense to say that a human hair has independent existence. The only reasonable point of view is to think of it as growing on the human body. Under no other circumstances can it exist; it cannot exist on its own. Everyone realizes that it is nonsense to speak of a hair as a reality in itself, or to attribute to it an independent existence, even in the ordinary, earthly sense; for a hair cannot come into being as a separate entity.

In the same way, a plant is often thought of as an individual, independent entity, but it is no more independent than a hair. For what a hair is on the head, a plant is in the organism of the Earth, and it is nonsense to think of a plant as an independent entity. . . .

It is important to remember the point at which an entity must cease to be regarded as a self-contained, independent entity. Indeed, in the most ultimate sense that human beings can grasp, nothing has an independent reality or existence that is not rooted in consciousness. Everything is rooted in consciousness—in different ways.

5. See *An Outline of Occult Science* (Hudson, NY: Anthroposophic Press, 1972).
6. See *A Road to Self Knowledge and The Threshold of the Spiritual World* (London: Rudolf Steiner Press, 1990).

Consider a thought, a human thought. These thoughts are in our consciousness but not only in our consciousness; at the same time, they are in the consciousness of the beings of the next higher hierarchy, the Angeloi. While we think, our whole world of thought is a thought of the Angeloi. Our consciousness is "thought" by the Angeloi. This shows you that to attain seership we must enfold a way of visioning the beings of the higher worlds that differs from our way of perceiving the world of ordinary, external reality. Seership cannot be attained if we continue to think in the same way as we think about the physical world of sense, about earthly existence. In the higher worlds we do not only think, but we must be thought and, moreover, know that we are "being thought." It is not easy to characterize what seers feel with regard to their vision, for no human words have yet been coined for it. But we can use a certain analogy.

Let us suppose we are making certain movements, not perceiving them directly but observing a mirror-image of them in the eyes of another person. By observing this image we know that we are making this or that movement with our hands or our features. This experience comes at the early stage of seership. We are aware in a general way that we are thinking, but we observe ourselves in the consciousness of the beings of the next higher hierarchy, letting our thoughts be thought by the Angeloi. We must know that we ourselves are not directing the thoughts in our consciousness, but that the beings of the next higher hierarchy are directing those thoughts. We must feel the consciousness of the Angeloi surging and weaving through us. Then enlightenment comes to us concerning the onward-flowing impulses of evolution. For example, we perceive the reality of the Christ impulse and how, once imparted, it works on and is working to this day. The Angeloi can "think" these impulses. We human beings can think of these impulses and characterize them if we surrender our thoughts to the Angeloi so that they think in us. We can achieve this through continual inner work, as described in my book *How To Know Higher Worlds*. . . .

from *The Fifth Gospel*, lecture 7

. . . .

LET US RECALL SEVERAL THINGS I HAVE DESCRIBED BEFORE. I have explained how authentic seership begins, how good seers have to acquire a totally different relationship to the spiritual world than they have to the physical world. I have said we perceive external beings and objects on the physical plane as existing outside us. We face these objects and take something of them into ourselves in the process of perception. Our I knows about the objects and creates mental images of them. This is the experiential basis of any kind of knowing and perceiving on the physical plane—we make mental images of the objects on the physical plane and recognize them.

But this basic experience changes as soon as we ascend to the spiritual worlds. There it is replaced with a different fundamental experience, the experience of oneself as object. Our I relates to the higher worlds in the same way that objects formerly related to the I. We no longer perceive, but experience that we are being perceived, that the spiritual beings of the higher hierarchies are observing us. This experience of being perceived and observed by the Angeloi, Archangeloi, and other spiritual beings is a total reversal of our former relationship to the physical world. We expand the awareness that our being has expanded to encompass the sphere of the hierarchies, and that the hierarchies are at work in us and are looking at us just as we used to look at objects on the physical plane.

Without this fundamental experience our whole relationship to the spiritual world is wrong, just as our whole relationship to the physical world would be wrong if we lacked the basic experience of perception and developing mental images. "I am observing" is true of the physical world. "I am being observed" is, in the final analysis, true of the spiritual world. . . .

. . . This is not something we can accomplish purely through our own efforts; all we can do is set out on the right path. The experience of being perceived by spiritual beings of the higher hierarchies comes to us as an act of grace on the part of the spiritual world itself. And it is not simply that higher beings look at us; we become perceptions, concepts, and thoughts for higher beings in the same way that objects on the physical plane are for us.

from *Community Life, Inner Development,*
Sexuality, and the Spiritual Teacher, lecture 3

PART ONE

The Spiritual Hierarchies
and the Physical World

1. The Renewal of Primeval Wisdom

APRIL 12, 1909, *Morning*

THIS CYCLE OF LECTURES WILL LEAD US into exalted regions
of spiritual life, will lead us as it were not only from our earthly dwelling place into the vastness of physical space, but even into the spiritual
worlds from which the physical aspect of space originates. At the
same time, however, precisely a lecture cycle of this kind will show us
that all knowledge and all wisdom aim to solve the greatest riddle of
all: the riddle of the human being. For, to understand the human
being, what illumines the riddle must be drawn from far distant
spheres. This is to say that anyone wishing to understand these lectures must be acquainted with the basic concepts of theosophy
[anthroposophy]—which happens to be the case with those present.[1]
Therefore, always taking care to make these matters gathered from
distant spheres as understandable as possible, we shall set the course
of our spiritual flight at an especially high level in these lectures.

When we speak of what are called the spiritual hierarchies, the
eyes of our soul should turn upward to those beings who exist above
earthly humanity. With our physical eyes, which perceive what is

---

1. These lectures were given to members of the Theosophical Society. The basic
concepts of anthroposophy (or Rudolf Steiner's "theosophy," as it was then) are
usually considered to be contained in Steiner's main written works, namely, above
all: *Intuitive Thinking as a Spiritual Path: A Philosophy of Freedom* (1894);
Christianity as Mystical Fact (1902); *Theosophy* (1904/5); *Cosmic Memory* (1904/8);
and *Occult Science—An Outline* (1910). Also note that, at the time that the lectures
contained in this book were delivered, Rudolf Steiner spoke as a Theosophist. To
avoid confusion, however, and following Steiner's own indications, *anthroposophy*
has been substituted for *theosophy* in this text.

visible, we can rise, as it were, only through beings representing four degrees of one hierarchy: the mineral, plant, animal, and human worlds. Beyond that, above humanity, begins a realm of invisible beings which, if we have developed the ability to do so, we can investigate with supersensible cognition. Then we rise toward beings and powers in the invisible, supersensible world who form a continuation of the four stages found on Earth. You are all familiar with the fact that knowledge and investigation of these realms arose not only in our own historical period of human development, and that research into them is not limited to the present. In truth, there exists what we might call a primeval world wisdom in which everything that we, as human beings, can fathom, know, and discern—all the concepts and ideas we can acquire, and all we can attain through clairvoyant imagination, inspiration, and intuition—has been prefigured in deed and in knowledge by the beings who stand above us.

To use a trivial comparison, we might invoke the metaphor of the watchmaker who first conceives the idea for a watch and then sets out to make it. The watchmaker constructs the watch according to ideas that have been envisioned prior to its construction. Later, we can take the watch apart, analyze it, study it, and thus reconstruct the watchmaker's thoughts from which the watch arose. In this way we can rethink—think through again—the watchmaker's thoughts. In fact, in our present stage of evolution, this relationship—that of "thinking through again"—is the only one we can have, as human beings, to the primeval universal wisdom; that is, to the spiritual beings who stand above us. Spiritual beings originally had the imaginations, inspirations, and intuitions—the ideas and thoughts according to which the world surrounding us was created. Human beings can recover these thoughts and ideas in the world, and if they rise to clairvoyant perception they can also discover the imaginations, inspirations, and intuitions through which one can gain access once more to the realm of spiritual beings. We may therefore say that, even before our world came into existence, the wisdom of which we are going to speak already existed. This wisdom is the plan of the world.

How far, then, must we go back, and still remain within the limits of reality, if we want to find this primeval, universal wisdom? Must we go back to some historical period when this or that great teacher was teaching? Indeed, we could learn much if we could go back here or there within historical epochs and become students of the great teachers. But, to gain access to the highest manifestations of primeval wisdom, we must go back to a time when there was not yet any outwardly visible Earth, when there was no world perceptible to the senses. For the world originated out of wisdom itself, and this wisdom, according to which the divine spiritual beings formed our world, was later bestowed upon humankind. Human beings in their thinking could then perceive the thoughts according to which the gods shaped the world. And after this primeval wisdom, this wisdom of cosmic creation, had evolved through several forms, it came, as you know, following the great Atlantean epochs, to the ancient, Holy Rishis of our first post-Atlantean culture, to the great teachers of India.[2]

The form in which the primeval wisdom appeared through the Holy Rishis is hardly conceivable to human beings today. For human capacities of thinking and perception have changed considerably since the great teachers of India first taught post-Atlantean humanity. If we were to repeat today what the Holy Rishis said, most souls—anywhere on Earth—would merely hear so many words. To understand the wisdom that was imparted to post-Atlantean humanity, quite other powers of comprehension are necessary than those we have in

2. Holy Rishis: see *Occult Science*, chapter IV (end). For instance: "These seven Initiates became the teachers and guides of those who in the time after Atlantis had settled in the South of Asia, more particularly in ancient India.... The power that could go out from the seven great Teachers of human beings such as these was tremendous. All that could be revealed through them entered deeply and livingly into the Indian soul.... Thus arose a civilization permeated through and through with supersensible wisdom."

Atlantean epochs and post-Atlantean culture: in *Occult Science* and elsewhere in countless lectures (see, for instance, *The Apocalypse of St. John*), Rudolf Steiner outlines the unfolding of earthly evolution through the Polarian, Hyperborean, Lemurean, Atlantean and Post-Atlantean epochs. There will be three post-Atlantean epochs, of which we are in the first. Furthermore, each such epoch is subdivided in turn into seven cultural ages. In the case of our post-Atlantean epoch these ages are: (Old) Indian, (Old) Persian, Egypto-Chaldean, Greco-Roman, and our own cultural epoch, which will be followed by the sixth (Slavic) and the seventh (American) epochs.

our time. All that has been recorded of this wisdom, all that is to be found in the best books regarding this original cosmic wisdom, represents only a faint echo of it. In many respects, it is obscured and darkened wisdom. No matter how sublime the Vedas appear to us today, or how beautifully the Songs (or Gathas) of Zarathustra sound to us, or how gloriously the ancient wisdom of Egypt speaks to us— indeed, we can never sufficiently express our admiration for such documents—they provide only a dull reflection of the original wisdom of Hermes, the great teaching of Zarathustra,[3] or the sublime knowledge proclaimed by the ancient Rishis.

Yet, this sublime wisdom was preserved and could always be found in certain small circles guarding the Mysteries—which is the term by which this knowledge is known. This primeval wisdom of humanity was preserved in the Mysteries of India, Persia, Chaldea, and Egypt, as well as in the Christian Mysteries, as these have existed up to our own time. Indeed, until recently, one could reach an understanding of *living wisdom*—not just of wisdom as it is found in books—only in these narrow circles. In the course of these lectures, however, it will become clear that what was kept alive in small circles must today penetrate into the masses of humanity to a greater extent than before.

The stream of the ancient wisdom, that of the Rishis, for example, never dried up. It continued to flow, as if through a renewing fountain, up to the time that we recognize as the beginning of our own era. This primeval divine wisdom, which streamed over humanity in ancient times, was transmitted by Zarathustra and his pupils, the Chaldean and Egyptian teachers. It streamed into the Mosaic revelation and came forth again with a new impulse, as if renewed in a rejuvenating fountain, in the earthly appearance of Christ. But, following Christ's appearance—that is, since the time of the outward proclamation of Christianity, indeed as a result of it—the stream of

---

3. For Hermes and Zoroaster, see Rudolf Steiner, *Turning Points in Spiritual History* (London: Rudolf Steiner Publishing Co., 1934). Also: *The East in the Light of the West* (Blauvelt, NY: Garber Communications, 1986).

primeval world wisdom became so deep, so inward in character, that it could flow into humanity again only gradually. In other words, we can see that, since the time of the outward promulgation of Christianity in the world, the primeval wisdom flowed slowly and gradually into humankind in a most elementary beginning.

Its message may be found in the Gospels and in other Christian writings that contain the wisdom of the Holy Rishis in a form that has been renewed in a rejuvenating fountain. But how was this message understood at the beginning of the Christian epoch, the time period created for its purification, its reformation? The least part of it was understood through proclamation of the Gospels, and only gradually did the Gospels work through to a broader understanding—indeed, in many ways, the Gospels worked more toward a darkening of understanding. Today, for most people, the Gospels are the most completely sealed of books. In the future, however, those who allow themselves to be renewed by the ancient cosmic wisdom will understand them. Because of this, the treasures lying in the shafts of Christian revelation, which are none other than the treasures of Eastern wisdom (except that they were born from restored powers) were preserved in narrow circles, and subsequently prolonged in various mystery societies, such as the Brotherhood of the Holy Grail and the Brotherhood of the Rosicrucians.[4] These treasures of truth have been closely guarded. They were accessible only to those who, having passed through stringent trials, had prepared themselves to receive this living wisdom. Thus, for centuries following the beginning of our era, the treasures of Eastern and Western wisdom were almost inaccessible to most human beings. Some small amount of this wisdom trickled here and there into the outer world, but, for the most part, it remained a secret of the new Mysteries.

Thus, the time has now come when the contents of the primeval cosmic wisdom may be brought in an appropriate form to many more

---

4. See, for instance, *Esoteric Christianity and the Mission of Christian Rosenkreutz* (London: Rudolf Steiner Press, 1984) and for the Brotherhood of the Holy Grail , *Karmic Relationships*, vol. VIII (London: Rudolf Steiner Press, 1975), lectures 3 and 6.

people. Since the last third of the nineteenth century, one may speak
of the primeval wisdom in a more or less unveiled form.[5] Because of
certain events in the spiritual world, the Guardians of the Mysteries
have been permitted to allow some of the ancient wisdom to flow out
into the world at large. You are all familiar with the evolution of the
Theosophical Society and must realize that the impetus for its development accompanied the proclamation of certain truths—in a form I
need not describe here— known as the *Stanzas of Dzyan*, which are
included in *The Secret Doctrine*.[6] These stanzas do, in fact, contain
some of the deepest and most significant fragments of wisdom. Much
of this wisdom originated in the teachings of the Holy Rishis that
flowed into the sacred lore of the East. There is also much in them
that streamed into Western Europe after the rejuvenating impulse of
Christianity had occurred. The *Stanzas of Dzyan* contain not only
wisdom preserved in the East, but also much that shines like a bright
light through the centuries of our era into the Middle Ages and the
Mystery Schools of the West. Much of what is to be found in the
Stanzas will only gradually be understood in all its depths. It must be
made clear that they contain a wisdom that cannot yet be understood
in the widest theosophical circles, nor fathomed with the exoteric
capacities of the present day. It is a hopeless task, indeed, to attempt
to interpret this important realm exoterically.

After the ice had been broken [by the development of theosophy],
one could speak more freely out of the wellsprings of Western occultism, itself a continuation of Eastern occultism that had been trans-
planted to meet the different spiritual and physical conditions of life

---

5. Rudolf Steiner is referring here to the heavenly-earthly event of the ascendance
of the Archangel Michael in 1879. See *The Archangel Michael: His Mission and Ours*
(Hudson, NY: Anthroposophic Press, 1994).

6. The *Stanzas of Dzyan*, deriving from Tibetan sources, provide the metaphysical
foundations for the cosmogenesis expounded in volume 1 of H. P. Blavatsky's *Secret
Doctrine* (1888). They are also available in a small volume with Blavatsky's *The Voice
of Silence*. Rudolf Steiner worked meditatively and profoundly with these verses.

For Steiner's view of the evolution of the Theosophical Society, see *The Occult
Movement in the Nineteenth Century* (London: Rudolf Steiner Press, 1973) and *The
Anthroposophic Movement* (Bristol, UK: Rudolf Steiner Press, 1993).

in the West. Today, however, the time has come to speak out of the sources of the living occultism faithfully guarded in the Rosicrucian Mysteries. There is no wisdom of the East that has not streamed into Western occultism. In the teachings and investigations of the Rosicrucians, indeed, you will find everything that has been preserved by the great sages of the East. Nothing, absolutely nothing, known through Eastern wisdom is missing in the wisdom of the West.

There is only this difference. The wisdom of the West had to illuminate this whole body of Eastern teaching with the light kindled in humanity by the Christ impulse, but without losing any of it. It should not be said that a single iota of Eastern occultism is missing from Western occultism, which is derived from the hidden Rishis of the West who are invisible to human eyes. Nothing is missing. It is simply that everything had to be renewed out of the rejuvenating fountain of the Christ impulse. The great wisdom of the supersensible worlds, as it was first uttered by the Holy Rishis, must resound again in what is now proclaimed about the spiritual hierarchies and their reflection into the physical world. Just as Euclid's geometry has not become other than it once was, though one teaches and learns it today with new human capacities, so the wisdom of the Holy Rishis has not become something other than it once was, even though we teach and learn it with capacities kindled by the Christ impulse. Much of what we have to say about the spiritual worlds may thus be called Eastern wisdom. There should be no misunderstandings in these matters. Unfortunately, however, misunderstandings occur all too easily.

Those who do not want to raise themselves from misinterpretation to genuine understanding may easily misunderstand what was said yesterday in the Easter lecture.[7] I mention this so that we can penetrate to a fuller understanding. Those, however, who do not wish to do so might say the following:

Yesterday, you spoke of the great so-called divine truths of

---

7. See lecture 8, Cologne, April 11, 1909, "The Event of Golgotha. The Brotherhood of the Holy Grail. The Spiritual Fire." in *The Principle of Spiritual Economy* (Hudson, NY: Anthroposophic Press, 1986).

the Buddha. You said that the Buddha taught and revealed the divine truths about suffering in one's life: that birth is suffering, illness is suffering, old age is suffering, death is suffering; that to be separated from loved ones and what one loves is suffering; that to be united with what one does not love is suffering; that to be denied what one desires is suffering. But you also said that if we were to consider post-Christian times and those who truly understood the Christ impulse, then we would become aware that through the understanding and penetration of this Christ impulse, the ancient holy truths of Buddha concerning suffering in human life would no longer be entirely valid. For with the Christ impulse comes healing for suffering in life. You have said, "Buddha teaches that birth is suffering." But one who understands Christ answers, "Through birth we enter a life which we share with Christ and through Christ's participation the suffering of life is extinguished." Even so, the healing power of the Christ impulse eradicates illness. For one who truly understands the Christ, illness, death, and so forth, are no longer suffering. Further objections to what you have said might also be made, but I can show you that the same words may be found in the holy writings of the Buddha and in the Gospels. There, too, it is said that life, illness, and so on, are suffering. Therefore, it might be assumed superficially that, although we possess these modern religious documents, their contents were already present in Buddhism. And from this one might conclude that there is no progress or development in the various religions, since they all embody the same truths. But you have spoken of progress and have told us that the ancient holy truths of Buddhism are no longer true because of Christianity.[8]

For someone to come to this conclusion from what I said would be a most grievous misconception, because this was not even implied. Certainly, all of the above was said—with the exception of the last

---

8. For Steiner on the Buddha, see above all, *From Buddha to Christ* (Hudson, NY: Anthroposophic Press, 1987).

sentence. In matters as subtle as these, it is important to develop a precise understanding. But this can be understood only by one who has developed a capacity for objectivity, certainly not by a fanatic.

One who speaks from the source of Rosicrucian wisdom and research will never attack the contents of the writings of the great Buddha, nor claim that anything in them is untrue. Such a person, speaking from the Rosicrucian source, supports Buddha's insights and the whole of Eastern wisdom, and denies none of it. What the Buddha beheld of the great truths of the suffering in life—through illumination in his inner being—is correct in every detail. Nothing, absolutely nothing, may be taken away from these truths. And precisely because everything that the Buddha said—that birth, illness, old age, death, and so on, are suffering—is true, the Christ impulse is for us such a powerful and important means of healing. For Christ puts an end to this suffering. This is true because, even though the sufferings in life exist, an even greater impulse above the world can lift them up out of the world. The Christ could be effective precisely because the Buddha proclaimed the truth. Humanity had to be led down from spiritual heights where primeval world wisdom was active in its purest form. Humankind had to be guided to independence on the physical plane. As a result, life and illness became suffering.

But a powerful remedy for these irrefutable facts had to appear in the course of evolution. Does a person deny the reality of the situation by claiming that, though the facts are true, at the same time a remedy has been given gradually to heal the situation produced by the facts? There is no question of Buddhism opposing Christianity or vice versa in the lofty heights of the spheres of the spiritual hierarchies. There the Buddha stretches out his hand to Christ, and Christ reaches out to the Buddha. But if we fail to recognize an ascending development in human evolution, we also fail to recognize the most spiritual deed that has occurred in earthly evolution— namely, the deed of Christ. Thus the wisdom of the East that brought us the wisdom of the Holy Rishis along with the primeval cosmic wisdom is not to be denied. But, over long periods of time during which this wisdom streamed into humankind, it became increasingly difficult for the masses of people who had no access to the sources of the Mysteries to understand this wisdom. Precisely the understanding itself became difficult.

In ancient Atlantean times, before the great catastrophe, the mass of humanity was still endowed with ancient, albeit dulled, powers of clairvoyance. When human beings turned their gaze to the heavenly expanses, to the spiritual hierarchies, they saw differently from humanity in later post-Atlantean times. For, by then, the old clairvoyance had disappeared for the great mass of humanity who now gazed into the physical expanses of the heavens with only physical eyes. Before the Atlantean catastrophe there was no point in speaking as we do today of heavenly bodies spread out in space. The clairvoyant human eye, which gazed into the expanses of space at that time, saw spiritual worlds. It would have been meaningless then to speak of Mercury, Neptune, Saturn, and so on, as astronomy speaks of them today. When astronomy today speaks of the cosmos and its contents, it can report only what the sense-perceiving, physical eye sees when it looks into the heavens. This was by no means the case for ancient clairvoyant humanity in Atlantean times. Human beings did not see physical, finite, shining stars then. What we see today with the physical eye is merely an outward expression of the spiritual reality that human beings beheld in former times.

Today when we look with our physical eye through a telescope to where Jupiter stands in the heavens, it sees, so to speak, a physical globe surrounded by moons. But what did the ancient Atlanteans see when they looked clairvoyantly at the same spot? During Atlantean times, the physical eye saw much as we do today when we try to see something through a thick autumn mist—the light is surrounded by a kind of misty aura and disappears in the colored rings that form around it. The eye of an Atlantean would not have seen the physical star of Jupiter; it would have seen something that is still today united with Jupiter, but which humanity can no longer see, namely, the aura of Jupiter, that is, the spiritual beings whose outward expression is the physical planet. Before the Atlantean catastrophe, the human spiritual eye swept the expanses of the universe and beheld spiritual beings everywhere. At that time, one could speak only in terms of a spiritual content. It would have been meaningless to talk about physical stars at an evolutionary stage when the physical eye was not yet open as it is today. Gazing into the vast, wide spaces of the universe, human beings then actually beheld spiritual beings, spiritual hierarchies. They saw beings.

The following comparison may help us to understand the course of evolution. Let us imagine ourselves in a thick fog where we cannot see each separate light, because everything is shrouded in a misty aura. Then the fog lifts suddenly, and individual lights become plainly visible, but as a result, the auras are no longer seen. In earlier epochs, the human eye beheld the aura of Jupiter; it saw in it the spiritual beings belonging to Jupiter at that particular stage of the planet's evolution. But, as humanity developed, the capacity of physical sight also developed. The aura remained, of course, even though human beings could no longer see it. At the same time, the physical center gradually became more clearly visible. Thus, the spiritual counterpart was lost as the physical aspect became manifest. But the knowledge of the spiritual beings who surround the stars was preserved in the Mysteries and spoken of by the Holy Rishis. When humanity was capable only of physical sight, the Holy Rishis still spoke of the spiritual atmosphere, of the spiritual populations in the cosmic bodies that are distributed through space.

Consider the situation that then arose. Within the sanctuaries of knowledge one could speak of the spiritual beings surrounding the cosmic bodies. Outside them, however, as sense perceptions became increasingly sharper, people came to speak more and more in terms of physical matter. Yet, when the Holy Rishis spoke the word Mercury—of course, they never actually used this word, but let us use it to make ourselves clear—did they mean the physical orb in the cosmos? No, not even the ancient Greeks, when speaking of Mercury, referred to the physical planet. When the Greeks spoke of Mercury in their sanctuaries of knowledge, they spoke of spiritual worlds, spiritual beings. When the disciples of the teachers in the sanctuaries of knowledge spoke the words *Moon, Mercury, Venus, Sun, Mars, Jupi-*

ter, and *Saturn* in their various languages, these words represented a gradation of spiritual beings. Anyone who refers to a physical planet with such a word today omits the most important aspect, and characterizes only the coarsest aspect of what originally was encompassed in the terms *Moon, Mercury, Venus*, and so on.

Spiritual teachers in ancient times sought to evoke the idea of a powerful spiritual realm. When they pointed to the place in the heavens where the Moon was, they were aware that the lowest rank of the spiritual hierarchies dwelt there. But when human beings, who had been cut off from spiritual vision by their increasingly sensory perception, looked up, they saw only the physical Moon, which they then called the "Moon"—one word for two things that, although connected, called forth quite different representations in human minds. When teachers in the stream of spiritual wisdom referred to *Mercury, Sun*, and *Mars*, they meant something quite different by these words than teachers do in the materialistic stream.

The two streams—the spiritual and the materialistic—drifted further and further apart. In the Mysteries, the words that later came to denote the external heavenly bodies had always referred to supersensible worlds, to a sequence of spiritual realms. The outer world always understands the words to mean the material aspect, and this is true even of the contemporary mythology—I use the word deliberately— we call astronomy. Spiritual science recognizes the full value of all mythologies. Thus, it also appreciates the worth of the mythology called modern astronomy which sees only space filled with physical cosmic bodies. This modern mythology is, for one who truly knows, merely a particular phase of all mythologies. A single thread runs through these mythologies from the ancient European sagas of the gods to the myths of the Greeks and Romans, the obscure myths of the Middle Ages, and the fully justified and admirable ones founded by Copernicus, Kepler, and Galileo.[9] A time will come when people will say of modern mythology, "In the past, there were human beings who

9. Nicolas Copernicus (1473-1543), Johannes Kepler (1571–1630), Galileo Galilei (1564–1642).

thought it correct to place the material Sun in the center of an ellipse and to rotate the planets in ellipses around it. They constructed a cosmic universal system even as earlier people had done before them. But today, we know that it is all mere saga and legend." Indeed, a time will come when, no matter how much the old mythologies are now despised by the modern world, it will be considered absurd to speak of a Copernican mythology. To realize this will help us to understand how words have been interpreted so differently over the course of time.

Nevertheless, the primeval cosmic wisdom flowed on exoterically; because it was increasingly interpreted in a materialistic way, it was understood less and less. True spiritual insight ebbed away. Yet, when ancient wisdom was restored at the beginning of our era, human beings were again directed to the starry realms so that humanity might not completely lose its connection with primeval spiritual wisdom. They were told in clear, direct words that, when they looked up to the heavens with their physical eyes, they would find there not only a material universe, but also realms filled with spirit.

The most intimate pupil of Saint Paul, Dionysius the Areopagite, clearly proclaimed in Athens that out in space there was not only matter, but that when the soul arose with inner awareness into the expanses of the universe, it would find spiritual beings who are above humanity in evolutionary development.[10] Dionysius coined different terms from those used previously, for otherwise people would have thought that he referred only to material entities. When the Rishis spoke of spiritual hierarchies, their words expressed what Greek and Roman wisdom expressed in their ascending universe of Moon, Mercury, Mars, Venus, Jupiter, and Saturn. Dionysius, the pupil of Saint Paul, had in mind the same worlds the Rishis spoke of. Dionysius clearly wished to emphasize that he was referring to spiritual matters. So, he deliberately chose words he knew would be taken spiritually—

---

10. Dionysius the Areopagite, whose works were not made public (or written down) until the sixth century and who is thought by scholars to have lived around then, wrote as if he were the intimate of St. Paul and St. John and is taken by Rudolf Steiner to represent authentic oral esoteric Christian teaching. Author of *The Mystical Theology*, *The Divine Names*, *The Celestial Hierarchy*, *The Ecclesiastical Hierarchy*, and *Letters*.

that is, he spoke of Angels, Archangels, Archai, Powers, Mights, Dominions, Thrones, Cherubim, and Seraphim. But people had completely forgotten what they once knew. If the connection between the terminology of Dionysius the Areopagite and the Rishis had been understood, one would have known that the "Moon" the Rishis referred to, and the "angelic realm" in other Mysteries, are one and the same thing. One might have heard the word *Mercury* on the one hand, and the word *Archangel* on the other, and would have known that they are one and the same. *Archai* and *Venus* refer to the same realm, as do *Sun* and *Powers*. On hearing the word *Mars*, one would have had the feeling of rising to the Mights. The word *Dominions* in the school of Dionysius corresponds to Jupiter, and the term *Saturn* to the Thrones.

In wider circles, this knowledge had disappeared and was no longer known. As science became more and more materialistic, the old names, which had once denoted spiritual realities, remained. But now increasingly they applied only to matter. In contrast to this materialistic stream, there did exist a spiritual stream that referred to Archangels, Angels, and so on. But this stream had lost the connection with the physical expression of these spiritual beings. Thus, we see how primeval cosmic wisdom penetrated into the school founded by Saint Paul through Dionysius and how it is a question now of permeating newfound knowledge with the spiritual impulse of the past. Indeed, it is the task of spiritual science or anthroposophy to renew the bond between the physical and the spiritual, between the world of the Earth and the spiritual hierarchies. For the spiritual aspect of knowledge must always remain incomprehensible to those who do not know the true origin of ideas about the outer material world.

This becomes particularly noticeable in writings that, although they contain only a faint echo of primeval cosmic wisdom, can be understood only by means of this wisdom. To exemplify the difficulties involved, take a passage from the Celestial Song, the Bhagavad Gita, which sheds considerable light on humanity's relation to the hierarchies—chapter eight, beginning with verse 23:

I will explain to you, Seeker of Truth [that is the usual translation], under what circumstances the exalted spirits of gods depart through the gate of death in order to be reborn or not. I say to you: Behold the fire, the day and the time of the waxing Moon, and the months of the increasing light of the Sun. Those who die at that time pass through the gate of death into *Brahma*. But those who die under the sign of smoke, in the night, at the time of the waning Moon, during the portion of the year when the sun rests low in the sky, they pass through the gate of death in the lunar light and return again to this world.[11]

Dear friends, here is a passage from the Bhagavad Gita telling us that our progress, our successive incarnations, depends on whether we die in the sign of light by day—by waxing Moon during the six months that the Sun is high in the heavens—or whether we die in the sign of the smoke by night, when the Moon is waning and the Sun is low. That is the literal meaning of the passage. It says that those who pass through the gate of death in the sign of fire by day, by waxing Moon, or when the Sun is high in the heavens need no longer return. But of the others—those who die in the sign of smoke by night, by waning Moon or during the six months when the Sun is low—it says that they cannot rise to the level of Brahma but only to the height of the Moon, and must therefore return again. This passage in the Celestial Song of the East presents untold difficulties to those who seek an exoteric interpretation. It can only be explained when light is shed upon it from spiritual knowledge. Indeed, the same light from which the passage was written continues to shine in the Mystery schools. Rejuvenated through Christianity, it is a light that illumines the bond between Moon and Angels, Mercury and Archangels, Venus and Archai, and so on. Through the light provided by spiritual knowledge, we shall find the key to this passage we have chosen as an example. It will be the starting point for our lecture this evening. Once we have discovered this key, we shall be able

---

11. Rudolf Steiner speaks extensively about the Bhagavad Gita in *The Bhagavad Gita and the Epistles of Saint Paul* (NY: Anthroposophic Press, 1971) and *The Occult Significance of the Bhagavad Gita* (Spring Valley, NY: Anthroposophic Press, 1968).

2. The Four Elements, Fire, and the Elemental Beings: the Lowest Realm of the Hierarchies

APRIL 12, 1909, *Evening*

THE KNOWLEDGE THAT FORMED THE BASIS of the teachings proclaimed by the Holy Rishis during the first post-Atlantean period was founded entirely upon the spiritual sources of existence. From the beginning of the post-Atlantean epoch, the most important aspect of this teaching or mode of investigation was that it penetrated deeply into natural processes and discovered the active, spiritual principles underlying them. Fundamentally speaking, we are continually surrounded by spiritual happenings and beings. Physical phenomena are merely the expression of spiritual facts. Things that appear to us in material form are but the outward sheaths of spiritual beings. Thus, when the primeval divine teaching spoke of perceptible phenomena in our surroundings, particular emphasis was laid on what was, to human beings of that time, the most important natural phenomenon surrounding humanity on Earth—that is, fire.

Ancient spiritual science regarded the phenomenon of fire as the most important expression in nature. Spiritual research into fire comprised the central focus of all explanations of what occurred on Earth. To understand these teachings concerning fire—so important in ancient times for all knowledge and life—we must first consider how other natural phenomena were regarded in the past by a teaching still valid in spiritual science today.

In those ancient times, all that surrounded human beings in the physical world was referred back to the four elements. Modern materialistic science no longer acknowledges the four elements of earth, water, air, and fire. But the spiritual science of that time did not understand these as we do today. When using the word *earth*, they did not mean what we mean by that word today. "Earth" denoted a condition of matter, the solid state. Everything we refer to as solid was called "earth" in ancient spiritual science. It did not matter whether it was a solid lump of arable soil, a crystal, a piece of lead, or a piece of gold. Everything of a solid nature was termed "earth." Everything fluid, not only water as we know it, was referred to as "watery" or "water." Iron, for example, when melted by fire so that it became fluid, would be termed "water" by spiritual science. All metals in the fluid state were called "water," while what we call gaseous was termed "air," regardless of the particular gas to which it was applied, whether oxygen, hydrogen, or some other gas.

Fire was considered the fourth element. Those of you familiar with elementary physics will recall that modern science does not regard fire as comparable with earth, water, or air. According to modern physics, fire is regarded merely as a condition of movement. For spiritual science, however, warmth, or fire, has an even finer substantiality than air. Just as earth, or solidity, can be transformed into the liquid state, so, according to spiritual science, all airy or gaseous forms gradually change into the condition of fire. Fire is so rarefied that it permeates all other elements. It permeates air, thereby warming it; and the same applies to water and earth. Whereas the three other elements are separate, the fire element possesses an all-pervading quality.

Now, both ancient and modern spiritual science agree that there is a still more important difference between what we term "earth," "water," and "air," and what we call "fire," or "warmth." How do we get to know the earth element or solidity? We might try touching it and experiencing its resistance. The same applies to water, though it offers less resistance. Nevertheless, we are aware of water as something external to ourselves, as a resistance. The same is true of air. We get to know it in relation to ourselves only externally. But this is not the case with warmth. Here we must emphasize an aspect that is regarded as unimportant by the modern way of looking at things, but we shall have to consider it if we wish to fathom the riddles of existence. The fact is, we become aware of warmth without touching it externally—this is the important point. Of course, we can become aware of warmth by touching an object that has been heated, in which case we become aware of it in the same way as we do the other elements, but we also feel the warmth within our own organism.

That is why ancient knowledge, even in ancient India, stressed that we become aware of earth, water, and air only in the outer world, while warmth is the first element that can be apprehended both inwardly and outwardly. Warmth, or fire, therefore, has a two-fold nature—an external aspect, which we get to know outwardly, and an inner aspect, which we feel in our own condition of warmth. It has an inner and an outer manifestation. Actually, we feel our own inner warmth—we are hot or cold—but we are little inclined to concern ourselves with what is gaseous, watery, or solid in our organism—that is, with what is air, water, and earth in us. We begin to be aware of ourselves only in the element of warmth. Therefore, both ancient and modern spiritual science proclaim fire or warmth to be the first stage at which matter becomes soul. In other words, we can rightfully speak of an outer fire, which we perceive as we do other elements, and of an inner soul fire within us.

For spiritual science, fire has always built a bridge between the outer material world and the inner soul world that can be perceived only inwardly. It was central to all observation of nature. The gateway through which we can penetrate from the outer to the inner—fire or warmth—is truly like a door. Standing before it, we can observe it from the outside, we can open it, we can behold it from within. This is how fire is to be understood in the context of natural phenomena.

Outwardly, we touch a physical object and encounter fire in the same way as the other three elements stream toward us, but we perceive and experience warmth as something that also belongs to us. With fire, we stand in the doorway and enter into the soul element. This is what spiritual science proclaims about fire. In fire, we see something that plays between the elements of soul and matter.

Let us consider an elementary lesson from the first human wisdom. In ancient times, a teacher of this wisdom would ask that one observe an object being consumed by fire. Then, the teacher would point out that two things could be seen. In those days, one was called "smoke," which still applies today, and the other was called "light." Both of these natural phenomena—on the one hand, light, and on the other hand, smoke—occur when an object is consumed by fire. A spiritual scientist saw fire as placed *between* light and smoke, and the teacher would say that out of the flames were born both light and smoke.

Here we should keep in mind a simple yet very important characteristic of light that is born of fire. Most people, asked if they see light, reply that they do, of course, see light. This is absolutely false, because, in fact, the physical eye cannot perceive light. Because of light, we see objects, be they solid, fluid or gaseous. But light itself we cannot see. Imagine all of universal space illumined by a light, the source of which is behind you where you cannot see it. Then imagine you were to look into the world-spaces illuminated through and through by that light. Would you see the light? You would see absolutely nothing. You would perceive something only when an object was placed within the illuminated space. We cannot see light but only the solid, fluid, and gaseous elements that we see through the effects of the light.

In truth, physical light absolutely is not seen with the physical eye. This is something that presents itself with great clarity to the spiritual eye. Spiritual science therefore says that light makes everything visible but cannot itself be seen. This is an important statement: light is imperceptible. It cannot be perceived by means of our outer senses. We can perceive what is solid, fluid, and gaseous, and we can also perceive warmth or fire outwardly, but at this point an inner perception begins. Light as such can no longer be perceived externally. If you think that you see light when you look at the Sun, you are quite mistaken. You see a burning body, a burning substance emanating light. If you were to test this out, you would find that you can experience what is gaseous, fluid, or solid, and that you do not see the light but only the burning object. So, according to spiritual science, we rise upward from earth to water, from air to fire, and then to light. That is to say, we pass from the outwardly perceptible and visible to the invisible—the spiritual etheric realm. Putting it another way, we could say that fire is on the boundary between what is outwardly perceptible and material and what is etheric-spiritual and therefore no longer perceptible.

Let us consider what happens to an object consumed by fire—that is, what occurs when something burns. On the one hand light is produced. At first, warmth is generated by an externally imperceptible aspect that is active in the spiritual realm and no longer merely material. This warmth, if it is sufficiently intense, becomes a source of light. A part of this light is then given over to the invisible world. But it must be paid for in the form of smoke. That is, out of the part that was first transparent and translucent, an opaque "smoky" portion is separated off. Here we see how fire or warmth is divided into two components. It portions a part of itself into light and thus opens a way into the supersensible. But, as a result, it also has to send something down into the opaque, perceptible, material world. Nothing arises in the world having only one aspect. Everything created has two forms. Therefore, on the one hand, warmth produces light and, on the other hand, it also creates opaque, dark matter. That is an ancient, basic teaching of spiritual science.

That is only the outer physical aspect of the process. At the foundation of the physical-material process lies something essentially different. In the case of warmth that does not yet produce light, one perceives warmth as outwardly physical, but this warmth also contains a spiritual element. When the heat becomes so intense that light arises and smoke is produced, a part of the spiritual component that was in the heat goes over into smoke. The spiritual component of warmth that was in the fire and then transferred to the gaseous element—that is, into a form beneath that of warmth—is transformed in the clouded smoke. Spiritual beings connected with warmth have to allow themselves to be made opaque, so to speak, to be enchanted in the smoke. Thus, everything of a clouding nature, of solidification connected with warmth, is associated with the enchantment of spiritual beings.

We can put it even more simply. Let us imagine that air is made liquid, a process that can be achieved today. Now, air is mere solidified warmth, densified warmth, as a result of the smoke that has been formed. The spiritual part, which should ordinarily be in the fire, has been enchanted into smoke. Spiritual beings, which we may also call elemental beings, are enchanted in the air. And when air is transformed into the liquid state, they are even more deeply enchanted in a yet lower form of existence. That is why spiritual science sees in all physically perceptible things an element that has proceeded out of an original condition of fire or warmth. As the warmth densified into gas, it became air—smoky or gaseous—the gas became liquid, and the liquid densified into the solid state. "Look backward," says the spiritual scientist. "Look at any solid substance. Once it was fluid. It has only become solid in the course of development. What is liquid was once gaseous, and the gaseous state arose from the smoke that proceeded from the fire. But an enchantment of spiritual beings is connected with each stage of densification."

Let us now look at the world that surrounds us. The solid stones, the streams, the evaporating water that rises as mist and fog, the air—everything solid, liquid, gaseous, and fiery—these are all, in fact, nothing but fire. Everything is fire—that is, densified fire. Gold, silver, and copper are densified fire. In the far distant past, everything was fire; everything was born of fire; but in all forms of densification, spiritual beings lie enchanted! How are the spiritual divine beings that surround us able to produce solid matter as it exists on our planet? How do they produce liquid and airy substances? They send down elemental beings that dwell in fire, and imprison them in the air, water, and earth. They are emissaries, elemental messengers of the spiritual, creative, formative beings. At first, elemental beings live in the fire and, to put it pictorially, they feel comfortable there. Then they are condemned to an existence of enchantment. We can say as we look around us, "The beings we have to thank for everything surrounding us had to descend from the fire element and are enchanted within the things of this world."

But can human beings help these elemental beings in one way or another? That is the great question asked by the Holy Rishis. Can we release them? Yes, we can. For human actions on Earth are nothing but the external expression of spiritual processes. Everything we do here is also important for the spiritual world.

Consider the following: Someone stands before a crystal, a lump of gold, or the like. He or she looks at it. What happens if this person simply stares, simply looks at some object by means of the physical senses? A continual interplay arises between that person and the enchanted elemental being. What are enchanted both in matter and the human being are in some way related to one another. Let us assume, however, that our person merely stares at the object so that he or she takes in only what is impressed upon the eye. The fact is, something is continually passing into human beings from these elemental beings, and this goes on from morning to night. As we look out into the world, hosts of elementals who were, or are, continually being enchanted in the processes of densification continually enter into us from our surroundings. Let us assume that, as we stare at objects, we have not the slightest inclination to reflect about what we see or to let the spirit of things live in our souls. We take the easy road; we go through the world but do not digest our experiences spiritually by means of thoughts and feelings. We remain mere spectators of the physical, material world. In that case, the elemental beings enter into us and remain there. They have gained nothing in the world process and have merely transferred their seat from the outer world into us.

But now let us suppose that we digest our impressions spiritually by thinking about them, and by forming concepts about the underlying spiritual foundation of the world. That is, we do not merely stare at the object but ponder its nature; we feel the beauty of things and ennoble our impressions. If we do this, what are we doing? As a result of our spiritual activity we redeem the elemental being that streams toward us from the outer world, thus raising it to its previous state. We release the elemental being from its enchantment. Thus, through our spiritual activity, we can release beings who are enchanted in air, water, and earth and lead them back to their former condition, or we can imprison them again in our inner being with no transformation having taken place in them.

Throughout earthly life, elemental beings stream into human beings. To the extent that a person merely stares at the things that hold elemental beings, these beings simply enter the human being untransformed. To the extent that a person tries to work on things in the outer world through ideas, concepts, and feelings of beauty, that person redeems and frees these spiritual, elemental beings.

What happens to the elemental beings who have entered human beings? To begin with, they inhabit us. Even those who have been released dwell in us until we die. When we go through the gate of death a distinction is made between those elemental beings who merely entered into us but have not been led back to the higher elements, and those who have been guided, through our activity, back to their earlier condition. Those who have not been transformed have gained nothing by wandering from the outer world into the human world; but the others, who were transformed through human activity, are able to return to their original sphere after the human being's death. During earthly life, human beings build a crossroad for elementals. After having passed through life in the spiritual worlds and returning through the gate of birth into a subsequent incarnation, a person is accompanied into physical existence by all the elemental beings who were not released. Those who have been released no longer accompany the person, but return to their original element.

Thus we see how human beings have the capacity in the course of their development, and in the way they establish a relationship to external nature, to free the elemental beings necessary for the creation of our Earth, or to bind them even more to the Earth than they were previously. What happens when someone looks at a material object and fathoms its true nature so that the elemental being is released? Spiritually, the course taken is the reverse of what occurred before. Whereas smoke originally arose from fire, the person now spiritually creates fire from smoke. At death, the fire is released. Now, in the light of this primeval, divine spiritual science, we can understand the profound spiritual meaning of ancient rituals of sacrifice. Imagine a priest at the sacrificial altar in those ancient times when religion was based on true knowledge of spiritual laws. Imagine a priest kindling the flame, the smoke rising and actually becoming a sacrifice in that it is borne upward with prayers.

What really happened in such sacrifices? The priest stood at the altar where the smoke was produced. There, where the solid emerged from the warmth, a spirit was enchanted, and, because a human being accompanied the process with prayers, the spirit was taken into the person and was released again when the human being died and entered into the higher world. What did the disciples of the ancient wisdom say to those who were to understand such a ritual? They explained that if you look at the external world so that your spiritual activity does not remain attached to the smoke, but rises spiritually to the fire element, then after death you free the enchanted spirit that dwells in the smoke. Those who had gained an understanding of the process would reply, "If the spirit that dwells in the smoke remains unchanged, it will have to accompany me in a next incarnation; after death it cannot return to the spiritual world. But if I have released it, if I have led it back to the fire, after my death it will rise into worlds of spirit and no longer need to return to Earth at my birth."

Here we have explained a part of the profound passage from the Bhagavad Gita spoken of in my last lecture. There is no mention of the human I. The text refers, rather, to nature spirits, to elemental beings that enter into us from the outer world. Therefore it says:

Behold the fire, behold the smoke. What we turn into fire through our spiritual activity are spirits that we liberate at our death. What we leave untransformed in the smoke remains connected with us after death and must be born when we are reborn.

Here the destiny of elemental spirits is described. Through wisdom, which we develop within ourselves, we continually liberate elemental beings when we die; but through lack of wisdom, through materialistic attachment to the world of the senses, we bind elemental spirits to us and force them into this world to be reborn with us over and over again.

These elemental beings are not connected only with fire. They are emissaries of higher divine spiritual beings and are involved in everything occurring in the external perceptible world. The interplay of forces that bring about day and night, for example, could not have arisen unless hosts of elemental beings had been active in rotating the planets in the universe in the appropriate manner. Everything that happens is affected by hosts of lower and higher beings of the spiritual hierarchies. We have been speaking of the lowest order—of the messengers. Such elemental beings live in the processes that transform night into day and day into night. Again, we are closely connected with these beings of the elemental world whose function it is to bring about day and night. When one is apathetic and lazy, and lets oneself go, the human being affects those elemental beings quite differently than one does when one is creative, active, diligent, and productive. When a person is lazy, he or she becomes united with certain kinds of elemental beings and this also happens when he or she is active, but in a most peculiar way. The elemental beings of the second class, whose lives unfold during the day and who, so to speak, tumble through the day, are in their higher element. But just as fire elementals of the first class are bound to air, water, and earth, so are certain elementals bound to darkness. Day could not be separated from night unless elementals were imprisoned in night. Human beings can enjoy daylight thanks to divine spiritual beings who have driven forth elementals and have chained them to night. These elementals continually flow into a person who is lazy, but they are left as they are. Through one's idleness one leaves unchanged those elemental beings who are chained to darkness at night. The elemental beings who enter into us when we are active and industrious are led back into the day. We thus continually release elementals of the second class.

Throughout the whole of our lives we carry elemental beings in us who have entered us during periods of idleness and during periods of industry. As we go through the gates of death, those beings whom we have led back to the day can enter the spiritual world. Beings, whom we have left in the night as a result of our apathy, remain chained to us and return with us at our next incarnation. What we allow to flow into us through the mere illusion of the senses by means of outward elemental beings, what we through laziness and apathy allow to flow into us from the night beings, all that will be reborn with us in our next incarnation. This brings us to the second point in the passage from the Bhagavad Gita. Again, it is not the human I that is referred to in the following words but a type of elemental being: "Behold day and night. What you redeem, what you transform from a being of night into a being of day, enters into higher worlds when you die. What you take with you as a being of the night, you condemn to accompany you in a succeeding incarnation."

The implications of all this must by now be clear. That is, the same holds true of more encompassing natural phenomena, such as the twenty-eight-day rhythm that brings about the waxing and waning Moon. Hosts of elemental beings had to be active to bring the Moon into movement so that the Moon rhythm and everything connected with it might arise visibly for us on Earth. This again meant that certain of those elementals had to be enchanted, condemned, and imprisoned by higher beings. Supersensible cognition always notices that during the time of a waxing Moon, spiritual beings of a lower realm rise into a higher. But then, for order to prevail, other spiritual elemental beings must then be enchanted into lower realms. These elementals of the third kind are also connected with humanity. Human beings, who are bright and cheerful, who are satisfied with life and of a cheerful disposition because of their understanding of the world, are continually liberating beings who are chained because of the waning Moon. These beings enter into such people, but are continually released because of their serene soul disposition, inner contentment, and harmonious view of life. Beings who enter into us when we are sullen, peevish, completely discontented, depressed, and pessimistic remain in the condition of enchantment in which they were at the time of the waning Moon. There are human beings who, through the fact that they have achieved a harmonious feeling about the world and a cheerful disposition, work, in a wonderfully liberating way, on large numbers of elementals, who come into being in the way described. The human being, through a harmonious perception of the world, through inner contentment with the world, frees spiritual elemental beings. Through moroseness, ill humor, and discontentment, a person imprisons elemental beings who could be freed through serenity.

Thus, we see that one's mood is not only of significance for oneself, but a cheerful or a morose attitude can bring about forces of liberation or of imprisonment that stream out from one's being. The effects of a person's moods stream out in all directions into the spiritual world. Here we have the third point in the important teaching of the Bhagavad Gita: "Behold the one, who, through mood of soul, releases during the time of the waxing Moon, spirits, which, when the person passes through the gateway of death, then return to higher worlds."

If, through ill humor and hypochondria, a person leaves the spirits that had to be called into oneself for the order of the moon to be fulfilled, then these spirits remain bound to that person and must be born with him or her when the person enters a new existence. Thus we have a third kind of elemental spirits, which either are freed at the time of a person's death and return to their homeland, or which must enter this world again with the human being.

There is, finally, a fourth kind of elemental being. These activate the course of the Sun during the year and participate in bringing about the wakening, fruitful activity of the Sun during the summer so that the ripening that occurs from spring to autumn may happen. As a result, during the winter period, certain spirits must be chained, enchanted. Here, too, the human being works as we have described for the other degrees of spiritual beings of the elemental realm. Consider a person who says at the approach of winter, "The nights are growing longer; the days, shorter. We are approaching a time of year when the Sun withdraws its ripening forces from the Earth. Outwardly, the Earth is dying, but as this process takes place, I feel all the more the need to awaken spiritually. I must now, ever more and more, receive the spirit into myself." Consider a person who, with the approach of Christmas carries an ever greater feeling of devotion in his or her heart, one who understands the true meaning of this festival; namely, that, when the outer perceptible world is most fully in death's grasp, the spirit must be all the more alive. Let us assume such a person lives through the winter season and at Easter realizes that the time of sleep for the spirit is connected with the enlivening processes in nature. He or she then experiences the Easter festival with understanding. Such a person does not merely possess an external religiosity but a religious understanding of the processes in nature, and of the spirit that dwells in nature. By means of this kind of devotion such a person is able to liberate elementals of the fourth class that continually stream in and out of the human being and are connected with the course of the Sun. A person not endowed with this kind of devotion, one who denies or does not perceive the spirit and is caught up by our materialistic chaos, is entered by elementals of the fourth class who stream into the person, remaining as they are. At one's death these elementals are either released, or chained so that they must reappear in the world at one's rebirth. Those who connect themselves to the winter spirits without transforming them into summer spirits—that is, without redeeming them through their spiritual activity—condemn them to be reborn with them. If the opposite is the case, the winter spirits will not have to return with them.

Behold the fire and the smoke! If you so connect yourself with the outer world that your soul-spiritual activity is akin to the process that brings about fire and smoke—if you spiritualize the things around you through your knowledge and your feeling—then you assist spiritual elemental beings to ascend again. If you connect yourself with the smoke, you condemn them to rebirth. If you connect yourself with the day, you liberate the corresponding spirits of the day.

Behold the light, behold the day, the waxing Moon, the summer season of the year! If you are active in such a way that elementals are led back to the light, the day, the waxing Moon, and the summer season of the year, you free those elemental beings whom you need so much; at your death they rise into the spiritual world. If you connect yourself with the smoke, staring at solid matter, or if you connect yourself to the night through apathy, to the spirits of the waning Moon because of your ill humor, and to the spirits who are chained in the winter through godlessness or lack of spirituality, then you condemn elemental beings to reincarnate with you.

Now we begin to understand what is really meant by this passage of the Bhagavad Gita. Whoever thinks it refers to human beings does not understand it. But whoever knows that all human life is a continual interplay between human beings and the spiritual beings that live around them, that these four groups of elemental beings are enchanted and need to be liberated, recognizes their ascension or their need to reincarnate. The mystery regarding the lowest rung of hierarchical beings has been preserved for us in this passage of the Bhagavad Gita. When one has to draw forth from primeval wisdom what is proclaimed in ancient religious documents, one begins to realize their true greatness and how wrong it is to take them superficially and thereby avoid plumbing their depths. One gains a right relation to them only when one says that no wisdom is too exalted to fathom what is contained there. Then the ancient records become permeated by the magic of devoted feelings. Only then do they become what they truly are: ennobling and purifying means for human development. Still, they point to fathomless abysses of human wisdom. Only when that which springs from the occult schools and mysteries begins to stream from human beings outward to humanity at large, only then will the reflections of primeval wisdom (and they are but reflections) be seen in their true greatness and appear in their true light.

By means of a comparatively difficult example, we have tonight tried to show primeval wisdom's understanding of the interplay that exists between human beings and the beings that surround and stream in and out of them. We have also tried to show something of what primeval wisdom knew of the interplay that arises between the spiritual world and the inner world as a result of human deeds. The riddle of humanity becomes important for us when we begin to realize that we influence the whole cosmos in all we do, even down to our moods—that our little world is of infinitely far-reaching importance for all that comes into being in the macrocosmos. A heightened feeling of responsibility is the finest and most important fruit that can be gained from spiritual science. It teaches us to grasp life in the truest sense and to take it so earnestly that this life which we cast upon the stream of evolution may be meaningful.

3. Planetary Evolution:
Saturn and Sun Stages of Evolution
and the Spirits of Personality

APRIL 13, 1909, *Morning*

AT THE END OF THE PREVIOUS LECTURE, about the lowest realm of the spiritual hierarchies, questions arose in your minds. This is quite natural. According to contemporary thinking, much of what was said must seem at first problematic and incomprehensible. Light will be shed on several points during the following lectures. To give you general guidelines to this way of thinking, however, one thing should be made clear at this point.

A person today might ask: If I do, in fact, release an enchanted being from a stone through my thinking, what remains in the stone? Does the being remain in the stone? What has happened to the stone? Suppose a second person comes along and goes through the same process. What results? Such questions can easily arise. Some will be dealt with in the course of these lectures, but it should be borne in mind that earthly thinking cannot grasp such matters. Everything on Earth is veiled and cloaked in *maya*,[1] and reality is other than it appears to our thinking. We need not blame the things themselves that such questions remain unanswered. The questions are wrongly put.

In time, we shall acquire a vantage point from which to put the questions correctly. That is, as we gain insight into situations not as deeply shrouded in illusion, matters will be seen to be radically different. On Earth, things are jumbled together, and, as a result, our thinking is continually led astray. Purer concepts can be gained by looking back into ancient times.

---

1. Literally that which can be measured. In philosophy, that which is subject to change by decay and differentiation; thus termed the illusory world, illusion.

Just as a human being passes from one incarnation to another, from one metamorphosis to another, so all the beings of the universe, small or great, go through re-embodiments. The Earth, a planetary being, also passes through incarnations. In the beginning of its existence, our Earth did not appear in its present form. Other states preceded it. This subject has often been dealt with in our circles.[2] Just as a human being in his or her present existence is a reincarnation of a previous life, so the Earth, too, represents a re-embodiment of an ancient planet. We call that former planetary incarnation *Moon,* but we do not mean our present Moon, which is only a part, a residue of the ancient Moon. By Moon, we mean a former state of the Earth that existed in the past and then, just as a human being passes through a spiritual state after death, went through the spiritual state called *pralaya.*[3] Just as a human being reincarnates, so this lunar planet reincarnated as Earth. Further, what we have characterized as this lunar planetary state is, in fact, the reincarnation of a still earlier state, which we call *Sun.* This Sun is not the present Sun but quite a different planetary state; it is the first reincarnation of the primeval planet we call *Saturn.* This is what we look back to when speaking of the incarnations of our Earth. Thus, we have four successive planetary incarnations: Saturn, Sun, Moon, and Earth.

Each planetary state has a special task. What is the task of the Earth? To make human existence possible. All effecting circumstances on Earth are such that, through them, human beings can become I-beings. This was not the situation during previous planetary states. Humanity only became human, in the present sense of the word, on Earth. Earlier planetary states of the Earth had similar objectives. Beings who are now above humanity reached their human state on earlier planets. From my book, *Christianity as Mystical Fact,* you may recall that an Egyptian sage once pointed out to Solon, the Greek, a remarkable intimation of an important truth that was

---

2. See, mainly, *An Outline of Occult Science* (Hudson, NY: Anthroposophic Press, 1972), also *Theosophy of the Rosicrucian* (London: Rudolf Steiner Press, 1966) and *At the Gates of Spiritual Science* (Hudson, NY: Anthroposophic Press, 1986).
3. Literally, "dissolution," indicating a period of rest.

known in the Mysteries.[4] The sage told Solon that the gods had once been human beings. In ancient times, a pupil of the Mysteries had to accept the truth that the gods who dwell in exalted regions had not always been gods, but had once been human beings, had risen from the human state to their present exalted heights. Of course, some students of the Mysteries immediately inferred the perilous "truth" that at some time in the future human beings would also become gods. This "truth" was viewed as dangerous because it absolutely required that one add to the former truth the fact that human beings can become a god only when they are ripe for that condition. If human beings imagine that they can find the god within, at any moment, before they have reached the necessary stage of maturity, they do not become gods but merely fools. Two paths are therefore open to humanity. Either a person can live patiently in anticipation of what Dionysius the Areopagite calls deification [*theosis*], or one can imagine oneself prematurely already a god. The first path leads to a true deification; the second, to folly and madness.

In our time, misunderstandings of the sayings of the ancients abound because we no longer differentiate between various degrees of divine spiritual beings. The Egyptian sage who spoke of the gods did not mean simply one degree of gods but whole sequences of divine spiritual beings. Dionysius the Areopagite and the wise sages of the East always differentiated between various degrees of divine spiritual beings. It matters little whether we speak of Angels or Dhyan-Chohans.[5] Those who grasp the unity of cosmic wisdom are well aware that they are merely different names for the same beings. But one must differentiate within this realm.

In Christian esotericism, the invisible beings immediately above humanity are called Angels, *Angeloi*, or messengers of the divine spiritual world. The beings one stage higher—that is, two ranks above humanity—are called Archangels, *Archangeloi*, or Spirits of

4. See *The Spiritual Guidance of the Individual and Humanity*, (Hudson, NY: Anthroposophic Press, 1992), lecture 2. Also, Plato's *Timaeus*.
5. Collective hosts of spiritual beings; see *The Secret Doctrine*.

Fire. Beings who, when they have accomplished their normal development, are at a still higher stage are called Spirits of Personality, Primeval Beginnings, or *Archai*.

To begin with, then, we have three ranks of beings above humanity. All of these were once human and passed through a human stage. Beings who are Angels today, when seen from the aspect of universal time, passed through their human stage relatively recently. They were human on the Moon. Just as we, as human beings, can inhabit the Earth because of the conditions here, so the Angels could pass through their human stage on the Moon. The Archangels went through their human evolution on the Sun. The Spirits of Personality (Archai or Primeval Beginnings) went through their human evolution on ancient Saturn. Such beings rose beyond humanity by degrees. Today they are higher beings at higher stages of the hierarchy than human beings.

Thus, as we begin to enumerate the stages of the cosmic realms from a spiritual aspect, we can simply say that, first, we have the visible, earthly kingdoms—the mineral, plant, animal, and human realms—and then, above these, the invisible realms of the Angels, Archangels, and Archai. In the course of the spiritual ascent of these beings, as they develop from human beings to gods—or, more exactly, to messengers of the gods—as they ascend in spiritual existence, the conditions of the planets they lived on also change. If we look back to ancient Saturn when the Archai were at the human stage, we find that conditions were totally different from those of Earth.

Yesterday, we said that on our Earth we distinguish four elements: earth, water, air, and fire or warmth. The first three elements were not present on ancient Saturn. Only fire or warmth existed on Saturn. A modern materialistic philosopher would say that we can become aware of heat only through outer objects—warm, solid bodies, warm water—and that heat cannot exist by itself. The materialistic philosopher believes that. But it is not true. If we could have observed ancient Saturn with our present senses, what would have been presented to us? Let us assume—hypothetically, of course—that you could have flown through universal space at the time of old Saturn. You would not have seen where ancient Saturn was. There was nothing to see. You would only have been aware of heat! Flying through ancient Saturn would have felt rather like flying through a heated oven. There would not have been the slightest breeze. You would not have been able to swim because air and water did not exist. You could not have stood up, because there was no Earth. Your hand could not have touched anything. There was only a huge ball of heat. Ancient Saturn came into existence from the element of warmth or fire. Our Earth's metamorphosis began with a planet of heat, and this shows how correct Heraclitus was when he said, "Everything is derived from fire." Yes, truly, the Earth is only a transmutation of ancient Saturn—everything on Earth arose from fire. Heraclitus knew this truth from the ancient Mysteries. This is indicated when it is said that his book, containing this truth, was dedicated to the Goddess of Ephesus, and that he placed it on her altar there.[6] In other words, Heraclitus acknowledged that he owed this truth to the Mysteries of Ephesus, where the teaching of the primeval fire of Saturn was proclaimed in all its purity.

You will have deduced also that the beings called *Primal Beginnings*, the Archai or Spirits of Personality, passed through their human stage under quite different conditions than we live under today. In bodily constitution, in their blood and bony system, human beings today can assimilate solids, liquids, and gases. The humanity of Saturn, the Spirits of Personality, had to build their whole bodies from warmth and fire. That is exactly what they did. On Saturn they had a body of fire consisting entirely of warmth.

In my previous lecture, I told you that there are two sides to warmth. One we feel inwardly. We feel warm or cold without contacting solids in the outer world. We can also become aware of outer warmth when, for example, we take hold of a heated object.

---

6. For Heraclitus, see Rudolf Steiner, *Christianity as Mystical Fact* (new edition forthcoming 1997 from Anthroposophic Press) and *Riddles of Philosophy* (Spring Valley, NY: Anthroposophic Press, 1973). Also, Philip E. Wheelwright, *Heraclitus*, and Sri Aurobindo, *Heraclitus*.

The distinctive aspect of Saturn's development lies in the fact that warmth—which, at the beginning of the Saturn state, was experienced only inwardly—gradually and then increasingly became outwardly perceptible. This continued until the end of the Saturn period. If you had traveled through Saturn during the early phase, you would not have been aware of any outer warmth touching your skin, but you would have felt inwardly warm; you would have sensed a comfortable feeling of inner warmth. Something of what we call today an inner warmth of soul would have been your experience as you traveled through Saturn during its early phase of evolution. You can imagine the experience you would have had on Saturn if you consider the following.

You know there is a difference between looking at a red surface and looking at a blue surface. Red, when you look at it, produces a feeling of warmth, and blue, a feeling of coldness. Imagine the feelings released in the soul by the impression of something red. At the beginning of the Saturn state, you would not have had these feelings. Instead you would have felt somehow comfortably warm, as when today you look at something red. At the end of the Saturn period you would have sensed not only this pleasant inner warmth, but also something resembling outer warmth coming toward you. Inner warmth would have transformed itself gradually into perception of outer warmth. The evolution of Saturn goes from an inner soul warmth to an outwardly perceptible warmth, or fire. One might say that, just as the child grows to adulthood and experiences various stages, so the Spirits of Personality also developed on ancient Saturn. Initially, they felt comfortably warm inwardly, and then they gradually became aware of how this warmth was being externalized—indeed, one could even say, embodied. But what happened then?

You must imagine first the inner warming process of the globe of Saturn.[7] This enabled the Spirits of Personality (Archai) to embody.

---

7. *Globe*: in theosophical terminology what anthroposophy calls the "planetary stages" were referred to as "globes."

During their incarnation, outer warmth gradually formed. Had you journeyed through Saturn during the later phases of its development, you could have distinguished between warmer and colder outer areas. However, if you had made a drawing of these self-contained bodies of warmth, you would have produced a picture in which, at the surface of Saturn, you would have found clusters of "warmth-eggs" forming an outer crust. From outside, the surface resembled a blackberry or raspberry.

What were these "eggs?" They were the bodies of the Archai, the Spirits of Personality, and through their inner warmth the Spirits of Personality produced the outer warmth of these Saturn "eggs." It could be said of this state that, as the spirits brooded over the warmth, they really brought forth the first bodies of fire. From cosmic space inward, the first bodies of fire coagulated. If we may use the expression, the external "warmth-eggs" coagulated outwardly in space-warmth. On ancient Saturn, the Spirits of Personality, the Archai, who were also called Asuras, were incarnated in these bodies of fire. The state of Saturn consisted only of this element of fire.

The Spirits of Personality during the evolutionary phase of Saturn could transform outer warmth into inner warmth once again. The process was not fixed in any way. It was inwardly mobile. Indeed, the Spirits of Personality, the Archai, were continually producing "warmth-eggs" and letting them dissolve again. To picture this process more exactly, imagine that you traveled for some time through these regions. You would have noticed that there were times on Saturn when no outer warmth was perceptible, only a comfortable feeling of inner warmth. This would have been followed by periods when the "warmth-eggs" appeared. You would have become aware of a kind of breathing on ancient Saturn, a breathing of fire. You would have thought, "I am within ancient Saturn and feel as if all outer warmth has become inward, as if everything were only a feeling of inner well-being." Then you would have said, "Now Saturn has breathed in the warmth." On another occasion, you would have come across the many "warmth-eggs," and you would have said, "Now Saturn has breathed out its inner warmth and is all external fire."

The Holy Rishis conveyed this image to their pupils who were transported back spiritually to the time of ancient Saturn, and caused to experience how the whole planet accomplished something similar to our outbreathing and inbreathing. The Rishis showed their pupils that when the fire flowed out, it produced countless bodies of warmth, and that when the fire was drawn in, it became the inner I-nature of the Spirits of Personality. Therefore, the life of the planet was compared to a breathing-out and a breathing-in. But, in the Saturn state, there was only a fire-breathing. Air was not yet present.

Let us now imagine that all of these Spirits of Personality on Saturn would have continued to breathe fire in and out. They would then have gone through their regular Saturn stage of development. The result would have been that, after a certain period, everything would have been gathered up again into inner warmth. The external fire planet would have disappeared, would have been taken up once more into the spiritual world. This could have occurred, but in that case, there would have been no Sun, Moon, and Earth states, because everything breathed out would have been gathered up into inner warmth again and returned to the spiritual world.

A trivial expression can easily characterize what actually happened. Certain Spirits of Personality preferred to take back only a portion of the warmth breathed out. Something continually remained behind so that, when there was a breathing-in, all the Saturn "eggs" did not disappear. As a result, a duality arose on Saturn: inner warmth, and then outer warmth, were incorporated in the "eggs." Not everything was taken back again. The Spirits of Personality left a part of the exhaled warmth to take care of itself, so to speak. They left it outside. Why did they do that? They had to, because otherwise they would never have reached their human stage on Saturn.

What does it mean to become a human being? It means to attain I-consciousness. But you cannot achieve this unless you can distinguish yourself from your surroundings. Only because of this are you an I. The bouquet of flowers is there, I am here; I differentiate myself as I from the objects around me. Had the Spirits of Personality not left something that offered outside resistance, they would have allowed their I to stream out eternally. They came to "I-ness" or self-consciousness because something was outside them; they differentiated themselves from the warmth element that had been made objective. They pushed a part of the Saturn beings outside, into a condition of external warmth, and said to themselves, "I must allow something to stream out of myself and leave it there so I can differentiate myself from it, and kindle my I-consciousness by means of this external part." Thus, they created a realm next to their own; and, at the same time, they produced a reflection of their inner life in the external. Consequently, when the Saturn phase of existence came to an end, the Spirits of Personality could not let the planet disappear. Had they breathed in all the fire, it would have disappeared, but they were not in a position to breathe in what they had previously externalized. They could not intervene in the sphere that had offered them the possibility of self-consciousness.

A condition of *pralaya* could not have arisen for Saturn only through the Spirits of Personality. Higher beings had to intervene to dissolve Saturn again and cause a state of transition, of disappearance, of sleep, or *pralaya*. Higher spirits, the Thrones, stepped in and dissolved everything that had existed. Thus, as the life of Saturn drew to a close, the Spirits of Personality had attained self-consciousness and absorbed a part of the warmth again. They had developed a consciousness of self at their center, and left behind a lower realm. The Thrones now dissolved what the Spirits of Personality had left behind. Saturn then entered into a kind of planetary night. This was followed by a planetary dawn when everything was to awaken again by means of laws that we shall get to know later. Had ancient Saturn disappeared through a complete breathing-in of the warmth, the whole of Saturn existence would have been gathered up into the spiritual world. In that case, an awakening simply could not have occurred.

Now, the Thrones could dissolve only temporarily what the Spirits of Personality had externalized as "eggs." These had to be given over to a lower stage of existence for further development. As a result, a planetary dawn ensued and the second metamorphosis of Saturn, the Sun state, arose. What came to life then? The Spirits of Personality, who had attained self-consciousness and no longer needed to go through what they had previously experienced, came over from ancient Saturn after the planetary sleep. The "warmth-eggs," which they had exhaled, now differentiated themselves again from the general mass. The Spirits of Personality were now bound, so to speak, to what they had previously left behind. Had they been able to gather everything into the spiritual world, they would not have been bound to the Sun existence—they would not have had to descend. But they had to do so, because they had left a part of their own being behind. They had to concern themselves with it. Indeed, it drew them down into a new planetary existence.

That was the destiny of Saturn: it was world karma, cosmic karma. Because the Spirits of Personality had not taken everything into themselves on ancient Saturn, they prepared the karma that obliged them to return. Down below, they found as a heritage of ancient Saturn what they themselves had brought about. What happened as the Spirits of Personality took up the karma they had created? I characterized these results yesterday in general terms when I explained that warmth divided itself into light and smoke. On the one hand, there arose out of the "warmth-eggs" on the reborn Saturn, a new planet, composed of gas, air, or smoke. On the other hand, there arose light, which appeared because warmth returned to higher conditions. So, on transformed Saturn, inwardly we have smoke, gas, and air, and, on the other hand, we have *light*.

Had you now traveled through the universe and arrived at the place of the old Sun, you would have been aware, from afar, of the light that had formed there because there was smoke behind it. You would not have seen the light, but a shining globe, just as you would have perceived a globe of heat on Saturn. You would have encountered a shining ball. And, had you penetrated beneath the surface of this ball, you would have experienced not only warmth but also winds, air, and gases, blowing in every direction. The globe of heat had transformed itself into a globe of light. *A Sun had come into being.*

We are quite justified in calling it a *Sun*. The orbs that are Suns today are passing through the same process. Inwardly, they are streaming masses of gas, and, on the other hand, they cause the gas to turn into light, and they ray forth light into the universe. In other words, light appeared for the first time during the course of our planet's transformations.

In the warmth of ancient Saturn, the Spirits of Personality, the Archai, were able to become human. In the light that streamed from the Sun, the beings of the spiritual hierarchies called Archangels, or Archangeloi, could attain their humanhood. If you had looked at the Sun, not as human beings do today but with clairvoyant faculties, you would have beheld not only a shining radiance but also the deeds of the Archangels streaming toward you in the light!

In the process, however, the Archangels also had to take something. The old Spirits of Personality still found pure fire on Saturn. On the planet they now had to inhabit, the Archangels, who could become human only on the Sun, found a gas-like, smoky state. What did they have to do to gain a firm foothold on the Sun and make their abode there? They formed their souls—the inward part of themselves—out of the light and incorporated it into an outer body of gas. Just as today you have a body and a soul, so the Archangels, who attained their human condition on the Sun, consisted of an inner being who could ray out light and an outer body of gas or air. Just as today the human body is made up of earth, water, air, and fire, so the Archangels consisted of air and, inwardly, light. They had, of course, brought over the fire element with them, for it was precisely this that they developed into smoke and light.

Thus, these Archangels also contained fire. Their total organization consisted of light, smoke, and fire. You would have encountered the Archangels in bodies woven of gas, fire, and light. The light enabled them to have an outer existence, and they streamed a shining force into the universe. Through the fire, they had an inner life and experienced the well-being of warmth. Because they dwelt in a gaseous body, they were able to live on the Sun planet as such. They could now differentiate their own gaseous body from the general substance on the old Sun. They collided with this general substance, and this kindled a kind of consciousness of self. But this consciousness could be developed into higher stages only because the Archangels preferred to remain connected, so to speak, to their gaseous, smokelike bodies or at least to remain in the Sun substance. For, in the alternating conditions on the old Sun, the Archangels could have absorbed all of the smoke, all of the gas of their surroundings into themselves.

We now have a real breathing process on the Sun! You would have experienced the currents of gas on the old Sun as a breathing process. You would have found conditions of absolute stillness, and you would have said, "Now the Archangels have inhaled all of the gas." But then the Archangels would begin to exhale again. Inner currents would begin to flow, and, at the same time, light would appear. These were the alternating conditions on the Sun. The Archangels inhaled all the gas. Stillness and darkness, the night of the Sun, followed. The Archangels exhaled, and the Sun became filled with streams of smoke and shone forth. The Sun's day had begun. The whole of the Sun's body went through a real breathing process. During exhalation—that is, the Sun's day—the surrounding world became illuminated; during inhalation—the Sun's night—everything became dark.

Here you have the difference between the old Sun and the present Sun. Our present Sun is always shining, and darkness is produced only when an object is placed in front of the light. Such was not the case on the old Sun. It had the power to produce alternating conditions of light and darkness that consisted of a breathing-out and a breathing-in. Let us imagine very vividly what happened outwardly.

Take the condition of exhalation, that is, when the light rays out and, at the same time, the Sun fills itself with smoke. These forms of smoke, these currents of smoke, have a regular configuration. At each exhalation, a sum of regular forms is imprinted upon the Sun's substance. What had previously been mere egg-shaped warmth bodies was transformed into various regular forms. Quite remarkable smoke forms containing an inner life and regularity now arose. It was as if the "eggs" had hatched. This might be compared to a process of densification. Much as the chicken comes out of the egg, so had the "warmth eggs" been split asunder; regular smoke forms emerged, which were the Archangels' densest bodies. These inhabited the Sun in bodies of smoke, gas, and air, and thus moved about as human beings. This gives us the spiritual idea of a fixed star, a universal Sun that produces the alternation of day and night by virtue of its own inherent power. Light and darkness came about through breathing out and breathing in, because at that time the old Sun was a kind of fixed star. Everything that of itself shines forth into our universal space sends the life of spiritual messengers, the Archangels, out with the light.

What did the original Archai or Primal Beginnings, the Spirits of Personality, accomplish through their own development? They made it possible for a Sun to appear. If it were not for them, there would have been only a Saturn stage in evolution. Because the Archai left external "warmth-eggs" on Saturn, the metamorphosis into a Sun could be achieved. On the Sun, the Archangels had the opportunity to pass through the human stage. They became the heralds of the cosmos who proclaimed that the Primal Beginnings—the Spirits of Personality—had preceded them: "As messengers of the universe, we proclaim in radiating light the former existence of the warmth-permeated ancient Saturn. We are the messengers, the heralds of the Archai." *Angeloi* means messengers, *Archai* means beginnings. The Archangels are, in fact, the messengers of the accomplishments of the Primal Beginnings, or Archai, in ancient times. That is why they are called the *Angels of the Beginnings*, *Archai*, and *Angeloi*, which gave rise to the English word *Arch-Angels*. These Arch-messengers achieved their humanhood on the Sun.

4. The Work of the Spiritual Hierarchies and the Zodiac

APRIL 13, 1909, *Evening*

WHEN WE CONSIDER, as we did this morning, the conditions on ancient Saturn that are more transparent and less shrouded in illusion or maya, we can better understand the redemption or further imprisonment of those beings we encountered yesterday in relation to the profoundly significant passage in the divine Gita. You will recall that Saturn's development would have come to an end and everything would have been reabsorbed into the spiritual world if the Spirits of Personality had completely drawn into themselves the egg-shaped heat bodies and left nothing behind on ancient Saturn. Yet, as I pointed out, this did not happen. The Spirits of Personality compressed more intensively than they should have, and left their seal on all of Saturn. They did not take everything back into themselves—indeed, they left behind outwardly perceptible warmth bodies.

What was the power working in the Spirits of Personality on ancient Saturn? It was the force we know today as the human power of *thinking*. The Spirits of Personality did nothing on ancient Saturn but exercise their power of thought. The "warmth-eggs"[1] were formed because they were able to call forth the idea of these "eggs." The power of conceptual thought in the Spirits of Personality was thus far greater than in human beings today. For what kind of power does the conceptual capacity of contemporary humanity have? If we have an idea or thought today, we create a form only in the astral world; it goes no further. That is why the form cannot be

---

1. See previous lecture.

verified in an outer physical way. But, on ancient Saturn, the Spirits of Personality were mighty magicians. They formed and left behind the "warmth-eggs" of Saturn through the power of their thinking. It was the power of the Spirits of Personality that caused the residue of ancient Saturn to be left behind, and this residue reappeared repeatedly, even during the solar phase of evolution. Since what was formed into "eggs" was made out of the surroundings of Saturn ("eggs" that were then enchanted and chained to a further existence), we can now grasp the fact that an entity or being, at the human stage, creates forms from its surroundings.

On this basis—the conditions are not yet so complicated—we can now present comprehensively what was said yesterday. Thus we can say: Consider the Saturn fire; consider what was repeatedly spiritualized from the ancient Saturn fire and then repeatedly retracted as inner soul fire, warm comfortableness, and then ascended to higher realms. In other words, consider how what was perceptible external warmth, that is, what densified into external warmth, had to be reborn so that it could reappear on the Sun.

Let us now look at the rest of what was described this morning. The beings of the spiritual hierarchies, whom we call Archangels (Archangeloi or Fire Spirits), achieved their human stage on the old Sun. On the one hand, the warmth element densified itself to smoke or gas so that the Sun was a gaseous globe; on the other hand, it burned the gas so that light streamed out into universal space. The Archangels or Fire Spirits, who lived in the streaming light, absorbed and then streamed out light, and lived in this process. I mentioned before that, if you could have journeyed through the universe, you would have beheld the old Sun shining toward you from a great distance. In the inner part of the old Sun, you would have perceived various currents of gas permeating the whole body of the planet like a breathing process. Let us now once more hold this ancient Saturn and ancient Sun before our souls. We have seen that life and activity ruled in both of these planetary bodies. On old Saturn, there was a forming and dissolving of egg-shaped structures. There were also residues left behind. Had one observed this internal activity on ancient Saturn, one would have said that Saturn was really a single living being. It really is as though it were a fully living being. It was alive, and lived in and of itself, producing forms continuously out of its own life. This was even more so on the old Sun. We meet this planet as a unit with conditions alternating between the Sun's day and the Sun's night, a breathing in and out of light. If one could have observed it, everything would have given the impression of a universal body permeated with life, not of something dead.

Everything that lives, however—that is, permeated with activity and thus inwardly lively and constantly moving—owes its motion to the spiritual beings who direct and guide it. We mentioned that the Spirits of Personality produced the egg-forms through their power of thought, thus implying that there must have been a substance available out of which the "eggs" could be shaped. But the Spirits of Personality, the Archai, were unable to create the substance. We should bear in mind that something must exist to furnish the substance—that is, the undifferentiated warmth, the fire itself. The Spirits of Personality could only shape the warmth. The substance had to be provided from elsewhere. We must ask: What conceived the whole realm of Saturn, especially the Spirits of Personality? And what was the source of the warmth substance, or fire element? It came from much higher spiritual beings who had achieved their human stage so far back in the past that they were already well beyond this stage on ancient Saturn. To form a clear image of the exalted beings who were necessary for the warmth-fire element on ancient Saturn, we must consider, by way of comparison, how the human being evolved, for human beings will also eventually become divine beings.

We know, and have often mentioned, that human beings today consist of four members or bodies—physical, etheric, astral, and I. This is the key to all spiritual science. We also know about humanity's future evolution. We know how the I, working from within, gradually transforms the astral body so that the I finally gains complete mastery over it. We know, too, that, when the astral body has been thus transformed, we say that it contains *Spirit Self* or *Manas*. An astral body ruled by the I is Spirit Self or Manas. The same applies to the ether body. When the I works even more powerfully still, it can overcome the opposing forces of the ether body. The transformed ether body then becomes the *Life Spirit* or *Buddhi*. Finally, when the I gains mastery over the physical body—when the most powerfully opposing forces of the physical body are also overcome—the human being bears within it the *Spirit Human* (*Spiritual Body*) or *Atman*.[2] In transforming one's physical body into Atman or Spiritual Body, one thus becomes sevenfold. Outwardly, the physical body appears as a physical body, but inwardly it is completely controlled and permeated by the I. At this stage, the physical body is both physical body *and* Atman. The ether body is both ether body *and* Life Spirit, or Buddhi, and the astral body is both astral body *and* Spirit Self, or Manas. The I has now become ruler over all of the other members.

Thus, out of its own forces, humanity evolves to higher stages of development. People strive toward their own deification, as the friend and pupil of St. Paul, Dionysius the Areopagite, called it.[3] But this is not the end of human development. Once human beings have reached the stage of complete mastery of the physical body, still higher stages of development await them. The process continues higher and higher. We can look up to sublime beings who, dwelling in exalted spiritual heights, become ever mightier. How do such beings become greater? At first, they need something, require something from the world. Later, they develop so that they can give something. *The fundamental spirit and purpose of development is that one proceeds from taking to giving.* We can find an analogy in human development between birth and death. Children are helpless and must accept help from individuals in their surroundings. But, gradually, they outgrow this helplessness and become helpers in their own circle. The same is true of the grand span of human development in the universe.

---

2. *Manas, Buddhi,* and *Atman* are the fifth, sixth, and seventh of the seven members of the self. See Rudolf Steiner, *Theosophy: An Introduction to the Spiritual Processes in Human Life and in the Cosmos* (Hudson, NY: Anthroposophic Press, 1994).
3. *Theosis,* in the teachings of the Eastern Church.

Humanity was already present in its earliest physical form on ancient Saturn, where this being received only the first foundation of human nature. This continued during the old Sun and old Moon periods. On Earth, however, humanity was given the I. And now human beings are gradually preparing themselves so that the I can work within the astral, etheric, and physical bodies. In this way, we become beings who can give cosmically. As beings, we gradually grow into the cosmic and develop the capacity for universal giving; that is, we develop from taking to giving. You have an example of this in the beings we spoke of this morning—the Archangels or Archangeloi. On the old Sun, the Archangels had already developed to where they could produce light in the universe.

The course of development moves from taking to giving. This activity of giving, in fact, can assume considerable proportions. When some beings, for instance, merely give their thoughts, this still denotes a somewhat restricted activity of giving. For whoever gives thoughts—even if one has many thoughts—and goes away leaves the situation as it was before. In a higher sense, nothing visible, nothing substantial has been produced. But then a time came when beings could give more than thoughts or the like. They were able to bestow far more. Indeed, they could give what the Spirits of Personality needed on old Saturn, the substance of warmth-fire. Who were the beings who had reached such an exalted stage of development that they could let the warmth-fire substance on ancient Saturn stream from their own bodies? They were known as the *Thrones*.

We can see how ancient Saturn was formed. From the periphery of the universe, the Thrones gathered into one point. Their activity could be compared on a larger scale to what the silkworm does in a lower realm when it spins silk threads out of its own body. The Thrones spun the warmth substance and sacrificed it on the altar of ancient Saturn. We have seen that on ancient Saturn the Spirits of Personality gave only "personality" or I-consciousness to warmth. But the warmth-fire substance itself streams out of the universal— out of the cosmos—from high, exalted spiritual beings, the Thrones. Now we know the origin of the "eggs" that we find on Saturn. They were spun from the bodies sacrificed by the Thrones. But the coop-eration of the Spirits of Personality and the Thrones alone does not account for the inner liveliness and activity on Saturn. The Spirits of Personality had the power to shape the warmth substance, but they could not achieve this by themselves. This inner liveliness and activ-ity required still other beings—lower than the Thrones but higher than the Spirits of Personality or Archai—to inhabit ancient Saturn. These beings had the task of helping the Spirits of Personality.

We can form an image of the nature of this assistance when we remember that above us we have the Angels or Angeloi, then the Archangels or Archangeloi, then the Primal Beginnings—the Spir-its of Personality or the Archai. These beings belong to the hierarchy immediately above humanity. The Thrones are not the next highest beings after the Spirits of Personality. Between the Spirits of Per-sonality and the Thrones are the intermediary ranks. One of these, the *Exusiai* (as Dionysius the Areopagite called them), or the *Powers* (as they are called in English), is one degree higher than the rank of Spirits of Personality. On ancient Saturn, these Exusiai had the same relationship to the Spirits of Personality as the Angels have to us. One stage higher, we have the beings we call *Mights*, the *Dyna-mis*. On ancient Saturn, the Dynamis had the same relationship to the Spirits of Personality as the Archangels have to us today. Still another stage higher than the Mights or Dynamis are the *Domin-ions*, or *Kyriotetes*. They held the same relationship to the Spirits of Personality on ancient Saturn as the Spirits of Personality hold to us today. Only after we have reached the Dominions or Kyriotetes, do we come to the Thrones.

On ancient Saturn, therefore, we have a progression of beings: the Spirits of Personality, who awaken and bring about I-consciousness; and the Thrones, who stand four stages higher than the Spirits of Personality and give forth the fire-substance. Between them, so that life on Saturn may be ordered and guided, we have, from below upward: the Powers, the Mights, and the Dominions; that is, the Exusiai, Dynamis, and Kyriotetes. These, so to speak, are the inhab-itants of ancient Saturn.

In our characterization of evolution from ancient Saturn to the old Sun, the beings just mentioned evolved one degree higher; the Archangels went through their human stage. Outwardly, warmth is physically densified into gas. The old Sun is a gaseous body, and, whereas ancient Saturn was a dark body of warmth, the Sun begins to shine forth and alternates between Sun-days and Sun-nights. It is particularly important to note this alternation between Sun-days and Sun-nights, because a considerable difference exists between these two conditions in the life on the old Sun. If nothing further had occurred on the old Sun, other than what I have described so far, the Archangels—human beings on the old Sun—would have rushed out with the light rays, spread into the universe during the Sun-days, and would have had to return to the Sun during the Sun-nights. There would have been a breathing-in and a breathing-out of light. There also would have been creatures weaving in the light. But this was not the situation.

Let me characterize the nature of the Archangels quite simply, almost trivially: they enjoyed floating out into the cosmos; they even preferred floating out and merging into the spirit of the universe rather than contracting and drawing themselves back together, which seemed narrowing—an inferior state of existence. It suited them better to dwell in the light ether. But their existence in the light ether could not have extended beyond certain limits if something had not come to their assistance. Had these beings been totally dependent on themselves, they would have had no choice but to return docilely to the Sun during the Sun-nights. Yet this is not what they did. Increasingly, they prolonged their stay in the universe, remaining longer and longer in the spiritual world. What came to their assistance?

Let's imagine a circle that represents the globe of the old Sun. The Archangels sped outward in all directions from the globe—spread out spiritually into the cosmos. Beings from the cosmos came to help the Archangels in their outward movement. Just as, on ancient Saturn, the fire element was previously brought from the cosmos by the Thrones, so now other beings, higher than the Thrones, came to meet the Archangels in their outward movement. These beings helped the Archangels to remain longer in the spiritual world than would otherwise have been possible.

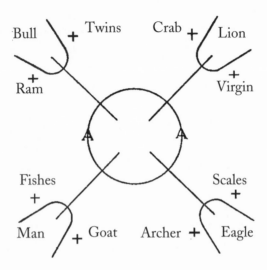

The beings who came to meet and receive the Archangels out of the spiritual expanse of space are called the *Cherubim*. The Cherubim are especially sublime spiritual beings, for they have the capacity to receive the Archangels, so to speak, with open arms. As the Archangels spread out, the Cherubim come to meet them out of the universe. Around the globe of the old Sun, we thus have the approaching hosts of the Cherubim. We could say that, just as the Earth is surrounded by the atmosphere, so was the old Sun surrounded by the realm of the Cherubim for the benefit of the Archangels. The Archangels, as they went forth into cosmic space, beheld their mighty helpers.

How did these great helpers meet them, and what was their appearance? Naturally, this can only be seen by looking with clairvoyant perception into the Akashic Record. These great universal helpers appeared in quite definite etheric forms. Our ancestors, still conscious of these important facts through tradition, represented the Cherubim as strangely winged beasts with variously shaped heads: the winged Lion, the winged Eagle, the winged Bull, and the winged Human. Indeed, at first the Cherubim drew near from four sides. They approached in shapes that could be represented afterward, and thus become known, as the forms of the Cherubim. In schools of the first post-Atlantean initiates, the Cherubim, who approached the old Sun from four sides, were given names from which the names Bull, Lion, Eagle, and Human were derived later on. More will have to be said on this subject, but this evening we shall consider further the four types of Cherubim who went out to meet the Archangels. The Archangels, who dwelled as human on the old Sun, beheld the four different types of Cherubim approaching from four sides as they moved out into cosmic space. Because of this, the Archangels could remain in the spiritual realm around the old Sun longer than otherwise would have been possible.

The influence of the Cherubim on the old Archangels was most enlivening. Further, because the Cherubim drew closer to the old Sun, they made their influence felt in yet another way; influences are never one-sided. Imagine, for example, two people in a room. One wants the room heated quite warmly; the other does not share this preference but, because the other person must also be there, they must both experience the warmth. The same is true of the Cherubim who streamed in from universal space. The Cherubim affected the beings of the ancient Sun who had soared up to the light element, and they knew how to live in the light element in the manner described. But this process could only occur during a Sun-day as light streamed out into cosmic space.

The Cherubim, however, were also in the heavens during Sun-nights when the light did not stream out. During these periods, the Sun planet was darkened and there was only warmth-gas—no light; currents of warm gases streamed inside the Sun globe. The Cherubim were all around it and sent their activity downward into the dark gas. Therefore, when the Cherubim could not influence the Archangels in the normal way, they sent their activity into the dark smoke, the dark gas of the Sun. During the period of ancient Saturn, influences were exercised on the warmth; but, influences now streamed from the universe into the densified warmth and the gaseous body of the old Sun. This accounts for the fact that the first seeds were established for what we today call the animal kingdom out of the Sun mist on the old Sun. Just as the first foundation of the human realm in the physical human body arose on ancient Saturn, so the first foundation of the animal kingdom was formed out of the smoke, out of the gas of the old Sun. The earliest beginnings of the human body were formed out of the warmth of ancient Saturn. On the old Sun, the first outlines of smokelike, independently moving, physical animal bodies were formed by the configuration of Cherubim reflected in the Sun gases.

On the one hand, therefore, the ranks of Cherubim—that totality of higher beings who spread themselves out around the Sun—received the approaching Archangels with open arms. On the other hand, they also magically brought forth the first physical manifestation of the animal kingdom out of the Sun's gas in the Sun-nights. The animal kingdom emerged in its first physical framework out of the Sun-mist. Our ancestors, who were familiar with these important facts of spiritual cosmology from the Mysteries, thus called the beings who manifested their influences from various sides of the universal space on the old Sun, the *zodiac* (animal circle). That is the original meaning of *zodiac*.

On ancient Saturn, then, the first beginnings of humanity were laid down. The substance that constitutes our physical body today was poured out, sacrificed, by the Thrones. On the old Sun, the beginnings of the animal kingdom arose. The first animal forms were conjured forth by the self-reflecting figures of the Cherubim out of the gas generated from the densifying warmth substance. Thus, the first animals became the Sun's reflections of the zodiac. There is a true inner relationship between the zodiac and the first animals on the old Sun. Our present animals are caricatures of the beings who were in the process of becoming animals on the Sun. Names were not given arbitrarily in ancient times. One must never presume that in those ancient times names were devised arbitrarily. What do astronomers do today who have the good fortune to discover a new star or planet in the chain of the planetoids? They open a dictionary, choose among the Greek mythological names one that has not been appropriated, and give it to the newly discovered star.

Names were never given in this manner when the Mysteries still flourished, for a name expressed the true nature of the thing it named. It was filled with meaning.

The shapes of our present animals, even if they are caricatures, were drawn from the periphery of the cosmos, from the forms of the zodiac that existed at that time. You may have noticed that I have written out here only four names of the zodiac. They represent the four principal expressions of the Cherubim, but, in reality, each of these cherubic beings has, to the right and the left of it, a kind of follower or companion. Thus, seeing that each of the four forms of the Cherubim is supplied with two companions, we have twelve forces or powers in the Sun's periphery that were already present in a rudimentary form on ancient Saturn. The twelve powers belonging to the realm of the Cherubim accomplished their task, their mission in the universe, as I have indicated.

But how are these powers belonging to the realm of the Cherubim related to the usual names of the zodiac? We shall talk about this in the next few days, for there has been a change in the sequence of the names. One generally begins with the Ram (Aries), the Bull (Taurus), the Twins (Gemini), the Crab (Cancer), and the Lion (Leo); then comes the Virgin (Virgo) and the Scales (Libra). The Eagle has had to take the name Scorpio for a definite reason, due to a later transformation. Then come the two companion signs: the Archer (Sagittarius) and the Goat (Capricorn). The Human is called Waterman (Aquarius) for a particular reason we shall come to later. Finally, we have the Fishes (Pisces). The true forms from which the Zodiac originated appear only in the Bull and the Lion; they appear less in the Human, who is referred to exoterically as the Waterman or Aquarius. In the coming days, we shall discuss why this transformation of the zodiac came about.

We have seen how exalted spiritual beings—the exalted hierarchy of the Thrones—separated the fire matter out of their own substance on ancient Saturn, and how even higher beings, the Cherubim, were able to receive into themselves the light that arose from this fiery substance and to transfigure and ennoble it. But a corresponding compensation, a lowering process, must take place each time an uplifting process arises in the universe. For the Archangels to have the opportunity of extending their spiritual existence by day, the Cherubim had to continue their activity at night and to produce— from the mist, smoke, and gas of the densified warmth substance— animal beings or forms that stand below the level of humanity. We have now set out the conceptional framework, according to primal cosmic wisdom, for showing how certain spiritual beings of the universe work together with our own planetary body and how what comes before us as outwardly physical, always leads back to spiritual beings. What is today known materially as the zodiac has its origin in the Cherubim's sending their influence down from the encircling cosmos to the old Sun that let its forces stream forth into the universe as the power of light.

Today we traced one important concept pertaining to the zodiac. Tomorrow, we will move forward with our considerations. Gradually we shall come to another characterization of the planetary bodies, and thereby throw increasing light on their relationship with the spiritual hierarchies.

5. Cosmic Evolution
and the "War in Heaven"

APRIL 14, 1909, *Evening*

WE HAVE CONSIDERED the working of higher spiritual beings in the cosmos by means of two examples: the development of ancient Saturn and the development of old Sun—which is the re-embodiment of Saturn. Today, we must penetrate into the spiritual realm of the higher supersensible beings and consider their activity from yet another aspect. In the first half of these lectures I referred to things that most of you are already familiar with. Besides assuming that there are listeners who have not yet heard some of this, I also thought it necessary to again lay certain foundations, because in this lecture cycle we shall ascend high into the regions of spirit-life.

You will gather from what has been said so far that the most divers spiritual beings are active in the development of an evolving cosmic system. But what, in fact, is the nature of ancient Saturn? Let us try to gain an accurate conception of it. It has, of course, nothing to do with our present Saturn. Rather, you must imagine that everything belonging to the totality of our solar system was already present embryonically on ancient Saturn. This includes our Sun, Moon, Mercury, Venus, Mars, and Jupiter. These bodies were within ancient Saturn and have developed out of it. Imagine a planetary body that has our Sun as its center and stretches so far out into space as to include our present Saturn. Only after having done this would you imagine correctly the size of ancient Saturn compared to our present solar system. The whole of our present solar system developed from ancient Saturn. One might even compare it, though only approximately, with the whole of the Kant-Laplace universal primeval mist out of which, according to many of our con-temporaries, our solar system has been formed.[1] However, the comparison is inadequate, because most people imagine some kind of gas as having been the starting point of our solar system. We have seen that it was not gas but a warmth-body. Ancient Saturn was really a gigantic body of warmth.

Yesterday we mentioned that where ancient Saturn transformed itself into the later Sun [old Sun], the Cherubim worked into the universe from the periphery. You must now imagine that these Cherubim, who were at work in the circumference of the old Sun, were already present around ancient Saturn, but had not yet been called to play their part. To put it trivially, although they were present at the periphery of ancient Saturn, they had not yet come to the point of accomplishing a high task.

But other beings were also present in the environment of ancient Saturn, beings of a more elevated rank than the Cherubim. These are the Seraphim. The Thrones come from the same realm. We have seen how the substance of the Thrones—who stand one level below the Cherubim—streams down, forming the warmth substance of Saturn. Therefore we can imagine ancient Saturn as a gigantic globe of warmth, surrounded by choirs of extraordinarily exalted spiritual beings. In Christian esotericism, these are called Thrones, Cheru-bim, and Seraphim. They are the Dhyanic beings of Eastern wis-dom.[2] What is the origin of these choirs of exalted beings? Everything in the universe is in the process of development. Every-thing evolves. Therefore, when we want to imagine where the Cher-ubim, Seraphim, and Thrones come from, it is best to begin with our own solar system and ask what it eventually will become. So let us briefly sketch the development of our solar system.

---

1. The philosopher Immanuel Kant (1724–1804) wrote his mechanical cosmology, *Allgemeine Naturgeschichte and Theorie des Himmels* in 1755. It was his first work. It was then taken up by the French astronomer and mathematician Pierre-Simon, Marquis de Laplace, who used it as the basis to set forth his nebular hypothesis in his *Exposition du système du monde* (1796). Hence: Kant-Laplace.
2. Again, this is the language of theosophy (see *The Secret Doctrine*).

The starting point was ancient Saturn. This transformed itself into old Sun, which transformed itself into old Moon. However, at the time of this transformation of old Sun into old Moon, we reach a particular evolutionary stage. The Moon leaves the Sun, and thereby we have for the first time, in the instance of the old Moon, a cosmic body existing outside of the Sun. Because it had cast off its coarsest substance, the Sun could now go through a higher stage of development. Then the whole system developed into the system of our present Earth. Our Earth came about when the Moon and the Earth—as the coarser substances and carriers of the coarser beings of the Sun—separated out of the Sun. But development goes on. The beings who must live their separate existence on Earth, those who have, so to speak, been cast off from the Sun, continue to develop their Sun singularity to even higher stages. Cut off though they are from the Sun, they continue to develop. They still have to go through the evolutionary stage of Jupiter. Then they must gradually mature so that they will be able to reunite with the Sun. When the Venus stage of evolution is reached, then all the beings who today surge and live on our Earth will be incorporated into the Sun again.

The Sun itself will then have reached a higher stage of development, because all the beings that had formerly been cast off will have been redeemed. This is followed by the evolutionary state of Vulcan, the highest stage in the development of our system. The seven stages in the development of our system are therefore: Saturn, Sun, Moon, Earth, Jupiter, Venus, and Vulcan. During the Vulcan stage, all the beings who have evolved out of the small beginnings of Saturn will have been spiritualized in the highest degree. Together they will have become not just Sun, but the *Over-Sun*. Vulcan likewise will be more than Sun, it will have reached a maturity capable of sacrifice, the maturity necessary for self-dissolution.

The next level of development, for a system whose starting point is a Sun, arises in the Sun, which is at first weak and has to throw off its planets, so that it can itself develop further. The Sun then grows stronger, reabsorbs its planets, and becomes a Vulcan. Then the whole is dissolved, and the Vulcan globe later becomes a hollow globe, that is, similar to the round of the Thrones, Cherubim, and Seraphim. The Sun will dissolve into the cosmos, sacrifice itself, send forth its being into the universe, and thus become a choir of beings like the Seraphim, Cherubim, and Thrones, who advance to new creative tasks in the universe.

Why could the Thrones give forth their substance, which was needed by Saturn? They could do so because they had prepared themselves in an earlier system through seven conditions such as those through which our solar system is now passing. Before a system of Thrones, Cherubim, and Seraphim comes about, it must first have been a solar system. This means that a Sun must have reached the stage when it could reunite itself with its planets; then it could become periphery. The Sun itself becomes a zodiac. *What we have come to know as the exalted beings in the zodiac are the remnants that have passed over to us from a previous solar system.* What previously evolved within a solar system can now work creatively into cosmic space and give birth to a new solar system from its own forces. For us, the Seraphim, Cherubim, and Thrones represent the highest hierarchy among divine beings, because they have already accomplished their development as a solar system and have risen to an exalted rank of cosmic sacrificial service.

As a result, these beings have come into the closest vicinity of the most exalted divinity we can speak of, the threefold divine power, or the Trinity. We must, therefore, picture the Godhead as beyond the Seraphim. We find this threefold divinity among almost all peoples as Brahma, Siva, and Vishnu, and as the Father, the Word, and the Holy Spirit. The creative source of every new cosmic system also arises within this exalted Trinity. Looking back, we could say that before anything of ancient Saturn came into existence the plan for it had to ripen within the divine Trinity. But the divine Trinity needs beings to execute its plan, and these beings must first prepare themselves for the task. The Seraphim, Cherubim, and Thrones are those beings who are, so to speak, closest to the Godhead. In Western Christian esotericism, they are appropriately described as "enjoying the unveiled countenance of the Godhead." The Seraphim, Cherubim, and Thrones receive the plans of a new cosmic system from the divine Trinity through whom they originated.

You will readily understand why I express these things figuratively. We are forced to convey exalted events with human words that simply are not created for this purpose. Human language was not created to express the exalted activity that took place at the beginning of our solar system when, from the Holy Trinity, the Seraphim received the highest plans that contained the whole future evolution of our solar system through Saturn, Sun, Moon, Earth, Jupiter, Venus, and Vulcan. The name Seraphim, correctly understood in the ancient Hebrew esoteric sense, is always interpreted as referring to the beings who receive the highest ideas and aims of a cosmic system from the Trinity. The Cherubim, belonging to the second rank of the hierarchies, have the task of elaborating in wisdom the aims and ideas received from the Gods. The Cherubim are thus spirits of exalted wisdom, capable of transposing into workable plans what is indicated by the Seraphim. The Thrones, who are in the third hierarchical rank from the Holy Trinity (counting from above), have, figuratively speaking, the task of putting into practice the high cosmic thoughts that have been conceived in wisdom, thoughts received by the Seraphim from the Gods and pondered over by the Cherubim.

Beholding with the soul, we actually see how the first stage of the realization of the divine plan is achieved by the Thrones in the flowing down of the fire-substance. The Thrones appear to us as beings endowed with the power to transpose into a primary reality what has been first conceived by the Cherubim. This occurs because the Thrones allowed their own substance of primeval cosmic fire to flow into the space allotted to the new cosmic system. We can picture it very clearly by saying that an ancient solar system disappeared—died away. The ranks of the Seraphim, Cherubim, and Thrones attained their highest perfection within this ancient system. According to indications of the majestic Trinity, they then selected a sphere within cosmic space: "Here," they said, "we can make a beginning."

At this moment, the Seraphim received the aims of this new solar system, the Cherubim worked them out, and the Thrones gave forth primeval fire—their own substance—into the appointed sphere. Thus we can grasp the origin of our solar system.

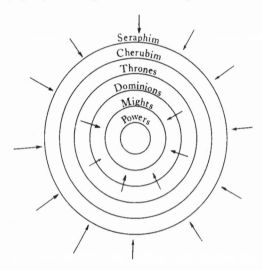

Other beings, however, were also present in the former solar system of which ours is the successor. They are not as exalted as the Seraphim, Cherubim, and Thrones. These other beings remained at a lower stage and came over in a condition in which they still had to pass through further stages of development before they could be creatively active, before they could offer sacrifice. These are the beings of the second threefold hierarchy. We have just been considering the first threefold hierarchy. The name of the first beings of the second hierarchy are the Kyriotetes (or Dominions or Spirits of Wisdom). They are followed by the Mights, the Dynamis (or Virtues, as Dionysius the Areopagite and, following him, the teachers of the West, named them). They are also called the Spirits of Movement. They are the second degree of the second hierarchy. The third rank consists of the Exusiai, also called the Powers or Potentates by the teachers of the West. These are also known as the Spirits of Form.

As we glance back to ancient Saturn, let us ask then where the beings of the second hierarchy were. We have seen that the beings of the first hierarchy surrounded Saturn. But where were the Dominions, Mights, and Powers? We shall find them within ancient Saturn. If the Thrones approached, so to speak, as far as the periphery of ancient Saturn, then the Dominions, Mights, and Powers were within its boundary. Thus, in ancient Saturn, within its mass, the Dominions, Mights, and Powers were at work. The threefold ranks of active spiritual beings were inside the Saturn substance.

Let us now come to terms, at least to some extent, with the fantastic modern theory of the world's origin as formulated in the Kant-Laplace theory. This theory claims that a mass of mist was the starting-point of our solar system. It then imagines that this huge mass of gas began to rotate, to whirl. The theory apparently finds it easy to account for the splitting off of the outer planets during that rotation. At first, rings are formed and then contract. The Sun remains in the center while the other planets rotate around it. The process is pictured mechanically. A nice school experiment is devised to show in miniature how such a solar system arose. One takes a vessel full of water, throws in a large drop of oil, then cuts a piece of paper representing the equator, and puts a pin into it from above. The drop of oil is then made to rotate. Small drops of oil split off and circle around, and the teacher making the demonstration says to the pupils, who are often quite mature, "Now, here you have in miniature the formation of our solar system!" And then the whole thing suddenly becomes obvious! For how could it be more obvious than to see with your own eyes how a solar system comes about? Why shouldn't one be convinced that once upon a time, out there, there was a gigantic cosmic mist that rotated and the planets split from it to form miniature Mercuries and Saturns, just like the small drops separating from the large drops of oil?

Amazement is the only response to the naivete of those who, to make it as concrete as possible, demonstrate the Kant-Laplace theory in this way. The fact is, they have forgotten one important thing, which on other occasions it is good to forget, but in this instance may not be forgotten: those doing the demonstration have forgotten themselves, their own presence. After all, they set the thing in motion. Indeed, it is an incredible piece of naivete, but the simple-mindedness of our modern materialistic mythology is considerable. It is far greater, in fact, than that of any other mythology. This will be realized only in the future. So, we have someone who sets the whole thing in motion. Therefore, we shall have to presuppose, if one can think at all—if one has not forsaken all of the good spirits of logic—that spiritual powers were involved in the rotation of the cosmic globe.

Aside from the error of placing primeval gas at the beginning instead of primeval fire, it cannot be assumed that the primal mass of gas began to whirl of its own accord. We should rather ask where were the spiritual forces that moved these masses—for us, masses of primal fire—so that something could happen within them? We have just spoken of these spiritual forces—the spiritual powers worked from the periphery and from within. Those who acquired their faculties in former cosmic systems worked from outside, while beings of lesser maturity worked from within. The latter brought about differentiation in the inner structures of warmth, as we have already seen. These beings were endowed with the highest intelligence and arranged everything that occurred there.

What kind of task belongs to the first beings of the second hierarchy? The Spirits of Wisdom (Kyriotetes or Dominions) receive what the Thrones bring down from the universe. They regulate it so that a harmonious relationship comes about between the separate cosmic body that is beginning—that is, Saturn—and the rest of the universe. Everything within Saturn must be arranged so that it corresponds to what is outside it. What the Seraphim, Cherubim, and Thrones bring down to Saturn from the hand of God must be regulated so that these commands and impulses are translated into reality. From the periphery of Saturn, through the intermediary of the highest hierarchy, the Kyriotetes (or Dominions) receive what is to be transformed and harmonized with Saturn's interior.

A further transformation occurs through the Mights (or Spirits of Motion, Dynamis). Whereas the Dominions are concerned with the highest arrangements within Saturn, it is the Mights who carry out their directives, as it were. The Powers, on the other hand, ensure that what has been constructed according to the intentions of the universe should endure as long as is necessary without disappearing immediately. We shall refer to this more specifically later. For the moment, we only want to characterize the matter in broad terms. The Spirits of Form (Powers) are the maintainers. In summary we may say, then, that within Saturn the Dominions are organizers; the Mights carry out directives; and the Powers preserve what has been formed by the Mights.

Today we shall not consider the workings of the next hierarchy— the Spirits of Personality, the Spirits of Fire, and the Angels—let us rather, with the knowledge we have newly acquired, turn our attention to the passage of ancient Saturn to old Sun. The most important aspect of the process was described in the previous lecture. When ancient Saturn changed into old Sun, the primeval fire was transformed into gas or air, so that old Sun consisted of the residue of the primeval fire. But the primeval fire was intermingled with what had densified into gas or smoke. Two substances were present then: primeval fire and a part of the primeval fire that had been densified into gas, smoke, or air—whichever you wish to call it. That, in essence, was the situation with the old Sun. As we shall see, things went a little differently for our Sun which, in fact, developed through various stages up to the present into something different than the old Sun— although, of course, there are people who assert that the interior of our Sun merely consists of some kind of gas.

If we look into the various theories of materialistic natural science, we certainly do find astonishing things! In a small popular book, much in demand because of its low price, we find the assertion that the Sun's interior is not solid but gaseous. But, incredible as it may seem, this popular handbook states quite specifically that this gas has the consistency of honey or tar. Now, I will gladly grant a fool's paradise in which to move about in air made of honey to the individual who believes that, under certain conditions of pressure, a gas can look like honey or tar; but I would never wish that individual to move in air as thick as tar! Materialistic theories bring forth strange aberrations indeed!

However, we are not speaking of our present Sun but of the old Sun that really consisted of primeval fire and of a fire-mist or fire-air. You will find the expression "fire-mist" in *Faust*, for Goethe was familiar with it.[3] You also will find it in theosophical literature.[4] We must imagine the old Sun as consisting of a mixture of these two substances, but this did not happen of its own accord. Cosmic bodies do not simply condense; spiritual beings must bring about densification. The beings who transferred the condensation of substance from ancient Saturn to the old Sun were the Kyriotetes (Dominions). The Dominions, working from outside, compressed the gigantic mass of Saturn so that it became smaller. The Dominions continued to exert pressure until the old Sun became a globe whose mass, if you place the Sun at its center, extended as far as Jupiter. Ancient Saturn was as large as a cosmic globe, having the Sun at its center and extending as far as our Saturn. It was a mighty globe, as large as our entire solar system and reaching out as far as the present orbit of the planet Saturn. The old Sun was a globe that extended as far as the present Jupiter. That marks the boundary of the old Sun. One can imagine the orbits of our planets as boundaries for the extension of former cosmic bodies.

You see, we are gradually gaining a conception of the nature of planetary bodies by tracing their origin back to the activity of the hierarchies. Let us now continue. The next stage is, again, one of condensation. The third condition of our cosmic system is known as old Moon. Those familiar with what can be learned from the Akashic Record[5] know that the Moon arose through a further condensation—as far as the watery state—of the substance of old Sun.

---

3. *Faust*, Part One.
4. See *The Secret Doctrine*, vol. 1; for instance: "The Worlds, including our own, were of course, as germs, primarily evolved from the ONE Element in its second stage...whether we call it, with modern Science, cosmic dust and Fire-mist, or, with Occultism—Akasa, Jivatma, divine Astral Light or 'the Soul of the World.'"
5. See *Cosmic Memory* (Blauvelt, NY: Steinerbooks, 1990).

There was no solid "earth" on the old Moon yet, but there were fire, air, and water. The old Moon introduced and regulated the watery element—it densified gas or air into a watery element. The second group of the second hierarchy, that is, the beings known as the Mights or Dynamis, brought this about. These beings also compressed the mass of old Sun up to the boundary of the present Mars, and Mars represents the boundary line for the size of old Moon. If you imagine a sphere with the Sun at its center, extending to the orbit of the present Mars, you have the size of the old Moon.

We must now keep in mind that when the old Moon arose out of Saturn and Sun, something completely new occurred. A part of the dense substance was thrown out and two bodies came into being. One body took up the finer substance and beings; it became a more refined Sun; the other body became a more dense Moon. The third condition of our system developed in such a way that it remained a single planet only for a time. Then it threw off a planet that remained in its vicinity. At first, so long as it formed a single body, the Moon extended to the orbit of the present Mars. Then the Sun contracted and was circled by a body more or less along the orbit of the present Mars, in other words, at the periphery of the original unified body.

What brought about the division of the two cosmic bodies? By what means did one cosmic body become two? It happened during the reign of the Mights or Dynamis. Many of you will be familiar with the fact that a process occurs in the cosmos that is similar to the one we know in everyday human life. Wherever beings develop, there are always those who progress and others who remain where they are—as many a father knows who complains that his son at school languishes behind while others forge ahead. It is a matter of different rates of development. This is also true in the cosmos.

At this point, then, when the Mights (Dynamis) had begun their task, an event occurred—we shall learn later why it took place—that is known in esotericism, as in all the Mysteries, as the "War in Heaven." The teaching of the "War in Heaven" forms an integral part of all Mystery wisdom and contains a primeval secret concerning the origin of evil.[6] At a certain time in old Moon evolution, the Mights or Dynamis were at different stages of maturity. Some longed to rise spiritually as high as possible; others lagged behind, or had at least progressed at a normal stage of development. Thus, on old Moon, there were Mights or Dynamis who had progressed far beyond their companions. As a result, the two classes of Mights separated from one another. The more advanced drew out the Sun and the ones who stayed back formed the Moon that revolved around it. This gives a sketchy description of the "War in Heaven," the splitting asunder of the old Moon that resulted in the accompanying planet—the old Moon—coming under the rulership of the Mights, who remained behind, while the old Sun was under the authority of the advanced Mights.

Something of the "War in Heaven" rings through the opening lines of the divine Gita where, symbolically, at the beginning of the battle, we find echoes of this mighty struggle. It was an immense battle indeed! From the time that the Kyriotetes or Dominions effected the establishment of the old Sun until the time of the creation of the old Moon, when the Mights or Dynamis began their mission, a huge battle, a gigantic "War in Heaven" raged. The Kyriotetes contracted the whole system to the boundary of the present Jupiter. Then the Mights contracted the whole system to the boundary of the present Mars. In the middle, between the two planetary boundaries in the heavens, was an enormous battlefield. Picture to yourselves this battlefield in the cosmos. It was not until the nineteenth century that the devastation produced by the "War in Heaven" was discovered again with physical eyes, so to speak.

---

6. Cf. Revelations XII, "And a war flared up in the heavenly world. Michael and his angels fought against the dragon. And the dragon fought in the midst of his angels. But his strength failed, and so there was no longer a place for them in the heavens. The great dragon was overthrown, the primeval serpent who is of both a diabolical and a satanic nature, the Tempter of all humankind. Onto the earth he was thrown, and all his angels with him. "Wars in Heaven" are frequently referred to in *The Secret Doctrine*; for instance: "In their turn the Rosicrucians, who were well acquainted with the secret meaning of the tradition, kept it to themselves, teaching merely that the whole of creation was due to, and a result of, that legendary 'War in Heaven.'"

Scattered between the orbits of Mars and Jupiter is a multitude of small planetoids. These are the wreckage of the battlefield of the "War in Heaven" that was waged between two points of cosmic time. This was when our solar system was contracted first to Jupiter and then to Mars. Astronomers today, directing their telescopes toward the heavenly spaces, are still discovering planetoids— namely, the wreckage on the great battlefield of the "War in Heaven" between the advanced Mights and those less advanced that also brought about the severing of the Moon from its Sun. Thus, when we consider the actions of divine beings, we see that external things appear as the expression, the outer physiognomy of divine spiritual beings.

6. *Geocentricity and Heliocentricity in Cosmic Evolution*

APRIL 15, 1909, *Evening*

YESTERDAY, WE SAW HOW EVENTS in the cosmos are brought about by the beings above us in the spiritual world. At the close of the lecture, we drew attention to an especially significant event—the "War in Heaven," whose battlefield extended between Jupiter and Mars. Physical science today increasingly finds planetoids in that sphere. These are the "corpses" left behind on that "cosmic battlefield." We shall return to this event. We shall also see that this event in Heaven is reflected in certain events that occurred in the Earth's development. In fact, we shall find a reflection of the "War in Heaven" in the opening of the Bhagavad Gita. Today, we shall first continue our observations by describing briefly the other beings of the spiritual hierarchies we referred to in passing yesterday.

The beings that are closest to human beings, as we ascend, are known in Christian esotericism as Angels, Archangels, and Prime Powers, or Primal Beginnings. They are also known as Angeloi, Archangeloi, and Archai. In anthroposophical terminology, the Archangels are also known as Fire Spirits; the Primal Beginnings as Spirits of Personality.

The beings between us and the spiritual beings referred to yesterday as reaching out to Jupiter, Mars, and so on, are, of course, more closely connected to human life on Earth. Let us first consider the Angels or Angeloi. They reached their human stage during the old Moon period and are at present developed only as far as we shall be developed during our Jupiter evolution. Hence, they are one stage above us. What is the task of these beings? To deal with this question, we shall have to consider the development of humanity on Earth.

A human being develops from incarnation to incarnation. We can trace human evolution back through the ancient Atlantean period and the earlier Lemurian times. Human evolution, in fact, began during the ancient Lemurian era. This development by means of successive incarnations will continue until almost the end of earthly evolution. At that time, other forms of human development will arise. Now, you know that the eternal essence of our being, our individuality, endures from incarnation to incarnation. Most people, however, remain unconscious of having lived in a previous incarnation and do not remember what happened in a preceding embodiment. Only those who have developed a certain stage of clairvoyance are able to look back into previous incarnations.

Since we cannot yet remember previous incarnations, however, what kind of continuity could exist between our incarnations if there were no being to link together our individual incarnations and guide our progressive development from one incarnation to the next? We must presume, therefore, that for every human being who cannot remember, there is a being who is a level higher than humankind and leads the individual from one incarnation to the next. We should remember that these are not the beings who order karma. They are simply guardian beings who preserve the memory of one incarnation until the next as long as a person cannot do so. These beings are Angels or Angeloi.

In each incarnation, each of us is an individuality, but a being watches over us who carries the consciousness of what has occurred in our lives from incarnation to incarnation. This explains why, at certain lower stages of initiation, a person, even though he or she does not yet know of former incarnations, has the possibility of asking his or her Angel. This is absolutely within the bounds of possibility for certain lower levels of initiation. It is the task of the Angels, therefore, to stand watch over all the threads that an individual weaves from one incarnation to another.

Now let's consider the next group of beings, known as Archangels (Archangeloi, Fire Spirits). These beings are not concerned with single individuals. Their task is more encompassing. They bring the life of the individual and the life of broader groups of humanity—that is, peoples, races, and so on, into harmonious order. Within earthly evolution they have the task of bringing the individual soul into relationship with what we call folk-soul and race-soul.[1] For anyone who can penetrate spiritual knowledge, folk-souls and race-souls are quite different from what is generally understood by these terms today, especially by the abstract, modern scientist. A certain number of people live in a particular area—for example, in Germany, France, or Italy. Because our physical eyes perceive human beings as only so many outer physical forms, abstract thinkers merely conceive of the folk-spirit or folk-soul as the abstract sum total of so many people. For them, only the individual human being is real, not the folk-soul or folk-spirit. But for anyone who can look into the true workings of the spiritual world, a folk-soul or a folk-spirit is a reality. A Fire Spirit or Archangel manifests in a folk-soul, governing the relationship between individual human beings and the whole of a people or race.

Ascending one stage higher than the Archangels, we come to the beings known as the Spirits of Personality (Primal Beginnings, Primal Powers, Archai). These are still higher beings who have an even more exalted task in the interrelatedness of human affairs. Essentially, they govern all the interrelationships of the whole human species on Earth. They live in such a way that, from age to age, through the waves of time, they can, at a particular point in time, transform themselves and take on a different spiritual body.

You are all familiar with something that, for the abstract thinker of today's typical education, is just an abstract idea but is a reality for anyone who sees into spiritual reality. I mean the dreadful expression we use to refer to the "*Zeitgeist.*"[2] This expression refers to what constitutes the significance and mission of a given human epoch. Take,

---

1. See Rudolf Steiner, *The Mission of Folk Souls.*
2. Literally, "spirit of the times."

for example, the mission and significance of the first millennium following the Atlantean catastrophe. Such "Time Spirits" encompass something that goes beyond single peoples or races. The "Spirit of an Age," the *Zeitgeist*, is not restricted to a particular people. Its influence goes beyond the frontiers of any particular country. The true Spirit of the Time, or Spirit of an Age, is the spirit-body of an Archai, Primal Beginning or Spirit of Personality.

Such Archai, for example, are responsible for certain human individualities appearing on the earthly scene at the appointed times. You will readily understand that earthly tasks have to be accomplished largely by earthly individualities. Certain epoch-making personalities have to appear at particular times. Utter confusion would reign in earthly evolution if it were left to chance whether, for instance, a Luther or a Charlemagne were to appear arbitrarily in one era or another. Such appearances must be conceived of within the whole of human earthly evolution. The right souls must appear at a particular epoch within the overall significance of earthly evolution, as it were. This is regulated by the Spirits of Personality or Archai.

Beyond the Archai we find the beings mentioned yesterday, the so-called Powers or Exusiai, also known as the Spirits of Form. Here we come to tasks that reach beyond the Earth. In human development, we have distinguished the evolutionary stages of Saturn, Sun, Moon, Earth, Jupiter, Venus, and Vulcan. From all that occurs within the Earth itself we have seen how everything that happens to individual human beings on Earth is regulated by Angels. Archangels are responsible for the relation between individuals and groups. Spirits of Personality, by contrast, are responsible for human evolution, as it extends from the Lemurian period to a future period when human beings will be so spiritualized that they will virtually no longer belong to the Earth. But something else must be regulated too. Humanity must be guided from one planetary condition to another. There must be spiritual beings whose task, during the whole of earthly evolution, is to make sure that, when that phase comes to an end, humanity rightly passes over into a *pralaya*, and finds its way to the next goal, that of Jupiter. This task belongs to the Powers or Spirits of Form, the Exusiai. They are the spirits who ensure humanity's guidance from one planetary stage to another.

Yesterday, we characterized their tasks from above downward. Now we shall do so from below upward. So, let us acquaint ourselves with the cosmic position of these beings. In spiritual science, in what should be continued as anthroposophy today—indeed, in what is known as Mystery wisdom—the beings of the spiritual hierarchies have always been spoken of in the same way. Yesterday, we saw that the present Saturn represents the limit of the workings of the Thrones; Jupiter represents the boundary of the activity of the Dominions; and Mars is the frontier for the influence of the Mights, the Dynamis or Virtues.

Let us now characterize how the spheres of influence of these beings are distributed spatially in our solar system. Here we touch on something that—even for those of you who are prepared to a certain extent—will seem somewhat strange, although it absolutely corresponds with the truth. In school we learn that, from very ancient times until Copernicus, a concept of the solar system existed, known as the Ptolemaic system.[3] It is said that people then believed that the Earth was at the center of our [solar] system—as indeed it appears to ordinary visual perception—and that the planets rotated around the Earth. But since Copernicus, so it is said, we know at last what human beings formerly did not: that the Sun is at the center, and the planets circle around it in their respective elliptical orbits. In fact, however—and this must be made clear—if one is to present the matter "correctly and honestly" according to the current understanding of that standard, the true description of what occurred is something quite different. One should rather say: until the time of Copernicus, people knew only certain forms of

3. Claudius Oleaginous (Ptolemy), second century A.D. astronomer, mathematician, and geographer of Alexandria. His *Megale Syntaxis tes Astronomias*, known as the *Almagest* from the title of its Arabic translation, described the (Ptolomaic) system of astronomy and geography based on the theory that the Sun, planets and stars revolve around the Earth.

movement in the heavens, and according to these, calculated how our solar system might be organized. What Copernicus then did was not to take a seat, so to speak, outside of the universe to observe how the Sun was placed in the center of a circle or ellipse, and how the planets moved around it. Rather Copernicus contrived a mathematical calculation, and this formula corresponded more closely to what one saw than the previous explanation. The Copernican world system is nothing but the result of thinking.

Putting Ptolemy's view aside for the moment, let us place the Sun in the middle and calculate where the planets should be in relation to it. Then let us consider whether or not this corresponds to our immediate experience. Indeed, from mere physical observation, this experiment coincides completely with our experience. Various cosmic systems have been built upon this premise, including the Kant-Laplace theory; but in the light of subsequent discoveries, we come to a position that, scientifically, is not quite honest. Later, as a result of purely physical observation, two planets, Uranus and Neptune, were added to the system.[4] We shall speak of their significance for our solar system later. Indeed, in describing our solar system, one should point out that the appearance of Uranus and Neptune brings a considerable amount of confusion into the calculations.

If one wishes to accept the Kant-Laplace cosmic system, it follows that Uranus and Neptune should move with their corresponding moons, just as other moons rotate around other planets. But this is not the case. Among these outermost, more recently discovered planets, we have one that behaves in a singular way. If the Kant-Laplace cosmic system were correct we would have to imagine that, after all of the planets had split off, someone turned the axis about ninety degrees, because the courses of the outermost planets are different from the other planets. Neptune and Uranus differ considerably from the remaining planets of our solar system. We shall see

---

4. Uranus was discovered by English astronomer Sir William Herschel (1738–1822) in 1781; Neptune was discovered by French astronomer Urbain-Jean-Joseph Le Verrier (1811–1877) in 1846.

their situation later. For the moment, we merely want to point out that the Copernican view is the result of calculations, that it is a hypothesis, an assumption made at a time when human insight into the spiritual reality behind outer happenings had completely ebbed away. *The Ptolemaic view, on the other hand, is not merely a physical system.* It was derived from spiritual observation at a time when it was still known that the planets represented the boundaries of influence of higher beings.

To characterize the realms of influence of these higher beings, our planetary solar system must be drawn very differently. I will now draw this planetary system as it was made clear in the Mystery schools of Zoroaster. We could equally well draw from other Mysteries, but we have selected this particular system to bring out the characteristics of our solar system with its planets in relation to the spiritual beings active within it.

In the Zoroastrian system something was included that differed from our observation of the heavens. You are aware that, in the course of many years, one can observe a procession of the Sun, apparent or otherwise, through the zodiac. It is usually stated, and quite correctly, that beginning approximately in the eighth century B.C., the Sun rose in the sign of the Ram (Aries) at the spring equinox. Each year, however, the Sun advanced a little further so that in the course of long periods of time the whole of the sign of the Ram was traversed. Before 800 B.C., the Sun did not rise in the Ram, but in the sign of the Bull (Taurus). This lasted about 2,200 years, so that the Sun had traversed the whole sign of the Bull with its vernal point. Before this, the Sun rose in the Twins (Gemini). That is, the Sun rose in the Twins before 800 plus approximately 2,200 years B.C. If, therefore, we look back to the fourth and fifth millennia B.C., we find the vernal point in the sign of the Twins. This was the period when the Mysteries of Zoroaster flourished. They flourished in the distant past when all the appearances in the heavens were calculated in relation to the sign of the Twins. So, if we draw the zodiac as it was described yesterday, we would have to place the constellation of the Twins here at the top.

TWINS

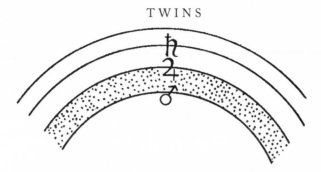

We would then have to draw what served as the boundary of the Thrones' sphere of activity in immediate relation to the zodiac—that is, we must draw what made up the boundary of Saturn. After that, we must delimit the sphere of activity of those spiritual beings known as the Dominions, or Spirits of Wisdom—the outermost boundary of Jupiter. Next, we delimit the sphere of influence of the Mights, or Spirits of Movement. This is delineated by the boundary of Mars. We have seen that the battlefield left by the "War in Heaven" is between those two.

TWINS

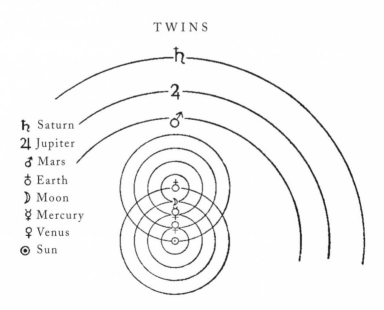

ħ Saturn
♃ Jupiter
♂ Mars
♁ Earth
☽ Moon
☿ Mercury
♀ Venus
☉ Sun

To differentiate correctly between the various realms of power, however, we must also draw the boundary line of the Sun. Just as Mars marks the outer boundary of the influence of the Mights, so the orbit of the Sun represents the frontier of the authority of the Powers or Spirits of Form. Here, then, is the boundary marked out by Venus that represents the sphere of influence of the Archai. Next, we come to the realm marked out by Mercury. This is the sphere of influence of the Archangels, the Fire Spirits. We are now coming quite close to the Earth. We reach the realm of influence bounded by the Moon. Therefore, here we must draw the Earth.

You must picture the Earth as the starting-point and, around it, a sphere of influence reaching to the Moon. This is followed by a realm reaching up to Mercury; then one to Venus; and then one to the Sun. You may be astonished at the sequence of the planets as I have given it here. You might think that, if the Earth is here and here the Sun, you would believe I should draw Mercury here, near the Sun, and here Venus. This is, however, not right, because both planets were, with regard to their names, mixed up by later astronomy. What is called "Mercury" today, was called in ancient teachings, "Venus"; and the planet referred to as "Venus" today was, in all of the old teachings, called "Mercury." Mark this well: *One does not understand the old writings and teachings if one applies what is said there about Venus and Mercury to what is meant today by the same names.* What is said about Venus has to be applied to present-day Mercury, and what is said about Mercury to Venus, because both of these designations were mixed up later. At the time when one turned the world system around, when the Earth was stripped of her central position, one not only changed the perspective, but allowed Mercury and Venus to roll around each other in relation to the old designations.[5]

Now you can reconcile what has been drawn here with the physical planetary system: Here is the Sun, and Venus revolves around it; beyond that, Mercury revolves around the Sun, then the Earth with

5. For background to this complex question of the relationship of Mercury and Venus, see Appendix, page 251.

the Moon; and beyond that, Mars, Jupiter, and Saturn revolve. You must imagine the physical movements in a way that each planet revolves around the Sun. But you can also think of an arrangement where the Earth is here and the other planets have revolved so that, on their paths, they are behind the Sun. If I wish to represent this diagrammatically, it would be as follows. First, we draw the physical system in the usual way; we place the Sun at one of the focal points and let Venus, Mercury, and Earth with its Moon rotate around it. Here are Earth, Mercury, and Venus according to the old designation; next is Mars; then, after the planetoids, Jupiter; and, finally, Saturn.

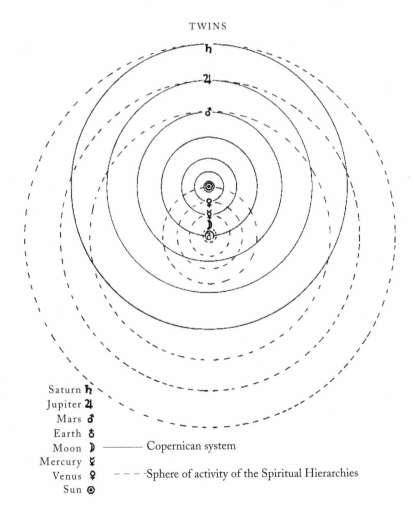

TWINS

Saturn ♄
Jupiter ♃
Mars ♂
Earth ♁
Moon ☽   ———— Copernican system
Mercury ☿
Venus ♀   – – – -Sphere of activity of the Spiritual Hierarchies
Sun ☉

You must imagine that the Earth is here below; then we have Mercury and Venus; and then Mars up there; and Jupiter, and so on. Now you have the Sun, Mercury, and the present Venus here. The planets can take up a variety of positions in relation to one another, and there is no reason why they should not stand like this. It is plausible. We have drawn the current physical system. To do so we have chosen a particular moment when the Earth, Mercury, and Venus are situated on one side of the Sun and the other planets, Mars, Jupiter, and Saturn, are on the other. That is all we have done, nothing more. Here are the Earth, Mercury, Venus, and on the other side of the Sun we find Mars, Jupiter, and Saturn. Is is simply a matter of changing perspective.

This system is imaginable, but it is valid only for this particular constellation. This actually was the case at a time when the Twins were above Saturn. At that time one could clearly observe clairvoyantly the spheres of influence of the spiritual hierarchies. Around the Earth, one could behold the sphere of the Angels—extending out to the Moon. Truly, if we do not take the physical system as our basis, but this unique constellation, we then find around the Earth a round of Angels extending to the Moon; beyond that, the sphere of Archangels extending to Mercury; outward to Venus, the Spirits of Personality; finally, the Powers, Exusiai, or Spirits of Form extending to the Sun. Then, as I told you yesterday, we come to the sphere of the Virtues, Mights, and, after that, the spheres of the Dominions and Thrones.

When speaking about the Copernican and Ptolemaic systems, we must be clear that the Ptolemaic system has preserved something of the constellation of the ruling spirits, and from that perspective the Earth must be taken as the starting point. A time will come when this cosmic system will again be correct, because humanity will again know of the existence of the spiritual world. It can be hoped that human beings will then be less fanatical than our contemporaries. The modern view holds that, before Copernicus, people talked nonsense and had a primitive cosmic system, but since Copernicus we know what is correct at last. Everything else is false. Today, people more or less think that, for example, because the Copernican system is right, it will be taught into the infinite future, even after millions of years. Human beings have rarely been as superstitious as modern theoretical astronomers, and hardly ever was there such fanaticism as there is in this field. We may hope that future generations will be more tolerant and say that humanity was no longer conscious of the spiritual world after the fifteenth and sixteenth centuries; and, further, that a spiritual world does indeed exist and that in the spiritual world one has other perspectives and must arrange heavenly bodies other than from simple physical observation.

Previously, such vantage points were useful. Then a time came when the arrangement of the heavenly bodies had to be established physically. People of the future will say it is understandable and that after the sixteenth century the physical view was also correct. For a while humankind had to ignore anything connected with the spiritual world, but then people began to think again in terms of a spiritual world and returned to the original spiritual viewpoint. One hopes that future generations will understand that astronomical mythology, as well as other forms of mythology, was once possible, and that they will not regard our age with the same disdain that contemporary humanity in its superstition shows toward its ancestors.

We see, therefore, that the Copernican system became a different one, because mere physical perceptions were considered. Before then, remnants of spiritual perception remained in the Ptolemaic system. But we can gain an idea of the working and weaving of spiritual beings in our cosmic and planetary system only by considering this other (Ptolemaic) system. Thus we are true to the spiritual context when we say that the Angels have authority extending to the Moon; the Archangels, to Mercury; the Spirits of Personality, to Venus; the Powers, to the Sun; and the Mights, to Mars. Then come the beings known as the Dominions and finally the Thrones. We merely have to draw other lines in the physical system to delimit the boundaries of the spheres of influence of the various hierarchies. As far as the spiritual influences are concerned, the Earth—not the Sun—is at the center of the cosmic system. The following therefore was maintained by people of all periods who placed emphasis on spiritual evolution: *Though the Sun is a nobler heavenly body, and beings who are superior to humankind have developed there, nevertheless, in evolution everything depends on human beings living on Earth.* Furthermore, the Sun separated so that human beings could develop further in the right way. Had the Sun remained united with the Earth, humankind could not have advanced at the right pace. That only became possible because the Sun withdrew, together with beings who could bear very different conditions. The Earth was left to itself, so to speak, so that humanity could establish the appropriate tempo for its evolution.

A cosmic system will assume this or that configuration according to its chosen starting point and perspective. If one asks where the center of our cosmic system is—viewed purely from the perspective of our physical senses—then the answer will be that the center is as found in the Copernican system. But if one inquires about the arrangement of our solar system in relation to the spheres of influence of the hierarchies, then the Earth must be at the center. In this case we use other boundary lines, because the planets are also something entirely different in this regard. They mark out the limits of the realms of the spheres of influence of each spiritual hierarchy.

You will now understand the relationship between the spatial distribution of the spheres of influence and what was said earlier about the task and mission of the various hierarchies. The beings closest to the Earth who are active in its immediate vicinity as far as the Moon are the Angels. From this realm they guide the lives of individual human beings from incarnation to incarnation. But more is required to distribute the masses of people appropriately, to allot their tasks on Earth. A simple reflection will show that here cooperation with the cosmos is necessary. Whether a group of people is endowed with this or that in its character does not depend on earthly but on the cosmic context. Consider how the conditions of skin and hair in one race is different from those of another race; cosmic conditions, which must be ordered out of heavenly space, affect these characteristics. That occurs out of a sphere of influence reaching to Mercury—in other words, to the boundary of the influence of the Archangels. The guidance of the whole of earthly human evolution is effected from more distant heavenly spaces, extending as far as Venus. When the task of the Earth itself needs to be directed and guided, this proceeds from the very center of the whole system.

Humanity develops through Saturn, Sun, Moon, Earth, Jupiter, Venus, and Vulcan. The Powers or the Spirits of Form are the beings of the spiritual hierarchy who direct the mission of humanity from one planet to the next. They must operate from a specially selected position. Their sphere of influence extends as far as the Sun. The Sun was already a special body when it was next to the ancient Moon. The Sun is now again in close proximity to the Earth. In the future, it will be near Jupiter. Its realm of influence extends beyond that of the individual planets. Therefore the existence of the Sun is connected with those spiritual beings whose sphere of influence goes beyond that of individual planets. The Sun is an extraordinary heavenly body, toward which each sphere of influence reaches and whose own sphere of influence reaches beyond those of the individual planets; this is to say that we find the external dwelling place of the hierarchies—their external sphere in space—not so much on the individual planets *as within the orbits marked out by the planets as if they were boundaries.* Imagine an entire sphere surrounding the Earth extending to the Moon. This space is filled with angelic activity, while the sphere from the Earth to Mercury is likewise filled with the workings of the Archangels, and so on.

Thus we are concerned with spheres in space, and the planets mark the boundaries for these realms of activity of higher beings. We find a continual progression of perfection from humankind outward. As human beings, we are chained to the Earth. But our eternal part that passes from incarnation to incarnation is guided by beings not bound to the Earth but who traverse the air-sphere and what lies beyond, extending to the Moon, and so on. Humanity has been developing on Earth since primeval times. Earthly human development is similar to the relationship between the small child and the mature adult. The adult teaches the child. The same is true of the hierarchies in the cosmic totality. Human beings bound to the Earth can struggle through to the knowledge needed for their necessary destinies on Earth only gradually. They must be taught by higher beings.

But, what must happen for this goal to be achieved? In the early phases of the Earth existence, beings not ordinarily bound to the Earth had to descend from higher spheres. This actually occurred! Beings who needed only to live in the sphere surrounding the Earth descended to impart to humanity what they already knew as older, more perfect members of the hierarchies. They did not have to incarnate into human bodies for their own evolution—they did not need that. Similarly when adults teach children, they do not spend time with the alphabet for their own progress; it is to teach the child. So we look back at Atlantean and Lemurian times when beings descend out of the sphere around the Earth, incarnate into human bodies and become teachers of humanity. These are beings belonging to the higher hierarchies of Mercury and Venus. Children of Venus and Mercury descended and became the teachers of a youthful humankind. Thus, within this youthful human species in its early stage of development, there were human beings who represented *maya* in their sojourn on Earth.

Truly, such beings existed. Let us suppose, in order to characterize it more clearly, that a normally developed Lemurian human being had met such a being. Outwardly, this being did not appear particularly different from other human beings, but a spirit dwelt in that body whose realm reached up to Mercury or Venus. Thus the outer appearance of such a human being represented *maya*, an illusion. This being looked like other human beings, but was something entirely different: a Child of Mercury or Venus. This phenomenon occurred throughout the dawn of human evolution. The Children of Mercury and Venus descended and sojourned among human beings, so that they also had, in an inner way, the character that the Mercury and Venus beings have. These Venus beings are *Spirits of Personality*. Such beings wandered on the Earth as human beings, who were narrowly limited human personalities externally, but guided humanity through their enormous power. Those were the forceful guiding relationships of the Lemurian time, when the Children of Venus piloted the entire human species. The Children of Mercury led portions of humanity, and were as powerful as what we call today the *race* or *folk spirits*.

Maya, or illusion, is not just in the world generally, but also in relation to human beings. People who stand before us can appear so that their appearance is true, so that what is external corresponds precisely to their souls. Or it could be maya. Then, the person has a task that corresponds to the task of a Child of Mercury or Venus. This is what is meant by saying that the leading individuals of ancient times, as they walked the Earth with their ordinary names, fundamentally represented maya. That is what H. P. Blavatsky meant when she indicated that the Buddhas represented a maya. You can find this expression in *The Secret Doctrine*.[6] Such things are derived from the teachings of the Holy Mysteries. We need only understand them correctly.

We must now raise the question: How does it come about that a Child of Venus descends to Earth? How can a Bodhisattva live on Earth? The being of a Bodhisattva—the being of a Child of Mercury or Venus—forms an important chapter in the evolution of our Earth in relation to the cosmos itself. Tomorrow, therefore, we shall consider the nature of the Children of Mercury and Venus, of the Bodhisattvas or Dhyani-Buddhas.[7]

---

6. See *The Secret Doctrine*, vol. 1, p. 574.
7. Ibid. p. 42.

7. The Constitution of Spiritual Beings and Humanity

APRIL 16, 1909, *Evening*

I WOULD LIKE TO BEGIN by making an observation about the end of yesterday's lecture. I noticed that some of you attached a certain amount of importance to the fact that, in the blackboard sketch, each planet was in line with the Sun, so that a kind of common conjunction was depicted.[1] I want to emphasize that this is of absolutely no importance in relation to what we are considering now—though we shall need such concepts later. Nevertheless, it is important that we do not give ourselves over to erroneous ideas.

To repeat: first, we drew the Sun according to the Copernican system; then Mercury (esoteric Venus); then Venus (esoteric Mercury); followed by the Earth with its Moon; then the orbits of Mars, Jupiter, and, finally, Saturn. This represents the Copernican cosmic system.

Having done this, as I said yesterday, I would now like to place before you the system taught in a school of Zoroaster. You must not think, however, that Zoroaster personally taught it. I am rather talking of elementary truths that were current in the schools of Zoroaster.

The constellation of the Twins (Gemini) is thus at the top. Then we take those points on the line from Gemini to the Sun. And, irrespective of whether there is such a conjunction or not, we connect the Sun with the constellation of the Twins. The positions of Saturn, Jupiter, and Mars do not matter. The purpose of the sketch is merely to show the orbits. They mark out the boundary of the various hierarchies.

---

1. See diagrams in previous lecture.

GEMINI

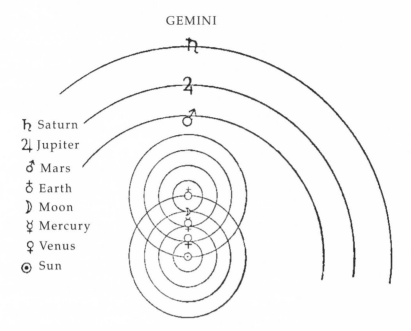

♄ Saturn
♃ Jupiter
♂ Mars
♁ Earth
☽ Moon
☿ Mercury
♀ Venus
☉ Sun

Now, to designate the realm of Saturn, we have to imagine the Earth, not the Sun, at the center. To do so, we must draw a circle with the Earth at the center. Actually, it is not really circular but egg-shaped. We proceed in a similar manner for the other heavenly bodies. Please discount aspects of secondary importance in this drawing and concentrate on what really matters. The aim here is to illustrate the corresponding figures for the realms of influence of the respective hierarchies.

Today, we shall consider in greater detail the nature of the members of the higher hierarchies immediately above humanity. The easiest way is to start with the human being. For only by becoming absolutely clear about what has repeatedly been said about the nature of the human being and human development can we rise to an understanding of the nature of the members of the higher hierarchies.

We know that human beings, inasmuch as they dwell and have developed on Earth, consist essentially of four constituent parts. These are the physical, etheric, and astral bodies, and the I. Let us depict these four members in a diagram.

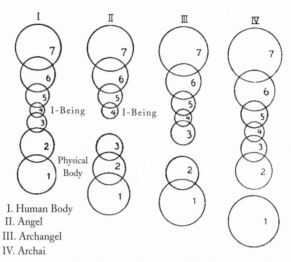

I. Human Body
II. Angel
III. Archangel
IV. Archai

Let us represent the physical body with a larger circle, the etheric and astral bodies with smaller circles, and finally, the I with the smallest circle. You know how human development proceeds. In the course of earthly development, the human being begins to work on the astral body through the I. In general we can say that, to the extent that a human being works upon the astral body with the I, so that this molded part of the astral body has come under the authority of the I, it is called *Manas* or Spirit Self. Thus the Manas or Spirit Self, as has often been emphasized, is not to be regarded as something newly added to the human being. Rather, it is simply the transformed product of the astral body. What I am describing here applies only to the human being. It is important that we don't simply extend generalizations without thinking, but realize that beings in the universe are very different from one another.

Therefore let us now draw the fifth member, the transformed astral body, or Manas, as a special circle. It should really be drawn inside the astral body. Above it, we draw the transformed etheric body, because insofar as the etheric body has been transformed, we characterize it as *Buddhi*, or Life Spirit. When the etheric body has been completely transformed, it is entirely Buddhi. Similarly, if we consider the human being in its ultimate perfection—a stage that can be attained by evolution through Jupiter, Venus, and Vulcan—

the physical body is transformed into *Atman*. Thus, when human beings in the Vulcan stage have reached the highest goal of perfection, they can be represented diagrammatically as follows: Atman, Buddhi, Manas, I, astral, etheric, and physical bodies. What is most characteristic in this scheme is the fact that *the seven members form a whole*, that *these seven principles interpenetrate one another*. That is the most important aspect.

But this is not the situation when we turn to the members of the next hierarchy, the Angels. We can apply this diagram to the human being but not to any angelic beings. Angels have developed a physical body, an etheric body, and an astral body in such a way that these, in certain ways, form a totality. But we must draw the I, Manas, Buddhi, and Atman of the Angels as separate from the rest of their being.

If you want to clarify an Angel's nature you must imagine the higher members, which the Angels have and can develop, hovering in the spiritual world above that part existing physically. Actually, the Angel has, however, only formed completely the Manas member—Buddhi and Atman will be developed later. An Angel, unlike a human being, does not have an accompanying I within an earthly body. Nor does an Angel develop Manas in the present stage of earthly development. That is why one would hardly think that the part of an Angel present in the physical world belongs to a spiritual being. When one meets human beings, it is obvious that they carry their members within them—everything is differentiated organically. But if you want to find an Angel, you must remember that an Angel's physical aspect here below is a reflection of the spiritual principles visible only in the supersensible world. You will find the physical bodies of Angels in flowing water, in mist rising from evaporating bodies of water, and in the wind and lightning flashing through the air, as well as other occurrences of this kind. One of the first stumbling blocks for the human being is the firm conviction that a physical body must have a definite boundary. As human beings we find it difficult to say to ourselves: I stand in a rising or falling mist or before a spraying brook. I am surrounded by the rushing, roaring wind. I see lightning flashing in the clouds. These are the revelations of the Angels. I need to see that beyond this physical manifestation, which is not as narrowly defined as the human one, is a manifestation of a spiritual body.

As human beings we develop all of the members of our being as self-enclosed entities. That is why we cannot imagine that a physical body can appear hazy and indistinct, that it may float and hover in the air, that it need not have definitely outlined contours. You must imagine, for example, that eighty Angels may have the densest part of their physical nature in one stretch of water. We should not imagine that the physical body of an Angel needs to be limited in any way. An Angel can belong to a portion of water here; far away is another segment. In short, we see that everything that surrounds us as water, air, and fire on Earth must be so conceived as to contain the bodies of beings belonging to the hierarchy immediately above humanity.

To behold the I and Manas of angelic beings, however, we need clairvoyant sight in the astral world. Angelic beings look down upon us from higher worlds. To find them, we must investigate the realm of the solar system that extends as far as the orbit of the Moon. Matters are relatively simple with regard to Angels. If, for example, we have the physical body of an Angel down here in a sheet of water or something similar, and if we investigate this portion of water or gust of wind clairvoyantly, we discover within it an etheric body and an astral body. That is why we have drawn these three members so that they are connected with one another. Of course, what we find in rushing wind, in flowing or evaporating waters, is not just the material image seen by common perception. The etheric and astral bodies of angelic beings dwell in everything belonging to water, air, and fire in the most varied ways. But if you wish to find the soul-spiritual nature of these Angels' being, you must investigate the astral realm clairvoyantly.

If we wish to consider the Archangels in the same way, the process is again different. Their astral body, as we have drawn it here, is not connected in any way with the physical and etheric bodies. We must draw their lowest members as the physical and etheric bodies. These are separate from the principles that dwell above in higher worlds.

To get a complete picture of the Archangels, we must look in two places. Their being is not like that of a human where everything is united into one being. An Archangel has a spiritual part above and a reflection of the spiritual down below. A physical body and an etheric body can be united only if the physical body consists of air and fire. For example, you could not sense an Archangel's physical body in rushing, roaring water. You could only perceive it in wind and fire, and you would have to look for the Archangel's spiritual counterpart, which is manifest in the rushing wind and fire, clairvoyantly in the spiritual world. That part is not even united with the physical, etheric body.

We now come to the beings we designate as Archai (or Primal Beginnings, Primal Powers, or Spirits of Personality). Here below we can draw only the physical body. All the rest is above in the spiritual world. Such a physical body can live only in fire. The physical bodies of the Archai can be perceived only in flames of fire. When we see the flashing fire of lightning, we can say that there we have something of the body of the Archai, but above, in the spiritual world, we can find clairvoyantly the spiritual counterpart that, in this case, is separate from the physical body. Indeed, the clairvoyant faculty can investigate the Archai with comparative ease. These Spirits of Personality dwell in a realm extending to the astronomical Mercury (esoteric Venus). Let us assume that someone has developed the capacity to observe what develops up there in the sphere of Mercury; such a person could then behold the highly developed beings known as Spirits of Personality—the Archai. Suppose this person gazes clairvoyantly up to Venus to observe the gathering of the Spirits of Personality, and then turns to the lightning flashing through the clouds. The person would see in the lightning the reflection of the Spirits of Personality, because the lightning contains their physical bodies.

Next, we reach the more exalted spiritual beings who extend their influence to the orbit of the Sun. These Powers (Exusiai) will concern us less today. It should only be pointed out that the Archai act through the instrument of Venus and Mercury beings, that is, through Venus beings who have their physical bodies in fire and

Mercury beings who have their physical bodies in fire and wind. You must imagine that, as the lower organs of their influence, the beings who dwell in the Sun make use of Venus spirits in flaming fire and of Mercury spirits in roaring wind. "And God makes the flames of fire into his servants and the winds into his messengers."[2] Sayings like this one in the Bible can be found in ancient religious documents. They are taken from spiritual facts and correspond to what can be observed with clairvoyant perception.

We have thus seen that the three hierarchies immediately above us are closely connected with our own existence. Human beings are the beings they are, because, in some measure, they partake of the solidity of the Earth. This separates us from all other beings; it makes a human being into a self-contained entity composed of separate members. On the Moon, a human being was still a being like others; there the human being went through transformations that were very much like water masses in a constant state of flux. It was on the Earth that, for the first time, so to speak, human beings were caught in their skins. They became self-contained beings consisting of a physical, etheric, and astral body, and an I. This occurred only comparatively recently. If we go back to Atlantean time, we find in the first epoch of that time human beings who did not experience their I fully within themselves. They were still waiting to receive their I into themselves. If we were to go back still further in earthly development, we find human beings who, we may say, consisted initially only of physical, etheric, and astral bodies. If we go back to Lemurian times, we find that a human being has no more of a physical, etheric, and astral body on Earth than the Angels have. From this point on, with the growth of the I from the Lemurian through the Atlantean epoch, the union of the different members begins. In Lemurian times, there were human beings on Earth who consisted of only physical, etheric, and astral bodies. These were not human beings in the present sense of the word, beings who could think and develop humanly as we understand it today.

---

2. Psalm 104:4.

Then something remarkable happened on our Earth. The human beings—who in Lemurian times sojourned on Earth and had only physical, etheric and astral bodies—couldn't help themselves; they could not manage their earthly existence and didn't know what they should do on Earth. Heavenly beings, inhabitants of Venus, now came down to those who lived on Earth, and, because the inhabitants of Venus had an affinity with the physical body, they could radiate into and inspire the physical body of the first Earth dwellers. Thus we have some of Lemurian humanity who went among the masses of human beings in a very remarkable way; they had a physical body different from the others. The physical body of such an exceptionally endowed human being was not ordinary, but was permeated, ensouled by a Venus spirit, a Spirit of Personality. Consequently, human beings who moved about in ancient Lemurian times—having a Venus spirit within the physical body—had a powerful impact on their entire surroundings. Outwardly, such Lemurians could not be distinguished fundamentally from their contemporaries, but because a Spirit of Personality was active in their physical bodies, these specially chosen individuals exerted a subtle yet powerful influence in the highest sense on their surroundings. They were objects of reverence, of awe, of obedience, unlike anything anywhere today. All of the migrations undertaken to populate the various regions of Earth were led by beings permeated with the Spirits of Personalty. Speech was unnecessary—there was no speech then—and no signs were necessary. The presence of such a personality was sufficient. If it was considered expedient to lead great masses of humanity from one place to another, the masses of humankind followed without reflecting upon it. Reflection was also nonexistent then and developed only later.

Thus, in ancient Lemurian times, the Spirits of Personality came down to Earth as Venus spirits. These Venus messengers who had taken on human countenances on Earth—such countenances possible then—were of special significance for the whole structure of the universe. Cosmically, they reached as far as Venus, and their activities were of significance for the entire interrelatedness of the cosmic system. They could lead humanity from one place to another because they knew the broader context that can be understood when one is acquainted, not just with the Earth itself, but also with its cosmic "neighborhood."

Human evolution continued, and it became necessary for Archangels, Mercury spirits, to intervene in this development. It was now their turn to ensoul and enliven what could be found below on Earth. This occurred mainly during the Atlantean period. Archangels, spiritual beings from Mercury, descended—beings who could ensoul and spiritualize the physical and etheric bodies of certain human beings. So, we also find human beings among the Atlanteans who could not really be distinguished outwardly from others, but who were, in their physical and etheric bodies, ensouled by an Archangel. Now, if you recall that yesterday it was said that Archangels have the task of directing whole peoples, you will understand that individuals who carried an archangelic being within them could give to the whole Atlantean race of people the appropriate laws as inscribed in the heavenly world.

When it was necessary to act more generally—the great leaders of ancient Lemurian times were ensouled by Venus spirits—those whose task it was in Atlantean times to direct smaller segments of humanity (the various peoples of the Earth) were ensouled by Archangels. The priest-kings of Atlantean times were really a maya; they were not what they appeared to be outwardly. An Archangel dwelled in their physical and etheric bodies, and this was the actual acting agent. We can go back into ancient Atlantean times and search for the hidden centers of these leaders of humanity. They worked from hidden places where they investigated the mysteries of the universe. Although the word originated later, we may call what was investigated and ordered from those ancient Atlantean Mystery centers, "oracles." The term *oracle* is very appropriate for the teaching and governing centers of Atlantean humanity, which the Archangels carried within themselves. From these centers great teachers carried out their work so that they could draw other human beings to them and could train them to become servants and priests in the oracles.

It is important to know that in Atlantean times human beings existed who were actually Archangels, that is, in whose physical and etheric bodies an Archangel was embodied. Clairvoyantly, one would have seen the physical body of such a being and behind him, a gigantic figure rising above and losing itself in indefinite regions— the inspiring Archangel. Such a personality was a twofold being, as if behind the physical human being, arising out of the indeterminate, there were the Archangel who inspired the person. At the death of such a being, the physical body was destroyed, according to Atlantean practice. The physical body, which had been inspired by the Archangel, dissolved, but the etheric body did not dissolve. There is a spiritual economy that requires exceptions to what must generally be represented as spiritual-scientific truth.[3] We usually say—and, in general, it is correct—that when someone dies, the physical body is laid aside and, after a certain time, the etheric body is likewise laid aside. Apart from an extract that remains, the etheric body dissolves. This, however, is only generally the case. There is an enormous difference between the etheric body of an initiate of the Atlantean oracles, which was permeated by an Archangel, and an ordinary etheric body. Such a valuable etheric body is not lost; it is preserved in the spiritual world. The seven most important etheric bodies of the seven great founders of the oracles were preserved by the mightiest leader of the Atlantean oracles. These etheric bodies had been woven through by archangelic beings who at death had naturally returned to higher worlds. Something was preserved, not in boxes, of course, but according to spiritual laws.

The Atlantean initiate of the Sun oracle is none other than the one—often referred to as *Manu*—who led the remainder of the Atlantean population over to Asia in order to establish the post-Atlantean cultures there.[4] He took a handful of people with him and

---

3. This topic is addressed in detail in Rudolf Steiner's *The Principle of Spiritual Economy in Connection with Questions of Reincarnation: An Aspect of the Spiritual Guidance of Man* (Hudson, NY: Anthroposophic Press, 1986), eleven lectures given in 1909 (GA 109).
4. See Steiner, *Cosmic Memory: Prehistory of Earth and Man*, (pp. 63–70).

led them across to Asia. Through generations he cultivated people, and, when the qualified seven had been produced and called to serve, he wove into their etheric bodies the seven etheric bodies that had been permeated by Archangels and preserved on ancient Atlantis. The seven, sent down by the powerful leader to found the first post-Atlantean culture, were the seven Holy Rishis of ancient Indian culture.[5] They bore within their sheaths the etheric bodies of the great Atlantean leaders who, in turn, had received them from Archangels themselves. Thus, past, present, and future work together. You would have found the seven Holy Rishis to have been simple people, for their astral bodies and I's had not reached the development of their etheric bodies. In the etheric body was woven their real capacity; thus they had certain times when inspiration worked in their etheric bodies. Then they said things that they could not have said out of themselves; what had been inspired through their etheric bodies flowed from their lips. They were simple people even by their own estimation; however, when they were inspired and their etheric body was active, they revealed the profoundest mysteries of our solar system and the whole universe.

Even in post-Atlantean times, human beings had not advanced sufficiently to dispense with ensoulment from above. We have seen that this ensoulment took place in Lemurian times because a Spirit of Personality permeated the physical body. During the Atlantean period, physical and etheric bodies were ensouled by archangelic beings, while, in post-Atlantean times, the great leaders of humanity were ensouled by angelic beings who had descended into their physical, etheric, and astral bodies. The mighty leaders of the first post-Atlantean periods had not just human physical, etheric, and astral bodies. Each leader was permeated by an Angel. This enabled the leaders to look back into their former incarnations. The ordinary person is not able to do so because he has not yet developed his Manas; he must first become an Angel. These leaders, born of ordinary people, embodied in their physical, etheric, and astral bodies an angelic

---

5. See Steiner, *An Outline of Occult Science.*

being who ensouled and penetrated them. That was again maya, for they were something very different from what they appeared to represent on Earth. The principle leaders of humanity in ancient times were quite different from what they appeared to be. They were personalities in whom dwelt an Angel, who inspired them with what they needed to be the teachers and leaders of humankind. The great founders of religions and religious leaders were persons possessed by angelic beings. Angels spoke through them.

Things in the world may be described as existing in a state of absolute regularity. Nevertheless, the stages of development are constantly overlapping. What is described as a process of complete regularity does not actually function with complete regularity. What has been said is mainly valid—namely, in Lemurian times, Spirits of Personality spoke through human beings, in Atlantean times, Archangels, and, in post-Atlantean periods, Angels. But even in post-Atlantean times, we still find human beings whose physical bodies are permeated by Spirits of Personality, and although they live in post-Atlantean times they are in the same position as those beings in Lemurian times through whom Spirits of Personality spoke. There can be human beings in the post-Atlantean era, therefore, who carry entirely the characteristics of the rest of the population, but who—because humankind also needs such great leaders—still carry within them one of the Spirits of Personality and are the outward embodiment of such a spirit. Furthermore, in post-Atlantean periods there were those who bore an Archangel—a Mercury spirit—in their physical and etheric bodies. Finally, there was a third category of human beings who were ensouled and inspired by angelic beings in their physical, etheric, and astral bodies. They were, in fact, human beings through whom Angels spoke.

According to traditions of the East, such personalities among human beings received special names. Thus, those who outwardly appeared like human beings of the post-Atlantean period, though they bore a Spirit of Personality in their nature—and were ensouled all the way into the physical body by such a spirit—were known in the teachings of the East as *Dhyani-Buddhas*, a general term for human individuals who are ensouled, even into the physical body, by a Spirit of Personalty. Personalities ensouled down to the etheric body by an Archangel in post-Atlantean times are known as *Bodhisattvas*. Those individuals, whose physical, etheric, and astral bodies are ensouled by an Angel, are called human *Buddhas*. Thus we have three degrees: the Dhyani-Buddhas, the Bodhisattvas, and the human Buddhas.[6] That is the true teaching of the Buddhas relating to the various categories of Buddhahood. We have to consider this in connection with the manner in which the hierarchies manifest themselves.

What we encounter is remarkable when we look back at earlier, undeveloped humanity. Among these human beings we find some through whom the mighty hierarchies of the cosmos came to speak to the planets. The spirits of the higher hierarchies, at work even before the creation of our Earth, gradually emancipated planetary human beings according to the degree of their maturity. Here we gaze into profound depths of wisdom. It is extraordinarily important that we discover how primeval universal wisdom was taught to humanity in ancient times.

You will hear about the Buddhas—the East teaches of not just one, but many Buddhas—among whom different degrees of perfection are represented. You should keep in mind that a Buddha sojourned on the Earth, but *behind* the Buddha, so to speak, came a Bodhisattva and even a Dhyani-Buddha. It could also occur in a particular instance that the Dhyani-Buddha and the Bodhisattva did not penetrate deeply enough to ensoul the physical body. The Bodhisattva may only have ensouled the etheric body, so that we can imagine a being who could not penetrate deeply enough to ensoul and inspire the physical body, but only the etheric body. A higher being, such as a Bodhisattva, who was physically invisible, since he appeared only in an etheric body, could inspire the human Buddha in a special way. So, we might have a human Buddha inspired by an angelic being who could still receive the inspiration of an Archangel into the etheric body.

---

6. Again, the background here is *The Secret Doctrine*.

Here we gaze into the profound complexities of the human being, and this is very important. Some individuals of former ages can be understood only when we realize that they represent focal points for a number of beings who work and express themselves through humanity. For, indeed, many periods do not possess enough great people who can be inspired by the spirits who have to be active. It is therefore often the case that various beings of the higher hierarchies have only a single person on Earth to ensoul. Sometimes, besides the inhabitants of Mercury, we have those of Mercury and Venus combined who speak to us through one person. Such concepts help us understand human evolution. We learn to recognize the true nature of the personalities who, when we meet them in their physical form, merely represent maya.

Tomorrow, we shall concern ourselves with the origin of the various physical planets, which until now we have considered only as boundary marks. We shall gain an understanding of them as the dwelling places of spiritual beings.

8. The Spiritual Hierarchies, the Zodiac, and the Human Being

APRIL 17, 1909, *Evening*

IN OUR PRESENTATION OF HIGHER BEINGS and their relation to our universe and solar system, we come today to the chapter that will be the most suspect to our contemporaries who receive their view of the world and their circumstances from ordinary popular scientific knowledge, because here we must touch on matters absolutely unimaginable to the modern scientist. It is not a matter of contradiction. Anyone firmly grounded in occultism can survey the facts of modern science from this vantage point. You will not find any contradictions between what has been said here and facts of modern science. It is just that the harmony between the two is not easily established. But, if you always have the patience to press forward, you will gradually see how individual facts unite to form the whole.

Perhaps I should also mention that some of what has been dealt with in these lectures has been considered from a different standpoint in the lecture cycles held in Stuttgart and Leipzig.[1] If you take them superficially, you can find some contradictions between this or that assertion. This is only because it is not my task in my lectures to speak about speculative theories, but about facts gained through clairvoyant consciousness, which appear differently when viewed from various aspects. To use a comparison, the picture of a tree drawn from one side will look very different when drawn from another; and yet, it is

---

1. *Universe, Earth and Man* (London: Rudolf Steiner Press, 1987), 11 lectures, Stuttgart, August 4–16, 1908; *Egyptian Myths and Mysteries* (Hudson, NY: Anthroposophic Press, 1971), 12 lectures, Leipzig, September 2–14, 1908.

one and the same tree. The same is true of descriptions of spiritual facts when illuminated from different sides. Certainly, taking a few particular ideas as a starting point, it is easy to set up an abstract system. But we are working from the bottom up: the crowning achievement of this approach will be a harmonious unity of the whole.

Above all, we must consider each assertion as to what sense and from which standpoint an assertion is made. For example: a popular scientific work states that air or gas on Jupiter must be as thick as tar or honey.[2] From the viewpoint of spiritual science it could be said that this is a grotesque notion, and the way I chose to express this emphasized the grotesqueness of the matter. Yet, from the modern scientific side, one could argue, "Don't you know that modern physics can produce liquid air as thick as honey or tar?" Although this is a self-evident scientific fact, it is irrelevant to our considerations. What science calls air can be densified to such an extent—there is no doubt about that. But, from the viewpoint of spiritual science this is as valid as saying water can be turned into something as hard as stone—namely, ice. Indeed, ice is water, but this is not the point. What matters is whether we learn to consider things in their various functions in a living way, or in the dead manner of modern science. It is obvious that ice is water, but what would be the response of someone who is used to driving a mill with water, if advised to use ice instead of water? The abstract concept that ice is water is irrelevant. What matters is that we come to understand the universe in its dynamic activity. This requires perspectives very different from abstract notions of a purely material metamorphosis related to density. We could no more breathe air as thick as honey or tar than drive a water mill with ice.

This distinction is important for spiritual-scientific observation. For we do not observe orbs in the universe as they are typically regarded today—namely, as some material lumps of a particular size that move around in cosmic space, which modern astronomical mythology views as simply material orbs. We observe them in their living soul-spiritual state—that is , we observe them in their entirety.

---

2. It is not known to what work Steiner is referring.

Thus, we must consider within this totality what we call, in a spiritual-scientific sense, the creation of the individual bodies of the universe.

For our first example of the creation of a cosmic body, let us take ancient Saturn, from which we know our evolution proceeded. To begin with, ancient Saturn was as large as our whole present solar system. What one calls old Saturn in its beginning stage was about as large as our solar system. But we should not simply imagine it as a material globe. You will remember that, on ancient Saturn, nothing existed yet of what we have today as the three physical states—solid, fluid, and gaseous. There was only warmth, or fire. Let us represent this primeval globe of warmth by a circle.

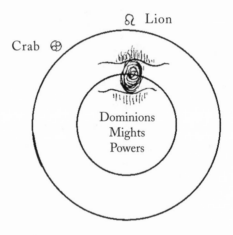

You will remember we said that, at the point where the primeval globe of Saturn develops into the Sun globe, those beings who form the zodiac appear surrounding the Sun globe. I indicated, however, that the zodiac already surrounded ancient Saturn, though not as compactly as during the evolutionary stage of the old Sun. Around ancient Saturn, therefore, we must picture the activity of Thrones, Cherubim, and Seraphim who spiritually represent the zodiac. The outer circle in the diagram represents the zodiac spiritually. You might ask, "How does this agree with the modern view of the zodiac?" It agrees completely with it, as we will demonstrate in the final lectures.

You should picture the situation as follows: Imagine placing yourself at a particular point on the Saturn globe. If you now raise your hand and point upward with your finger, above this spot on Saturn you will find the region of certain Thrones, Cherubim, and Seraphim. If you move from there and indicate the area beyond, you will point out another region of Thrones, Cherubim, and Seraphim, because groups of these three beings form a circle around ancient Saturn. Suppose you then wanted to point in the direction of certain Thrones, Cherubim, and Seraphim. Remember, these beings are by no means the same like a group of twelve identical soldiers. They differ considerably from one another. Each bears its individual stamp so that, depending on where one's attention is directed, one sees quite different beings. So, to point out a particular group of Thrones, Cherubim, and Seraphim, one denotes them as a particular constellation. The constellations are like signposts: in one direction, over there, are the Thrones, Cherubim, and Seraphim known as Gemini, the Twins; over there, Leo, the Lion; and so on. They are, so to speak, guideposts that indicate the direction where particular beings may be found. So we conceive of the constellations as guideposts or boundaries between these regions of beings. The constellations of the zodiac are more than mere signposts, but we must make it clear that, as a first stage, when we speak of the zodiac, we are referring to spiritual beings.

The Thrones are the first to exert their activity on the fiery form that we call ancient Saturn. They have reached a stage of development that enables them to pour forth their own substance. They cause their own warmth substance to seep into the mass of Saturn. That is how, as I have described, a series of "eggs"—perhaps a strange word to use, yet they have this form—appear all around this structure.

You might ask about the substance as such. Did a warmth substance already exist? What existed before can only be described as a neutral cosmic fire that was fundamentally one with universal space. *In other words, to begin with there was only space.* This was marked out, so to speak, and now the warmth substance of ancient Saturn was made to trickle onto the surface. As soon as the warmth substance was poured into ancient Saturn, spiritual beings became active from two sides. We have mentioned previously that, here in the inner part of the Saturn space, we find the Powers or Spirits of

Form, the Spirits of Movement or Mights, and the Dominions or Spirits of Wisdom. The Powers, Mights, and Dominions are active from within. The Cherubim, Seraphim, and Thrones work from outside and, as a result, a cooperation occurs between the beings working from the outside and those active within.

In the first lecture we said that one can distinguish inner soul fire, experienced inwardly as inner warmth and well-being, and outwardly perceptible fire. Between these two is a neutral warmth contained in the egg-shaped forms. Spread above them is soul warmth, as if streaming in from outside, but also holding itself back slightly. It is as if radiating soul warmth were held back because of the neutral fire within—the perceptible warmth is pushed back from within. Thus, what was previously delineated as a "warmth-egg" is enclosed by two currents—namely, an outer stream of soul warmth and an inner stream of warmth that would have been perceptible to the outer senses. Only the inner part, therefore, is composed of physically perceptible heat. Now, because of the working together of the outer and inner warmth, the Saturn "eggs" begin to rotate. Each single "egg" inscribes a full circle and comes, in turn, under the influence of the various Thrones, Seraphim, and Cherubim situated at the periphery.

Then something strange occurs. On its journey, this "egg" finally arrives again at the point where it came into being originally. (I am describing these facts according to spiritual-scientific observation.) When it reaches this point, it becomes stationary. It cannot go further and comes to a halt. Every "egg" is created at a particular point,

travels around the circle and is stopped at the point where it originated. This creation of "eggs" lasts only for a specific period of time;
after this, no further warmth "eggs" come into existence. When all
of these "eggs" have arrived and are stopped at one particular point,
they fall on top of each other, forming a single "egg." Thus, at their
point of origin, the "eggs" halt and come to rest. Naturally, from this
moment, after which no new "eggs" are formed, the "eggs" all gather
together and cover themselves. A globe is thus created on the circumference, but, naturally, only over the course of time. This globe
consists of the densest part of the fire substance, called *Saturn* in the
narrower sense of the word, for it occupies the position of our
present planet Saturn.

As previous stages are in a certain sense repeated, so were whole
processes repeated at the origin of our Earth. Our present Saturn
came about in a similar way. It, too, was held back at a particular
point, but, because things shift for various reasons, it was not held
back at the same point as in the case of ancient Saturn. However, the
process of origin is the same. In this way, as a result of the working
together of all the cosmic powers belonging to the hierarchies, a small
Saturn globe is born out of the mighty, voluminous original Saturn.

Let us consider more closely the moment on ancient Saturn when
all the globes came to a standstill. The sages of primeval wisdom
spoke of this moment as follows: The first foundation of the human
physical body was formed on ancient Saturn. This earliest foundation was formed only out of warmth, but within this warmth body
all future organs were already present in seed form. At that point,
where the initial movement again comes to rest, the seed is created
for that organ in the human body, which, when the body is later set
in motion, also ensures that all of the functions of the physical body
may be brought to rest again—that is, *the heart*. Here—from the first
impulse of movement—the germ of the heart appears, but it only
comes into existence in its first manifestation so that the movement
will again be brought to rest at this point. Thus the heart becomes
that organ through which the entire physical body in all of its functions is brought to rest when the heart itself stops beating.

In ancient languages, each member of the human body was identified with a very precise name. The heart was called the "Lion" in
the body. Thus the primeval world wisdom asked, "In which zodiacal direction must one point to find the region where the first seed
of the human heart was planted?" They pointed upward, and designated the Thrones, Seraphim, and Cherubim who worked on the
heart, the zone of the Lion. The human being projected elements of
the body into the cosmos, and the region of the body one is used to
identifying as the inner manifestation of the Lion was also identified
outwardly as the region of the Lion in the zodiac. This is how such
matters relate to one another.

All of the other aspects of the human being were also formed
through the zodiac. The heart was formed out of the region of the
Lion. The rib cage, which is near the heart and must exist for its protection, is referred to in the human body as the breast plate. Naturally, it must have been formed in the region next to and preceding
the Lion—that is, before the completion of the heart. Another name
for breast plate was assigned, and the descriptive element was sought
in an animal, which by nature also has such armor: the Crab. The
breast plate that appears in the zodiac is called Cancer, because the
Crab embodies a natural protective shield. Hence this region was
called Cancer and is to one side of the Lion.

The other regions of the zodiac were named according to the
same principle. Indeed, the names of the various regions of the
zodiac arose as a result of the human form being projected outward
into the cosmos. It is not always easy to discover the original inten-
tion from the frequently distorted or misrepresented names, as you
can see in an example such as Cancer. In several instances, the name
has not been handed down correctly, and so one has to go back to
the source to obtain a clear picture.

For the moment we shall not consider how Saturn disappears—
how it is dissolved again. We want to discuss how evolution proceeds
after a pralaya runs out. A new evolution begins. The first phase that
occurs is exactly the same as what previously occurred on Saturn.
After this, all of Saturn existence repeats itself: a second formation

begins again from the center point. We come now to the next stage of evolution, which we usually designate as the development of old Sun. Just as previously the Thrones sacrificed themselves, we now have the sacrifice of another rank of the spiritual hierarchies—the Dominions or Spirits of Wisdom. The Thrones are mightier beings; they were able to trickle forth physical and warmth substantiality, were able, out of their own bodies, to bring forth the substance of Saturn as we have described. The Dominions or Spirits of Wisdom are able to sacrifice only an etheric body, which is thinner. The human being already possessed the foundations of a physical body; to this the Dominions or Spirits of Wisdom now added an etheric body. This happened in a second circumference, as it were.

Eagle

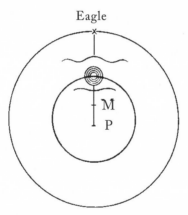

I draw here a second circumference. This represents the original size of the old Sun, shrunk in comparison to the former larger circumference. In this process of contracting, it has also become more dense. As a result, the possibility arises that inside the old Sun there is not only warmth substance but densified warmth substance, a gaseous, airy substance. Now, out of the periphery the beings previously mentioned, the Thrones, together with the Dominions, begin to work; and within the circumference of the Sun only the Powers and the Mights or the Spirits of Form and the Spirits of Movement remain. The other beings work from the periphery inward.

The following now occurs in a way similar to what occurred on ancient Saturn. Certain currents form, which were created by the spirits at the periphery (the Thrones), and now work in cooperation with the Dominions. As a result, these currents are somewhat denser than those the Thrones alone had earlier activated. Inside, this mass contracts, and one globe of mist after another is produced between the activity of the two currents. This globe is different from the Saturn globe in that Saturn, with all its beings, was composed only of warmth substance, and everything, so to speak, was astir in the space around it. But this globe is permeated by ether— an etheric bodily substance. Although the globe is only as dense as gas, it is interpenetrated by an ether body. As a result, the whole globe is a living being. It is inwardly alive. Saturn was an inwardly dynamic being, full of mobility until it was brought to a standstill by the Lion. But this globe that we can call Jupiter is inwardly alive. (We can call it Jupiter because the planet Jupiter, as seen in the heavens, is a repetition of a part that split off from the old Sun.) Thus, we have the old Sun; the globes around it are circling, living globes, grand living beings.

Instead of Leo, you must now think of another region of the zodiac—the region of the Eagle—where these globes were originally created. In this region lies the original impulse that led to the creation of the Sun globe, this living being in cosmic space. When this living globe has completed its journey along the entire circumference, it returns to the region of the Eagle. But now something different happens. Whereas before each globe was infused at this point with life, it is now killed on its return by the same influence that originally called it to life. One globe after another is slain. When all have been killed and no further globes come into being, the existence of the old Sun comes to an end. Life consists here of the creation of new globes; when they return to this place, they are killed by cosmic forces. The sting of death inflicted by the cosmos on the life of the old Sun was experienced as the "sting of the Scorpion." So, because that region inflicts death, it is called the region of Scorpio, the Scorpion. At this position may be seen the constellation of the Eagle, which brings dead matter to life, and the constellation that sends forth the forces of death, Scorpio. The forces in the zodiac that brought to rest primordial life in the physical organization of the human being are in the region of the Lion. The forces that have the capacity to destroy life as such are in the region of Scorpio. It remains for us to become acquainted with the context of conditions today, which are, of course, differently constituted, but can only happen gradually. A thick veil or maya has been drawn over the original conditions.

Let us proceed. We don't need to consider the next set of circumstances in such a thorough way, because the significance of these relationships and the entire process appears before us. The following, however, must be remembered. Basically, what kind of body is Saturn? It is a warmth body. When you look at Saturn, you would be very wrong if you assumed Saturn to be a body that can be compared with other planets such as Jupiter or Mars. What exists there is actually no more than an expanse of warmth. You only see it as you do, because you can look at it through an expanse of light; you glimpse it through illuminated space. Visualize how an unilluminated object appears when seen through a light-filled space. It would appear bluish. You can observe this in the flame of a candle. The flame appears blue in the middle and is surrounded by a kind of radiance. If you look at darkness through illuminated space it always appears blue. I am very aware that I am in danger of talking nonsense according to the modern, mechanistic school of optics. The fact is, this nonsense is correct. Modern physics does not know why the expanse of the heavens looks blue. It appears blue to you, because it is, in fact, dark, black, and you see it through an illuminated space. Darkness seen through the light appears blue. That is why Saturn, when you observe it, also appears as a somewhat bluish cosmic body.

Everything said here agrees with the facts of science, but not with the fanciful theories that have been contrived around them. It would lead too far astray if I explained to you, along the same lines, the cause of the rings of Saturn, because, with each Saturn one is concerned with three layers of warmth: a neutral layer, a layer of soul warmth, and a physically perceptible warmth. When looking at these various layers through an illuminated space, the illusion of a gaseous globe arises, surrounded by a kind of dust ring. We are simply experiencing an optical phenomenon. Saturn is still today a heavenly body consisting only of warmth substance.

These things can, of course, be said only in a context such as the current one—otherwise, one could not understand them. Each Saturn must be addressed while recognizing that it is composed in essence of warmth substance; everything regarding this Saturn is explained in this context. Every Jupiter, which is nothing more than a stage of solar existence, is a formation composed mainly of gas and warmth. So it is with today's Jupiter, which is a repetition of ancient Jupiter. Of course the relationships within space and concerning movement change somewhat. The present Jupiter is not at exactly the same position it was earlier, but basically it is.

Let us now proceed and elucidate the Mars phenomenon in the same way. Mars originated as a result of the cooling of a gigantic globe into the fluid state, until it finally separated from the general misty, watery mass into a compressed globe of water. Again, this occurred because the watery globes that arose at the periphery were held back at a particular point. Just as the Lion halted movement on Saturn, and Scorpio brought about death on Jupiter, so on Mars, the watery globes are brought to rest. To be sure, the details about Mars are somewhat different than those of Jupiter and Saturn. Mars today is a repetition of old Moon. The old Moon reached as far as the present position of Mars. Mars is the other piece of old Moon. One piece is the present Moon, which is dross. The living remnant, which represents the other pole, remained with the present Mars in the course of the repetition. In this sense, Mars is the third condition of our planetary evolution, and it corresponds to the stage of old Moon. Mars is essentially a water-body. During the period of the old Moon—or old Mars, if you prefer—human beings received their astral body—or, in other words, the first form of consciousness. The human body at that time consisted of a watery Mars or Moon substance. Just as the human body today is composed of earthly substances, so the human body at that time consisted of fire, air, and water. According to the densest substance they contained, human beings of that period could be termed water beings. The human being became a water being above all because the astral body had been implanted into the being. This human being was not yet an I-being. It was a human being endowed with an astral body. This occurred after an impulse was given at a particular point, moved around the course of the circle and came back to the same point from which it first set forth. This point became the region in the zodiac known as the Waterman (Aquarius). Here the significance of the zodiacal sign of "Waterman" can be found, for there humankind received consciousness on the old Moon, or old Mars, after having completed a single circuit.

We come now to the Earth, which represents the fourth stage of development. The three earlier stages are repeated. Saturn is formed; Sun is formed, and leaves Jupiter behind, which is a repetition of the Sun; Moon is formed, and leaves Mars behind; and finally the Earth emerges, as I have described it, severed from the Sun with the part that separated as lunar dross. You know that the I first began in the time of ancient Lemuria when the present Moon separated from Earth. That could happen only because, once again, an impulse came from the periphery that resulted in the completion of one rotation. Sufficient maturity had now been attained in order to receive the first beginnings of the I. This happened during ancient Lemuria. For this, we point to the position in the zodiac referred to today as the "Bull" (Taurus). When this designation was created humankind could still experience the reality of this name very clearly and concretely. In its most essential manifestation, the name originated in the secret doctrine of the Egyptians and Chaldeans. We can find its origins there, and a consciousness of the correct meaning of the word only exists today within the true mystery teachings.

The very first stirring, or tendency toward the I-am is expressed in speech, in sound. All sound-formation is connected in a certain way with the forces of procreation. This should not be touched on here, but it is familiar to every occultist. The breaking of the voice at puberty, for example, is connected in a definite way with the powers of propagation. There is a hidden relationship between them. Everything related to this human capacity and activity was summed up by ancient consciousness as the "Bull" nature of the human being. From that capacity arose the name of this particular zodiacal sign, which has the same meaning for the Earth that the Lion has for Saturn, that Scorpio has for Jupiter, and that the Waterman has for Mars. As the Egyptian period approached, so too came the third post-Atlantean culture. First came the ancient Indian; the second was the ancient Persian; and the third was the Egyptian cultural epoch. These periods of civilization represent stages of repetition of the development of the Earth as a whole. The Lemurian era was the third period of the Earth's development. Egyptian mystery teaching repeats, therefore, essentially a spiritual reflection of what occurred in Lemurian times. What happened in Lemurian times was best known to the priests of the Egyptian Mysteries for these occurrences were reflected in the particular culture of Egypt. That is why Egyptian civilization felt a particular kinship with the constellation of the Bull and with the cult of the Bull in general.

So, now you will understand that it is by no means easy to describe the real processes that led to the origin of our heavenly bodies and what occurred in relation to them. How does a heavenly body originate? Our Saturn, Jupiter, Mars, and so on, originated thus: first, sheaths formed themselves; one after the other was destroyed in turn, and, when the process of calling into life concluded, then the global formations that had previously shaped the sheaths coalesced to form a single creation of circumference. Celestial bodies such as Saturn, Jupiter, and Mars came about because, originally, a type of sheath existed: the heavenly bodies densified into a creation in that one globe was laid on top of another, so as to become visible in cosmic space. Here you have nothing of a mechanical process or the dreary theories of Kant-Laplace; rather, here you have a living picture of how, as a result of the spiritual workings of the hierarchies, heavenly bodies such as Saturn, Jupiter, and Mars originated.

9. Evolution and the Cosmic Human Body

APRIL 18, 1909, *Morning*

QUESTIONS NATURALLY ARISE following a talk like the one given yesterday. Also, if it is the first time one has heard such a presentation of broad cosmic truths, some things may not be understood. I emphasized yesterday—and I ask you always to remember—that what I am describing here is not based on speculation or theory. It arises out of the real facts we call the Akashic Chronicle. Such facts can be put together into a kind of system only later.

A question that might have arisen for some people should be anticipated here today: What is the status of the finished planets? Yesterday, from a certain perspective, we described the genesis of a planet to the point when it becomes an individual, visible planet. But now someone might say, "Yes, but were the planets we see in the heavens not in existence before the moment described yesterday?"

The answer is, no, they were not. We must be clear about the following. When the moment I spoke of yesterday was reached, a new epoch began. Assume, for example, that we want to describe the origin of a planet, not as it occurred at the time of ancient Saturn, when only Saturn existed, but as it occurred at the creation of the Earth. First, we have the repetition of the Saturn stage of development; then the stages of the Sun and Moon are repeated. The development of the Earth likewise begins with the formation of a tremendous warmth or fire body—just as I described concerning Saturn. Now, the time came when, at a certain moment, under the influences of the zodiacal region of the Lion, this great, revolving globe of fire divided itself off; that is, this single Saturn—what we call Saturn today—reached its peak at the moment of its separation. Thus the individual planet came into being.

You should not imagine, however, that the calming influences exerted through the Lion stopped Saturn's motion completely. Saturn became a being that absorbed everything previously distributed in its periphery. This occurred through the influences of the Lion. But now the large globe from which Saturn severed itself contracted, yet continued to exist as a smaller globe. Although the whole structure withdrew inwardly, Saturn nonetheless preserved some of its original motion. This was after a calming influence had been exerted and Saturn's movements inwardly came to rest. Previously, it had used its own momentum, because by necessity, so to speak, it had to keep moving as if swimming within the globe. Now that the globe had been withdrawn from it, however, a self-impelled motion continued, even though the inner movement had been broken. This self-impelled capacity to move after the first impetus was given is the current motion, the current rotation of Saturn.

A similar process occurred in the case of Jupiter—for, as the Earth began to form, what has been described had already happened. Differentiation took place in the globe—which had begun to contract inwardly. Under the sign of Scorpio, the slaying of the individual globes occurred. These globes interpenetrated one another and, as a result, each began its own inner life. After Jupiter as a mighty life-being had, as it were, been slain, the life of the several beings on the planet began. As the globe contracted again, Jupiter, finding within itself the impetus to do so, continued to move independently. What we observe as the present motion of Saturn, Jupiter, and so forth is a consequence. It began as the formative process I described yesterday was being concluded.

Another difficulty appears to have arisen, because I referred to Jupiter as the second planet and Mars as the third to detach themselves, whereas, chronologically, I mentioned first a Saturn stage of evolution, followed by Sun and Moon evolutions. This is totally justified. Our current planets arose during the recapitulation that occurred during the fourth stage of evolution—that is, during the development of the Earth. In the beginning, when Saturn was formed, only Saturn actually existed. When the Sun stage of development occurred, conditions in this second body that had formed require us to speak of a Sun. But when this Sun development advanced beyond the Saturn stage, the entire evolutionary process of the Sun ended. So, when we look back on these first planetary developments of our Earth we must be aware that they had also been completed.

This is not true of the development of Earth proper. First, Saturn came into being, then the Sun arose, albeit as recapitulation; but the process advanced inwardly; it was not completed. Jupiter is left behind as the remnant of the recapitulation of the Sun development. This is what we have to remember. Then the Moon stage of development is repeated on Earth. If we look back on this process of development as a whole, this Moon stage was brought to a definite conclusion at that time. But the Moon period within Earth development does not represent a conclusion. It continues, and Mars is left behind during the recapitulation.

The current planets that are visible to us in the heavens must be considered to have originated during the time we call the *fourth* stage of development—the time of earthly evolution—according to our Akashic Chronicle system. We have considered these things; it is impossible, however, to speak of the entire universe and mention every aspect of it. You may have noticed that first a kind of globe existed. I spoke, for instance, about Saturn, about a globe of fire or a large kind of fiery "egg," and after that we spoke of a rotating motion.

Indeed, we can think of a kind of "egg" or globe. And while each such globe, corresponding to the most primal condition of Saturn, rotates, increasingly a kind of belt is formed. It does not surround the whole of the "egg." It is more like a broad band. Within this belt, various forms assemble that were created around the globe. This belt formation represents a general cosmic law. You can see that the law, under which everything moves toward a concentration, refers to a kind of equator or belt and is manifest in the cosmos as far as you can survey; the Milky Way, for example, owes its existence to it. When you see the Milky Way as an outermost belt surrounding cosmic space with stars sparsely distributed in between, it is the result of the law that causes things to be gathered together into a belt as soon as rotation begins. Because of this, our cosmic system is lentil-shaped. It is not spherical as is usually presumed, but lentil-shaped, and at the broad equator, the belt draws together. You must also imagine such a band forming at the origin of a planet. To draw these stages schematically, take an "egg" and, possibly with red color, paint such a band around it. The whole "egg" must not be colored red, only the belt. The bodies selected to form a planet now assemble along this band. Here one would have to draw a point where everything comes together.

Thus, we see that the configuration, the distribution of the stars, as set in space around us, is the result of the activity of spiritual beings or hierarchies. For when we speak about the contraction of great masses, we must be conscious that this contraction does not occur by itself, but through the activity of the beings we have described as the higher hierarchies.

To sum up then, we can say that during the period when ancient Saturn—that is, when the grand fire-globe from which our whole solar system issued—was formed, the Spirits of Personality were going through their human stage of existence; during the formation of the Sun, the Archangels or Fire Spirits went through their human existence; during the development of the Moon, the Angels went through their human existence; and, on Earth, humanity now experiences its human stage. Yet it is also true that the human being was involved in all that previously occurred. What we call the physical body today received its first beginnings during the earliest phase of the formation of Saturn. The physical body was not yet permeated by an etheric or astral body then, but the physical body was already predisposed—once it had achieved the transformations that it would later experience—to become the bearer of the spiritual earthly human being of today.

Very slowly, step by step, the human physical body was prepared during the development of ancient Saturn. Member by member the parts of the human body came into being as ancient Saturn formed, passing through each sign of the zodiac. During the time when Saturn was in the sign of the Lion, the outline of the heart was formed. The beginnings of the rib cage came about as Saturn passed through the sign of the Crab. The predisposition to symmetry in the human physical form—the fact that the two sides of the body are alike— occurred when Saturn was in the sign of the Twins. In this way we can describe the origins of every part of the human body. Looking up to the constellations where the Ram is found, we could say: The foundations for the upper part of the head were established for the first time when ancient Saturn was under the sign of the Ram. The foundations of our speech organs were laid down when Saturn was in the sign of the Bull. If you now imagine the human being divided according to its various physical components, you will glimpse the creative forces in the zodiac that gave rise to each part of the human being.

In the ancient Mysteries, the zodiac was represented pictorially, much as we have it here on the ceiling of this hall. Indeed, by chance—but there is no chance—we are in a hall where the ceiling is decorated with the zodiac. Formerly, the zodiac was not depicted in terms of the respective animal forms; rather the various parts or members of the human being were assigned to their respective regions. The head was assigned to the sign of the Ram, the larynx area to the Bull, the arms to the symmetry of the Twins, the rib cage to Cancer, the heart to the Lion, and so on down to the lower part of the legs assigned to the Waterman, and the feet to the Fishes. Imagine the zodiac as the form of a human being inscribed in the cosmos; there you have what created the original forms for the members of the human physical body out of the cosmos—out of the corresponding powers of the hierarchies of the Thrones, Seraphim and Cherubim. This form is the great cosmic human being who strides forward in the wisdom literature and myths of the world, after which each individual human being has been patterned and created in the most varied manifestations.

Think, for example, of the giant Ymir spread out in the cosmos, for the microcosmic human being was formed from Ymir, the giant.[1] Everywhere you find the great macrocosmic human, the creator, who represents outwardly what the human being contains inwardly. A profound truth lies at the basis of such pictures, a truth that, depending on the clairvoyant capacities of the various peoples, comes more or less perfectly to light. It also shines through in the wisdom that found external expression in the Old Testament. It illumines the wisdom that, as the esoteric teaching of the ancient Hebrews, creates the foundation for the wisdom of the Old Testament in the Adam Kadmon of the Kabbala.[2] The macrocosmic human is none other than the human being we have seen inscribed in the constellations of the cosmos. We only have to form concepts about this in the right way.

What I have unfolded for you now, culminating in the instruction about the macrocosmic human being, are teachings containing the deepest secrets of the universe that will gradually flow into humankind's general education. Humankind is still far removed from understanding these teachings today, and if a conventional scholar listened to these lectures, that person would probably consider this audience as something other than a sensible group of people.

---

1. Ymir, the earliest being and progenitor of the ancient giants, was killed by Odin and his brothers. The Earth was made from his flesh, the waters from his blood, and from his skull the heavens were created.

2. According to Kabbala, Adam Kadmon is the name given to the first emanation from the "Eternal Fountain." It signifies the first Man, or the first production of divine energy or son of God, and other and inferior emanations are subordinate to it (Albert G. Mackey, *An Encyclopedia of Freemasonry and Its Kindred Sciences*, vol. 1, Chicago, 1912, p. 15. See also, Rudolf Steiner, "The Cosmic Origin of the Human Form," in *The Mystery of the Trinity and The Mission of the Spirit* (Hudson, NY: Anthroposophic Press, 1991).

Human beings are far removed from understanding these things today. But we are beginning an age when facts found to contradict the fantastic theories of modern science will urge people to seek the way to these encompassing truths of primeval wisdom. The mystery about the process of conception, for example, about which there is much childish speculation today, will not be unraveled until the teaching of the macrocosmic human is applied to it. Precisely what a real mystery is, and above all, what cannot be investigated by instruments and tools, will be illumined to the very minutest point of investigation. How small is the cell where conception takes place when compared to the cosmos! But only the mysteries of the great cosmos will solve the riddle of what is taking place in the smallest cell. Nothing else has the capacity to unravel the secrets of the processes within the cell. The contributions of exoteric scientific research to the problem of conception are by no means worthless, yet they strike one as mere child's play compared with the great mystery involved. This can only be solved when one understands how *the answer to what happens at a particular point can be found only in the periphery.* For this reason the ancient Mystery teachers said, "If you seek to understand the center, investigate the circumference, for only there will you find the answer." Here is the essential part of understanding: *You can grasp the point (what is at the center) only when you have understood the periphery (circumference).*

If you recall that the individual heavenly bodies remain in motion even after they have reached their own completion, so to speak, then you will also understand what is meant by the karma of these cosmic bodies. From the moment when the planet itself has come to completion, the beings who belong to it must consider its dissolution—that is, its disappearance from the cosmic environment. For example, to describe the development of ancient Saturn, we must say to ourselves: until the contraction of the whole globe of warmth, the process of the Saturn phase of development is an ascending one—or, if you will, a descending one—in that it is a process of densification. But, speaking of the first Saturn stage of development, once Saturn begins to rotate on its own, the globe is completed; everything having to do with it has been accomplished. The fact that, in the process of dissolution, the spirits involved must take into account the forces that were active in building it up—that is karma. It is an inescapable factor: Things have to be dissolved in accordance with how they have been built up. The karma of the first half of evolution fulfills itself in the second. What was built up in the course of the first half of evolution is step by step dismantled in the second. The cosmic process of becoming is the creation of karma. And the passing away of worlds, in the broadest sense of the word, is nothing other than suffering under karma and the dissolution of the karma related to it. This is so for every planet, in all aspects, great and small. For each planet faithfully mirrors back the conditions of the formation of its karma.

The same process can be observed in a people or a nation. Imagine a people striving in its youth and full of activity and energy. Imagine this people in successive ages bringing forward various elements of culture and civilization. At a certain point a zenith is reached, but also a certain amount of karma, a karma of a "nation," has been accumulated. Just as karma has been accumulated during the development of Saturn—and one must consider what has come into being—so a people also collects karma during the period of its cultural growth. This karma is at its peak, at its strongest, when a nation has given forth its original and most elemental forces.

We have seen that during every period there are guiding beings. We have seen in the case of the Earth how higher spiritual beings, Angels, Archangels, and Archai, descended, and where humanity could not make progress on its own, these higher beings guided humankind to a higher stage. These are the spiritual beings of the hierarchies who reached their maturity in earlier times. Once a particular stage has been attained, and once the beings who descended from heavenly heights to lead a nation have achieved their goal, other spiritual beings must take on the guidance of the nation. For a people to rise beyond its zenith, leading personalities must, of their own free will, allow themselves to become bearers of higher spiritual beings. Only in this way can a nation progress to certain stages beyond what was originally intended. But then, something further must occur—

namely, the beings who descend to guide a culture beyond a certain point in its development must take the accumulated karma of that nation on themselves. This is the important law of taking on the karma of nations or races. After a certain point in time, leading personalities must bear within themselves, must take on the karma of nations or races. Personalities, such as Hermes, took the karma inherent in their people, the accumulated karma, upon themselves. These things are reflections of great cosmic processes on individual planets.

We have still other such reflected images. We have seen that the Thrones reached their position only because they could make the step from the created to creator. The capacity to receive was transformed into a capacity to give. At some time in another cosmic system the Thrones developed to the point where they could stream forth their substance. Bringing and offering sacrifices indicates a higher stage of development than storing up what is present in the cosmos for oneself. This again occurs in a reflected form in the case of humanity. Look back spiritually through Atlantean and Lemurian times, and then look forward. Human beings receive their physical, etheric, and astral bodies; they receive the I. The I then begins the process of transforming the other members—the transformation of the astral body into Manas, the etheric body into Buddhi, the physical body into Atman, that is, into Spirit Self, Life Spirit and Spirit Body.

In every age, primal wisdom has taught the following: that people transform their astral bodies so that—to begin with, at least—a part of the old astrality remains, and the other part becomes Manas. In time, however, they will transform their astral bodies completely. The astral body will then be fully permeated by the activity of the I. Take a person who has not yet reached this stage of development when the astral body is completely permeated by the activity of the I. This, with very few exceptions, is actually the situation for the vast majority of human beings today. What we've already transformed accompanies us through all of eternity. The portion we have not yet transformed, and in which the I has had no part, separates itself like an astral sheath as the human being passes through kamaloka. It dissolves in the astral world, but not without causing considerable damage if the astral body encompassed bad appetites and passions. So, we could say that human development consists of leaving less and less of oneself behind in the astral world.

Let's follow this process through. A human being dies. Shortly after death, the etheric body is released, but a remnant remains behind. The person goes through kamaloka, and the untransformed sheath is detached. The transformed part is carried in the I through all eternity and is brought back in the new incarnation. The more perfected a person is, the less he or she will leave behind in the astral world in the form of remnants. Finally, one reaches the stage where none of one's astral body remains in kamaloka—that is, the human being has come so far that such a person cannot harm anyone living on Earth because of untransformed remnants left in kamaloka. Such a human being then also has the possibility of seeing into spiritual worlds. For it is not possible to reach this condition without also having achieved a certain level of clairvoyance in the astral.

The whole of the astral body is spiritualized at this point. It has become Spirit Self. This means that the whole astral body is then taken along. Previously, the untransformed portion had to be left behind; now the entire astral body can be taken into the entire subsequent time. At the moment the astral body has progressed so that it is completely transformed, the new form of the astral body, the Spirit Self, stamps itself into the etheric body so that it receives an imprint of the transformed astral body. It need not yet have been completely transformed itself, but what has been worked through in the astral body is imprinted into the etheric body. Briefly, we have described a particularly exalted being who has progressed to the most eminent degree, in that the being has developed the whole of the Spirit Self. Such a being is named *Nirmanakaya* in Eastern wisdom, for the being's astral body, the astral kaya, has reached the stage where no remnants are left behind. This is *Nirmanakaya*.[3]

---

3. *Nirmanakaya*, literally, "the body that is built," is considered the "vehicle" that is maintained by one who has renounced *Nirvana*, hence the body of a Buddha of Compassion or, in Mahayana Buddhism, a "Bodhisattva."

Let us proceed. As human beings, we can continue to work further and further; ultimately, we can also refashion our etheric and physical bodies. What happens when the etheric and physical bodies are transformed so that they come under our own mastery? Once the etheric body has been transformed—so that one has not only achieved Spirit Self in one's astral body but one has also gradually developed Life Spirit or Buddhi in one's etheric body—and once the Life Spirit is imprinted in the physical body, then the next higher stage of development has been reached. This is a kind of intermediary stage. Through this intermediary stage one reaches the point where one no longer needs to leave any part of one's etheric body behind. Such an etheric body transformed into Life Spirit or Buddhi continues to exist for all time in the same form.

Through such influences we shall become more and more capable of attaining mastery over our astral and etheric bodies. Such mastery will also enable us, in a certain respect, to direct the astral and etheric bodies. One who has not yet brought the astral body under the mastery of the I will naturally have to wait until this stage is reached. But those who have attained mastery over their astral and etheric bodies can dispose of them freely. They can say, "Because of what I have been able to experience with my I in many incarnations, which has taught me how to transform my astral and etheric bodies, I have gained the ability, when returning to Earth, to fashion new astral and etheric bodies as perfect as the etheric and astral substance out of which they are fashioned." As a result, such individuals can sacrifice their own astral and etheric bodies, transferring them to others. There are individuals who have achieved mastery in their etheric and astral bodies, have learned to reconstruct them, and thereby have become capable of sacrificing their etheric and astral bodies. When they want to return to Earth, they construct a new astral body and a new etheric body from available material. What they achieved in perfection, however, is passed on to others who have certain tasks to accomplish in the world. Thus, the astral and etheric bodies of earlier individuals are interwoven and assimilated into the astral and the etheric bodies of later individuals. When that occurs, those of a former time not only have an effect from where they currently are, they also work directly into the future through those who carry a portion of the astral and etheric bodies of earlier personalities within their being.

Zoroaster, for example, who could manage his astral body, which he later passed on to Hermes, could say, "I live, but I shall not only be effective as the outer person I am now; I will also permeate the astral body of the Egyptian Hermes who will be the founder of the Egyptian cultural epoch." [4] Such a person possesses a body, a *kaya*, that works not only at the place where one is, but also into the future, proclaiming the law for future development. The law that reaches into the future is called *Dharma*. Such a body is therefore termed a *Dharmakaya*.[5] Such expressions are common in Eastern teaching, and here you have the true explanation of it as it has always been given in primeval wisdom.

In surveying the many things we have considered during these days, a question may well arise in our minds as to what humanity really is. We have called the human being a particular stage of development. We have seen that the Spirits of Personality were "human beings" on ancient Saturn—even the Thrones must have been "human" once—and we have discovered that humanity continues to develop, that it will evolve into ever higher forms of being. We have come to know the first stages of this development in Angels and Archangels, and we have seen how such beings are able to sacrifice a part of themselves. We have seen the beginnings of sacrifice in the Thrones, who are beings who possess it to the highest degree. We see the first gleam of creative activities in the leaders of peoples and races, who knew how to refashion their own bodies so that something streamed forth from them. Just as the Thrones streamed their

---

4. Hermes Trismagistus (the Thrice Great) or Thoth was the great Egyptian initiate, legislator, priest, and philosopher. According to tradition, there were three Hermes, one of whom antedated the flood and the last of whom may have lived around 1100 B.C. The founders of the Egyptian cultural epoch would then have been the first two Hermes. For the anthroposophical view, see also Steiner, *Turning Points in Spiritual History* and *The East in the Light of the West*.

5. *Dharmakaya* means, literally, "the Body of the Law." *Law* has the general meaning of "the teachings of a Buddha," or "Supreme Truth."

being forth, so, to a different degree, the Nirmanakayas let their own bodies stream into the future for the benefit of individuals who would appear later, and could not have reached a particular point of development had they not assimilated what streamed from beings who lived before them.

Thus, the idea of development moves from the point where one *takes*, to the point where one streams out, *creates*. The concept of the "creator" arises before our spiritual eye, and we may say that every being evolves from creature to creator. Archangels achieved human-hood on old Sun; Spirits of Personality, on ancient Saturn; Angels, on old Moon; and human beings, on the Earth. So it will continue. There will always be beings developing into human beings. But does this process continue endlessly? Is it merely an eternal succession of cycles, such as that of the Sun, which repeats what occurred on Saturn—apart from the fact that some beings reach this stage only later?

The Spirits of Fire, for example, develop one cycle later than the Spirits of Personality. But is it really for beings who start as helpless creatures to develop so that they, too, can bring a sacrifice? No, that is not the case, most definitely not. Is the humanity of the Spirits of Personality on Saturn the same as that of the Archangels on the Sun and of the Angels on Mars (old Moon), and of humankind here on the Earth? If we take, for instance, the nature of the Angels, do we only see in them our own future image as it will be on Jupiter? Do we only see in the Spirits of Fire an image of what we ourselves shall become on Venus? Is there really evidence to say the following: "We here on Earth shall reach higher stages of development. We, too, shall advance within the hierarchies. Yet, the beings we shall become in the future already exist now, and our own stage previously was achieved by other beings in earlier times." Fundamental questions such as these must arise for those who let these lectures work on them impartially.

If we are, indeed, merely dealing with an ever-recurring human-ity, then we are identical with the Spirits of Personality on ancient Saturn, the Archangels on the old Sun, and the Angels on Mars (the old Moon). It may be important to us, but for the Gods, it would only involve an increase of creatures. No very appreciable progress would thereby have been achieved. It is another matter, however, if human beings, by developing their humanity on the Earth, thereby evolve into beings able to contribute something that Angels, Archangels, and Spirits of Personality cannot. Has the whole of creation learned something by creating human beings *after* the Archangels and the Angels? Has creation advanced? Is it feasible that, because humanity has agreed to descend further, it thereby has the prospect to ascend even higher? This is the question that logically follows.

We shall devote the final lecture to considering humanity's significance in the cosmos and our relationship to the higher hierarchies—that is: What will ultimately become of humankind in the ranks of the hierarchies?

10. The Christ

APRIL 18, 1909, *Evening*

APART FROM THE QUESTIONS RAISED at the end of the last lecture, there would be much to add to our present theme, but it is impossible in ten lectures to exhaust a consideration of the universe. Therefore, allow me, before I deal with our main question, to make some remarks that, in a certain sense, will relate to our concluding observations.

The first observation that I have to make is difficult, indeed hardly understandable at all for modern consciousness, but it is good if one is aware of it. It relates to the question of how planetary structures, once they have appeared, disappear again. From a spiritual point of view, it is clear how the course of development occurs. Beings ascend to higher stages, and, as they advance, they have to leave their previous places of activity, that is, they must leave their former dwelling places that enabled them, for a period, to develop certain faculties they would not otherwise have been able to acquire. When, in the course of evolution, that time we call the old Lemurian period drew near, humanity had come so far in its development that it had recapitulated all that could be achieved through the stages of Saturn, Sun, and Moon. Then humanity appeared in the environment of earthly evolution, which had just been made ready for our further development. We developed through Lemurian and Atlantean times on into our own period, and, moving from incarnation to incarnation, we will develop further in the future. Then, after a time, humanity will have to leave the Earth again. The Earth will have nothing further to give humanity; for it will not be able to offer further possibilities of development.

You could imagine that after the departure of humanity our Earth would become a desolate ruin. You could compare it with a city that had been deserted by its inhabitants. You know what such a city looks like after only a short time—how it gradually turns into a mound of earth. Seeing ancient cities taken over by the forces of nature gives us a graphic picture of the process. So it is today in reality. But this will not be true for the future of the Earth. The following observation can guide you toward an answer to the following questions: How will it be in the future of our Earth? What is the significance for the development of the Earth of such persons as Leonardo da Vinci, Raphael, or any of the other great geniuses in this or that field? What does it mean for earthly development that Raphael or Michelangelo produced wonderful works of art that are still enjoyed by thousands and thousands of people to this very day? Some of you may have felt a certain sadness on seeing Leonardo's *Last Supper* in Milan, and you may have wondered how much longer this magnificent work will last. We should remember that Goethe, on his first Italian journey, still beheld the work in its full glory, and that we can no longer see it in that state. From Goethe's time until today, the fate of this work of art within its outward material environment is such that it now calls forth feelings of sadness in us. And for people who will live as long after us as we live after Goethe, the work will no longer be in existence. So it is with everything that human beings have created and embodied in physical matter on Earth.

The same is also true for the Earth itself, and even for the creation of human thoughts. Imagine that period of time when human beings will ascend, spiritualized, into higher spheres. Thoughts, in the present sense of the word—I am not at all referring to scientific thoughts, for in three or four hundred years they will no longer have any significance—but human thoughts, as produced by the brain and meaningful on Earth, have no significance for higher worlds. They are only significant on Earth. But humanity will have left the Earth. What will happen then to everything that we have created on Earth in the course of centuries and millennia?

What must first of all be considered from a spiritual perspective is the evolution of the individual. Leonardo da Vinci has risen higher by means of what he accomplished. That constitutes his ascent. We ask ourselves: Are the great thoughts, the great impulses that the great creators imprinted on the substance of the Earth, of any significance for the future of the Earth? Will the future reduce the Earth to dust, and will everything that men and women have made out of the Earth disappear when the planet no longer exists? You admire Cologne Cathedral. Certainly, in a relatively short time, not one stone will rest upon another. Does this mean it is of no significance for the Earth as a whole that human beings embodied the idea of the Cologne Cathedral in stone? We are not now considering what a human being takes with him from the Earth; we are looking at the Earth itself. A planet actually becomes smaller and smaller in the course of its development. It contracts. That is the destiny of the material part of a planet—but that is not the whole story. It is, so to speak, only the part that can be observed by means of physical eyes and instruments. There is also an evolution of matter that proceeds beyond what can be so observed.

I now want to consider the evolution of matter beyond this point, and thereby I come to what I previously described as difficult, indeed almost incomprehensible, to contemporary understanding. The Earth is constantly contracting. Matter is being pressed from all sides into the center. Now I can say, and naturally with full awareness, that there is a law of the conservation of force, but I must also say in full awareness that there is another fact known to every occultist: that matter presses increasingly into the center and, remarkably, disappears into the middle point.

Imagine a piece of matter pressed more and more into the central point, where it disappears. It is not being pushed through to the other side. At the center, it actually disappears into nothingness! In other words, eventually the Earth, as its material aspect presses in upon the middle point, will disappear into the center. But that is not all. As much as disappears at the center, so much reappears at the periphery. It reappears at the extremity. Matter disappears at one point in space—the center—and reappears at another, the circum-ference. Everything that disappears into the center emerges again at the periphery. Everything has been worked into this matter. The beings who were at work on the planets impressed everything into the matter. Naturally, the matter is not in its present form, but in a form that it received by means of this process of transformation. So you will see Cologne Cathedral, whose material particles disap-peared into the middle point, reappearing from the other side. Nothing, absolutely nothing is lost of what has been accomplished on a planet; it comes back from the other side.

All that came to us during the earliest phase of earthly develop-ment before Saturn was thus transferred outside, beyond the zodiac. In primeval wisdom this is called "the Crystal Heaven." It is where the deeds of beings belonging to a previous evolution were deposited. They formed the basis on which new beings could become creative.

As I said before, it is difficult to understand these things with con-temporary understanding, because we are accustomed to considering only the material aspect. We are not used to acknowledging that matter can disappear from one position in three-dimensional space and come back again somewhere else after it has gone through another dimension. As long as you remain in your thinking in the context of three-dimensional space, you cannot grasp it, for this phenomenon goes beyond three-dimensional space. Thus, it cannot be seen until it again reenters three-dimensional space from the other side. In the intervening period, it is in another dimension. This is something that we must understand, for aspects of cosmic creation are bound together in the most complex manner. Some-thing in one place is connected in a complicated way to something else found in an entirely different place in three-dimensional space.

The formation of our planets began with ancient Saturn. That is how it really began. Then the formation continued until Jupiter. As the whole creation began on Jupiter, as you know, all of the beings of the periphery also participated in the process. But just as beings within worked to set out the planetary system and continue their own development, so, too, the outlying beings worked inward from the periphery. As certain beings from the center withdrew outward, those beings who were out in cosmic space did the same. Certain ones on the periphery also withdrew. As Jupiter itself contracted, beings who had withdrawn compressed to form Uranus. Similarly, during the development of Mars, beings who had withdrawn contracted to form Neptune. The names *Uranus* and *Neptune* are of course no longer chosen in the same way that the ancients chose appropriate names for these things—although there still remains something significant in the name *Uranus*. It was given at a time when one still had an inkling of the process of giving the right name. Therefore everything lying beyond our own planetary system was designated collectively with the name *Uranus*.

Thus, we see that both planets—which our modern astronomy places on a par with the other planets—actually stand on quite a different basis, and, in fact, have nothing especially to do with the formation of our world. They represent worlds that came about because beings who still had something to do with us during the ancient Saturn period withdrew and established their dwelling place beyond the periphery of the universe. Many facts can be deduced from this; for example, that these planets have retrograding moons, and so on.

We have now surveyed in rough outline the process through which our solar system came into being, and we have raised the question: What position does the human being have in relation to the beings of the higher hierarchies, who are actually our human ancestors? We can begin with the most exalted—the Seraphim, Cherubim, and Thrones. Indeed, in characterizing their nature we can arrive at a good idea of the human being. But once we go beyond the Seraphim, we enter into the region of the Holy Trinity. That is what the Seraphim, Cherubim, and Thrones have that is extraordinary, beyond what other beings in the universe have: they enjoy what is called "the immediate gaze of the Godhead." They are endowed from the beginning with what human beings must gradually seek over the course of their development. As human beings we say, "To attain higher and higher powers of cognition, will, and so on, we must begin where we are today. If we do this we shall draw nearer and nearer to the Godhead, who will be increasingly present with us. Thus we must develop ourselves toward what is still veiled from us; we must draw toward Divinity." Such is the difference between the Seraphim, Cherubim, and Thrones on the one hand, and humanity on the other. From the beginning of their development, these highest beings of the spiritual hierarchies were immediately present with the Godhead, the Divine Trinity. From the very beginning, they enjoyed being within sight of the Divinity. For the Seraphim, Cherubim, and Thrones, the condition that human beings ought to progress toward, existed from the very beginning. It is extremely important to recognize that, from the time of their origin, these beings beheld God, and that, as long as they live, they will always behold God. They accomplish everything through gazing upon God, and God works through them. They could not do otherwise than to act as they do. It would be impossible for them to do otherwise. The sight of God is such a powerful force, has such an influence upon them, that they accomplish what the Godhead ordains with unerring certainty and immediate impulse. Nothing resembling deliberation or judgment exists in the sphere of these beings. There is only the beholding of the Godhead's commands in order to receive the immediate impulse to do what they have beheld. They see the Godhead in its original true form, as it really is. They consider themselves simply as those who fulfill the will and wisdom of the Divine. Such is the situation of the highest hierarchy.

Descending to the next hierarchy, to the beings called Dominions, Mights, and Powers, or Spirits of Wisdom, Movement, and Form, we must say that they no longer have the immediate gaze of the Godhead. They no longer see God in his immediate form, as He is, but they see God's manifestation, as God reveals Himself, if I may put it so, through his countenance. It is clear to them that the countenance is the Godhead. Like the Seraphim, Cherubim, and Thrones, they also receive a direct impulse to carry out the manifestations of the Godhead. The impulse is not quite as powerful, but it is, nevertheless, still direct. It would be impossible for the Seraphim, Cherubim, and Thrones to say that they would not do what they discern as ordained by the Godhead—it would be unthinkable because of their proximity to the Godhead. But it would be equally out of the question for the Dominions, Mights, and Powers to do what was not willed by the Godhead itself. For the evolution of the world to advance, however, something very extraordinary had to intervene.

We are now introducing a subject that has always been difficult to understand, even for those who have advanced to a certain degree of Mystery wisdom. In the ancient Mysteries one sought to make it comprehensible in the following way. At a particular stage of initiation into the ancient Mysteries, the neophyte was led into the presence of hostile powers who had a cruel and horrible appearance, and who performed the most dreadful acts before the eyes of the neophyte. Those who did these things were none other than masked priests, masked sages. To bring about the necessary temptations, priests disguised themselves in ghastly demonic forms, as dreadful beings, performing the most terrible acts that one could possibly imagine.

Why was this done? Why did the initiate, the priest, bring before the neophyte the guise of the wrongdoer, the mask of evil? To show the neophyte how far development could err from the right path. The neophyte was supposed to have the illusion of standing face to face with evil. Only when the unmasking occurred did the neophyte see the truth. The illusion was removed. Only then did the neophyte know that this scene was a means of creating a trial or test. To strengthen and arm the neophyte against it, evil was presented in its most hideous forms by priests who, of course, did not err. This was merely a reflection of something that actually took place in cosmic evolution.

During the period between the Jupiter and Mars stages of development, if I may express it somewhat trivially, a host of beings from the sphere of the Dynamis, or Mights, were "countermanded." Instead of acting as progressive influences, they were placed in the course of development to cause obstacles. We have come to know this as the "War in Heaven." The actions of these "adversely commanded" Mights (to coin a phrase) were thrown across the path of development, for the ruling cosmic powers of the hierarchies said to themselves that, if the path were smooth, what was intended to come into existence could never arise. Something greater must arise.

Now suppose that you have to push a cart; and because you push it forward, your powers of strength develop to a certain extent. If you loaded the cart with heavy freight you would have to push harder, but you would also develop greater strength. Suppose that the Godhead had permitted cosmic evolution to take its course up to and beyond the Jupiter stage. Humankind certainly could have developed well, but could become even stronger if obstacles were put in its path. For the good of humanity, therefore, certain Mights had to receive adverse commands. They were not evil to begin with—one need not regard them as evil forces—rather one could say that they sacrificed themselves in order to place an obstacle in the path of development. These Mights may, therefore, be called the "Gods of Hindrance," or "Gods of Impediment" in the broadest sense of the word. These are gods of obstructions or hindrances that have been placed along the path of development; and ever since that moment the possibility was created for everything that was to be accomplished in the future. These countermanded Dynamis were not yet evil in themselves; on the contrary, by running up against the normal course of development, they were the great promoters of evolution. Nevertheless, they were the originators of evil, because, out of the storms they produced, evil gradually arose.

The course of development for the "adversely commanded" Mights took a very different form from that of their fellows. The effect of their activity was very different, and, as a result, during the development of the Moon these Mights became the tempters of the beings we call Angels. During the evolutionary stage of the Moon the Angels were passing through their human phase. There were Angel-humans on the Moon who witnessed the effect of these obstacles on the course of development. They said to themselves, "We can now allow ourselves to assail these hindrances; we can plunge into the stream of the Moon's development. But we prefer to abstain. We do not want to plunge in, but choose to remain above with the good gods." These Angel beings, at a particular point during the course of the Moon stage of development, tore themselves away from the Mights who, down below, had introduced obstacles into the development of the Moon. But there were other Angel-humans on the Moon who said, "We will not follow our fellows, because, if we did, the pattern of development would be turned around and nothing new would happen." Indeed, just because the hindrances were present, from the development of the Moon stage on, something new was introduced. There were beings who said, "We wish to have absolutely nothing to do with what is happening down there. We remain with the Mights, who do not wish to be touched by the lesser."

These beings withdrew from the Moon mass during the development of the old Moon and became followers of everything that occurred in the Sun. They wanted nothing to do with what happened on the Moon, which had been cast aside because the hindrances were present. The others who plunged down, however, had to take into their bodily nature everything they had received of the existing developmental hindrances on the Moon. They had to harden themselves more than otherwise would have been the case. Their bodily sheaths became denser than they would have been, and they bore the consequence of the actions of the Mights in their bodies. We should remember, however, that the deeds of the Mights or Dynamis were well founded within the divine cosmic plan.

A further consequence of all this was that, when the development of the Moon passed over into that of the Earth, the whole process was, in a certain way, repeated. Those beings who hurled themselves into the full tide of the Moon development lagged behind those who would have nothing to do with it. Still others remained even further behind, because they were attracted by the retrograde development.

All of this therefore led to the presence of two sorts of Angel-humans during the development of the Earth. Some of the Angel-humans were those who had gone ahead, and some were those who had stayed behind. The advanced Angel-humans now set to work on humanity in the Lemurian time, as humankind became mature enough to receive the seed of the human I. They gave human beings the option, so to speak, of ascending immediately into spiritual worlds and having no more to do with what had mingled with the course of cosmic evolution since the Moon phase of development. The beings who had stayed behind, whom we call luciferic beings, went to work on the human astral body—they could not reach the I—and injected the results of the War in Heaven into the astral body. As the Mights were countermanded into participation in the War in Heaven and became Gods of Hindrance, the consequences of their actions crept into the human astral body, where they had a different and greater significance; for there they represent the possibility of error and the possibility of evil. Human beings were thus given the possibility of error and the possibility of evil, but at the same time they also received the capacity to rise above error and evil by their own strength.

Consider that beings such as the Mights or Dynamis, belonging to the second hierarchy, did not have the possibility at all of becoming evil by themselves—they had to be "adversely commanded." Only the beings of the third hierarchy, the Angels, who are closest to human beings, could follow or not follow the hindering Mights. Those who did not succumb are represented in pictures depicting the victories fought out in the Heavens. They are supposed to express what came to pass during the Moon stage of development, when human beings had advanced to the incarnation of the astral body—that is, to the human-animal stage. The Angel beings who remained pure, as it were, tore themselves away from the course of the Moon development. They escaped what was taking place below on the Moon.

This picture is represented in many different forms before our souls. Originally, we find it depicted in the battle between Michael and the Dragon.[1] We also find it expressed with great clarity in pictures of the Mithraic Bull. But the object of such representations was not to say that these Angel beings have forsaken their duty. They were intended to depict an ideal for the future. "These beings," it was said, "preferred to ascend into spiritual worlds. You, on the other

---

1. Revelations 12. See also Steiner, *The Archangel Michael, His Mission and Ours.*

hand, have descended, along with other beings who followed the Powers of Hindrance. It is now up to you to work through what you have taken in, and carry it upward into the spiritual world. On the upward path you are called on to become a Michael and a conqueror of the Bull." A symbol such as this must be interpreted in this two-fold way.

So we see that humanity received the possibility of reaching its goal by its own powers—something that even the Seraphim cannot attain through their own endeavors—only because the Mights were given adverse orders. That is the most significant fact. The Seraphim, Cherubim, and Thrones cannot do anything but follow the immediate impulses given them by the Godhead. The Dominions—indeed, the whole of the second hierarchy—must do likewise. Only among the ranks of the Mights were some commanded adversely. They could also not do other than follow the orders of the Godhead when they threw themselves across the path of development. Even in causing what could be called "the source of evil," they merely performed the will of the Godhead. By making themselves servants of evil, these Mights accomplished the will of the Godhead, who wished to strengthen the good by means of the detour through evil.

Let us now descend to the beings called Powers or Exusiai. They, likewise, could not have become wicked by themselves, and the same applies to the Spirits of Personality (Archai) and the Fire Spirits (the Archangels); for when the latter passed through their human stage on the Sun, the Mights had not yet been adversely commanded, and there was not yet any possibility of becoming evil. The first to have this possibility of becoming evil were the Angels, because this possibility existed only since the Moon stage of development. The War in Heaven took place during the transition from the Sun to the Moon. A number of Angels rejected this possibility—refused to be seduced, so to speak, by the powers destined to introduce hindrances. They remained true to their former nature. So that we have, down to the Angels, and also among some of the Angels, beings of the higher hierarchies who cannot do anything but follow the divine will. This is most important.

We now come to two categories of beings. First, there are those Angels who hurled themselves into what the Mights had brought about during the War in Heaven. These are beings who, on account of their later deeds, are called luciferic beings. They went to work on the human astral body during earthly evolution and introduced the possibility of evil, but also the possibility of developing oneself through one's own free activity. Thus, in the whole range of the hierarchies, it is only among a portion of the Angels and among human beings that we find the possibility of freedom. The possibility of freedom begins within the ranks of the Angels, but it is fully developed only in humanity. When humanity came down to Earth, human beings first had to fall prey to the mighty power of the luciferic hosts. These hosts permeated the human astral body with their powers so that the I became enmeshed in this field of forces. During the Lemurian and Atlantean periods, and also subsequently, we find the I wrapped in a cloud caused by Lucifer's influences. The human being was saved from being overpowered by these debilitating forces only because earlier beings—the Angels who had remained above, and the Archangels—overshadowed the person and incarnated in the individuals chosen to guide humanity. This continued until the time when something remarkable happened. A being, who had previously always been united with the Sun's existence, advanced so far that he could not only penetrate the human being's physical, etheric, and astral bodies, as previously had been the situation with higher beings, but could also permeate the human being as far as the I.

You will recall that I described how higher beings descended during former times, and ensouled human physical, etheric, and astral bodies. Now, at a special moment in time, an individual arose who had been chosen to receive the most exalted being into himself—a being who had been united with our Sun existence and who now worked inspiringly into the I, even down into all the forces of the I.

The I expresses itself through the blood. Just as the blood in its material substance is the expression of the I, so the warmth or fire of the blood, which is the remnant of the Saturn fire, is the expression of the I in the elements. This being had to express itself physically in a twofold way. In the element of fire the being proclaimed himself to Moses in the burning bush and in the lightning on Mount Sinai. One and the same being could penetrate the human I, and speak to Moses from the burning bush and from the lightning and thunder on Mount Sinai. This being prepared his advent and then appeared in a blood-permeated body—that of Jesus of Nazareth. This Sun-being entered into an earthly individuality. Because the human I will be filled and saturated more and more by the power that then penetrated it, this I will become more and more capable of overcoming, through its own forces, all of the influences that have the capacity to pull it down. For this being who penetrated the human I is of a different nature from those other beings who formerly descended to Earth and ensouled the physical, etheric, and astral bodies.

Let us consider the ancient Holy Rishis. As we have seen, the spirit of a high being lived in their etheric bodies, because the Holy Rishis had inherited the etheric body from great Atlantean ancestors in whom that exalted being had lived. It was passed on to them. But the Rishis could not comprehend with their I and astral bodies what streamed through the inspiration of their etheric bodies. And so it went from epoch to epoch. Human beings received inspiration. They always experienced something like a force within them when they were inspired. Inspiration was something that they captured, as it were, with a force. The individual withdrew somewhat from the ordinary human capacity to manage on one's own. So that one could improve, could advance, the person had to be inspired by a more perfect being. This was the situation for all founders of religions. Beings who had been exalted above the War in Heaven were infused into the religious founders; so human beings were not left to depend just on their own resources.

In the Christ, however, a Being of very different nature appeared. He was a Being, who did absolutely nothing, who exerted not the slightest compulsion to bring people to him. This is the main point!

If you consider the propagation of Christianity, you will find living evidence that during his lifetime Christ did not do what occurred in spreading Christianity. Consider the founders of religions of ancient times. They are the great teachers of humanity. From a certain moment in their development, they begin to instruct, and their teachings work on human beings with an overwhelming power. Now consider the Christ. Does the Christ actually work through his teachings? Anyone who thinks that Christ's main contribution lies in his teaching does not really understand the Christ. At least in the first instance, *the Christ did not work through his teaching but through what he did.* And the greatest deed of the Christ was the deed that ended with his death. It was, in fact, his death. That is the most important point! Christ worked through a deed. And when knowledge of this action began to spread through the world he was no longer physically present. That is the fundamental difference between the efficacy of Christ and that of other great founders of religions. This difference is hardly understood at all, but it is the most important one.

All of the teachings of Christianity—everything that is preached in Christianity, every Christian teaching—you can describe, you can find, in other religious systems. This cannot be denied. It can certainly be said that the essence of Christian teaching is also contained in other systems. But has Christianity been effective through the contents of its teaching? Did the person who did the most in spreading Christianity rely on its teaching? Consider the Apostle Paul! Did he allow himself to be transformed from Saul to Paul by what is written in the Gospels? Paul persecuted the followers of Christ Jesus until the one who died on the Cross appeared to him out of the clouds—that is, until Paul had his own personal, occult experience of the fact that Christ *lives.* The effect of that death, the efficacy of that act became the quickening impulse for Paul, and that is what matters. Other religious systems work through their teachings, and the teachings are the same as those found in Christianity. But in Christianity it is not a question of teachings. What matters is the *deed* that took place.

The act of Christ only works on a person when one decides to allow it to have an effect—that is, when the deed is united with the absolutely free nature of the individual I. It is not enough for the Christ to be present in the human astral body. To be truly understood, Christ must be present in the I. And the I must freely resolve to receive the Christ. That is the point. But as a result of the I uniting itself with the Christ, this human I acquires within itself a reality, a divine power, not just a teaching. Therefore, it can be demonstrated a hundred times that the teachings of Christianity may already be found here or there; but that is not the point. The essential aspect of Christianity is the act that can only be made one's own through a voluntary ascent into higher worlds. Human beings receive the power of Christ into themselves because they willingly accept it, and no one can receive it who does not voluntarily accept it. This has become possible for the human being only since the Christ became human on Earth, since he was called on to become a human being on the Earth.

The fallen Angels, who came to live on Earth as luciferic beings, are in a different position. Indeed, they should have become human on the Moon. But they remained behind in their development. As a result, they can penetrate the astral body, but they cannot gain access to the I. They are in an unusual situation, which we can only represent graphically—even if that seems pedantic. Let's assume—leaving aside the etheric and physical bodies—that the astral body of the human being during the Lemurian development is represented by this circle. The I would then be encased within this astral body, because it has gradually entered into the astral body.

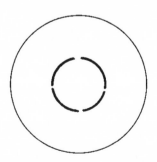

What happens next? During the Lemurian epoch the luciferic forces crept into the astral body from all sides and penetrated human beings with their activities. In human beings these are expressed as lower passions. The possibility for human beings to succumb to error and evil is embedded in the astral body; the luciferic spirits introduced that possibility into us. If they had not, we would never have had the possibility of erring, of doing evil. Instead, we would have been lifted up to a region where we would have received the I untouched by hindering influences. This is the situation. But the great leaders of humanity protected human beings so that we should not sink too low.

Then the Christ event occurred. Let us take a human being who has voluntarily received the Christ—of course, Christianity is only at its beginning, but let us take an ideal situation—a human I, in complete free will, has allowed the power of Christ to flow in. When the I has advanced so far that it is permeated by the Christ, then the power of Christ irradiates the astral body and streams into the actions of the luciferic powers that had been injected into it. And what will happen in the future? Because with Christ's help—and only with His help—we can extinguish those qualities in us that stem from Lucifer, at the same time, we can also gradually release the luciferic powers. The time will come when the luciferic powers, which had to sink to a lower stage of evolution for the sake of human freedom and therefore could not experience the power of Christ on Earth, will experience the power of Christ through human beings and so will be redeemed. Human beings will redeem Lucifer if they receive the Christ-power in the appropriate way. As a result, human beings will grow stronger than they would have been otherwise. Imagine if human beings had not received the luciferic forces, the Christ-power would have streamed forth but would not have encountered any luciferic obstacles. It would have been impossible for us to progress in goodness, truth, and wisdom to the degree that we now can once we have to overcome these countervailing forces.

The human being is one of the hierarchies, but distinct from the others. Human beings are different from Seraphim, Cherubim,

Thrones, Dominions, Mights, Powers, Spirits of Personality, Fire-spirits—and from some of the Angels as well. Looking into the future, a human being can say, "I am called to seek the impulse for my actions in the deepest recesses of my own inner being—not out of the contemplation of the Godhead, as the Seraphim do, for instance, but out of my own inner being." The Christ is a God who does not work in such a way that his impulses have to be followed. One follows the Christ only out of understanding and freedom. The Christ is the God who never seeks to hinder the free, individual development of the I in this or that direction. The Christ could say in the profoundest sense, "You shall know the Truth, and the Truth shall make you free." And the beings of the next hierarchy, who had the possibility of doing evil, the luciferic beings, will again be redeemed and freed through the power of human beings.

Thus, we see that cosmic development does not simply repeat itself. New factors enter in. A human stage, such as that experienced by human beings, was not to be found previously among the Angels, Archangels, or Primal Beginnings. Humanity has a completely new mission to fulfill in the world—the mission we have just characterized. Humanity descended into the earthly world in order to accomplish this mission. Christ came into the world as the free helper of humanity; not as a God working from above, but as the firstborn among many.

Only in this way can we grasp the full dignity and importance of humankind among the members of the hierarchies. Looking up to the exalted nature and glory of the higher hierarchies, we can say to ourselves, "However mighty, wise, and good these higher hierarchies may be—and hence unable to err from the true path—it is humanity's great mission to bring freedom into the world, and, along with freedom, what we call, in the truest sense of the word, love." For without freedom, love is impossible. Beings who absolutely must obey a particular impulse, merely do so; but for those who can do otherwise, there is only one power that enables them do so, and that is love. Freedom and love are two poles that belong together. If love is to enter our cosmos, it can do so only through freedom—that is, through Lucifer and the one who conquers Lucifer—the one who is also the redeemer of human beings—the Christ. This is why the Earth is the cosmos of love and freedom, and it is important that, without wishing to tempt human beings away from humility, we should learn to familiarize ourselves with the sequence of the hierarchies as this has always been known in the esotericism of the West.

Seraphim, Cherubim, and Thrones obey the direct impulses transmitted under the gaze of the Godhead. The Dominions, Mights, and Powers are still so closely bound up with the higher powers that they have to receive countermands so that the development of humanity can move forward. Even the Archangels and the Spirits of Personality cannot err, they cannot sink into evil of their own free resolve. The hierarchies immediately above humanity were called Messengers and Arch-messengers to indicate that they were not accomplishing their own tasks but merely fulfilling orders received from above. But humanity is a hierarchy that is gradually maturing so that it will carry out its own tasks. Throughout the development of Jupiter, Venus, and Vulcan, human beings will mature gradually toward the accomplishment of their own impulses. Even if this goal is still distant today, in time humanity will attain it.

What are the hierarchies? We begin with the Seraphim, Cherubim, and Thrones. They exercise their authority by carrying out the impulse received from the Gods. Then come the Mights, who owe their strength to what is received from above, and the same is true of the Powers. Were they to become evil, they could do so only as a result of a decision of the divine world. And now, we come to the Spirits of Personality and the Arch-messengers, and Messengers, who descend to the immediate proximity of humanity. How should humanity be integrated into the ranks of the hierarchies? After the Archangels and Angels (Arch-messengers and Messengers), we must place among the hierarchical ranks those we may call the "Spirits of Freedom" or the "Spirits of Love." Counting from above downward, this is the Tenth Hierarchy. This Tenth Hierarchy, although still in the process of development, nevertheless belongs to the spiritual hierarchies. It is not just a matter of repetition in the universe. Each time a cycle has been completed, a new element is introduced into cosmic evolution. And the integration of the new element is always the task of the hierarchy that is at its human stage of development.

In these lectures, we have endeavored to fathom the meaning and significance of humanity by considering the significance of our cosmos. Today, to some extent at least, we have raised the spiritual question of the significance of the human being. And we have tried to establish the significance of the human being, the point at the center of the universe, according to the teachings of the mysteries. In so doing, we tried to solve the riddle of the center, the human being, from the periphery—the riddle of the point from the perspective of the circumference! In doing so, we place our knowledge within the sphere of reality. This is the essential point—that true spiritual scientific knowledge is also real, concrete knowledge. In other words, spiritual scientific knowledge itself directly produces a picture of the cosmos and the spiritual hierarchies.

We are at the center of our universe. Everything around us loses its significance because we have to acknowledge that the outer, sense-perceptible world cannot solve the riddles that confront us. It is as if everything were concentrated at a single point. But just as everything compresses altogether, the solution of the cosmic riddle comes back from the periphery as powerfully real as matter itself, which is a reflection and image of the spiritual. Matter gathers itself together, disappears at the center and reappears at the periphery. That is reality. Our knowledge is real when it steps in front of our eyes as the structure and process of the entire cosmos. Such knowledge is no longer a form of speculation—a weaving of fanciful theory—for such knowledge is born out of the cosmos. This is the feeling we should develop. Wisdom must become an ideal for us, born out of the periphery of the cosmos and capable of filling us with great strength, with the strength that enables us to fulfill our own destiny and to achieve our own cosmic ideal. With this strength, we shall also be able to realize the human ideal that awaits us in the future.

PART TWO

Reality and Illusion:

The Inner Aspects of Evolution

1. The Inner Aspect of the Saturn Embodiment of the Earth

BERLIN, OCTOBER 31, 1911

IF WE WISH TO CONTINUE to explore the reflections we worked on last year in our branch evenings, we shall have to master some concepts, ideas, and perceptions other than those we have spoken of so far.[1] For what we have to say about the Gospels and the other spiritual documents of humankind would not by itself be enough, unless we presume the development of our entire cosmic system. We have described this evolution as the embodiment of our planet itself through Saturn, Sun, and Moon existences up to the present Earth existence. Whoever remembers how often we have referred to these fundamental principles also knows how necessary they are for all esoteric observations concerning human evolution.[2] However, if you look at the account of the developmental stages of Saturn, Sun, Moon, and Earth described in *Occult Science—An Outline,* you will have to admit that what is given there is only a sketch—even if it had been expanded, it would not be otherwise. It is only a sketch from a certain point of view so that an explanation could then be given from a particular perspective. For just as Earth existence offers an immense wealth of details, so, too, it stands to reason, there are likewise an endless number of details to record about the Saturn, Sun, and Moon existences. Even so, it is always only possible to give a "rough sketch" or "outline" of these details. In these lectures, then,

---

1. See Rudolf Steiner, *Background to the Gospel of St. Mark* (Hudson, N.: Anthroposophic Press and London: Rudolf Steiner Press, 1985).
2. See, for instance, Steiner, *Cosmic Memory; Theosophy of the Rosicrucian; Universe, Earth and Man.*

we shall have to portray a characteristic of evolution from yet another side.

When we ask ourselves where all of these accounts originate, we know that they come from so-called entries in the Akashic Chronicle.[3] We know that whatever once occurred in the course of cosmic development may, to some extent, be read by means of an impression in a delicate spiritual substance called the Akasha substance. Everything that has happened has left an imprint of this kind from which one can elicit how things once were. In the physical world, when we look at something, we can assume that things nearer to us are generally clear and distinct in their details, and that the farther away things are, the less clear and distinct they appear. Things that are closer to us in time also reveal themselves more exactly than things that are farther removed in time. It is the same when we look back in a supersensible sense: the Saturn or Sun existences, for example, will have less distinct outlines than the Earth or Moon periods of development.

But why do this at all? Why do we consider it important to "track down" a time that lies so far distant from our own? Someone might well ask: "Why do these anthroposophists bring up these ancient matters today? We certainly do not need to concern ourselves with such things. We have enough to do with what is going on in the present."

It would be wrong to speak in such a way. For what was once set into the stream of time continues to come to fruition even today. What was brought into being in the time of Saturn development did not exist simply and exclusively in and for that era. What occurred then continues to affect our time, but it has become veiled and invisible in relation to what exists externally in the physical plane around human beings. Indeed, what occurred so long ago during ancient

---

3. Cf. *Theosophy of the Rosicrucian*, lecture 4: "What is the Akashic Chronicle? We can form the truest conception of it by realizing that what comes to pass on our earth makes a lasting impression upon certain delicate essences, an impression that can be discovered by a seer who has attained Initiation. It is not an ordinary but a living Chronicle. Suppose a human being lived in the first century after Christ; what he thought, felt, and willed in those days, what passed into deeds—this is not obliterated but preserved in this delicate essence. The seer can behold it—not as if it were recorded in a history book, but as it actually happened."

Saturn existence is barely visible today. Nevertheless, ancient Saturn existence is still significant for humankind. In order to imagine why it is significant for us, let us place the following before our soul.

We know that the innermost core of our being stands before us as what we call the "I." This I, the innermost core of our being, is truly an immaterial, imperceptible entity for humanity today. Just how imperceptible it is can be inferred from what is said about the soul in the so-called "official" psychologies. These no longer have any notion of what constitutes the being of the I, or, indeed, that such an I may even be intimated.

I have often drawn attention to the fact that, in nineteenth century German psychology, the expression "soul theory without soul" gradually came into use. The world-famous school of Wilhelm Wundt,[4] which is influential not just in German-speaking countries, but is greatly respected wherever psychology is discussed, made this "soul theory without soul" fashionable.[5] This "soul theory without soul" describes soul qualities without presupposing an independent soul entity. Instead, all qualities of the soul first come together in a kind of focal point, that is, gather themselves in the I. That is the greatest absurdity that has ever been linked to a theory about the soul. Yet psychology today stands completely under its influence; today, this notion is celebrated throughout the world. Cultural historians studying our era in the future will have their work cut out for them if they wish to explain plausibly how such a theory could ever have been regarded as the greatest achievement in the field of psychology in the nineteenth century and well into the twentieth. I say this only to point out how unclear "official" psychology is with regard to the I, the middle point of the human being.

If we could grasp the I in its true nature and set it before us in the way we can set the physical body before us, and then tried to discover the environment upon which the I depends—in the sense that the

---

4. Wilhelm Wundt (1832–1920), German physiologist, psychologist, and philosopher, founded the first Institute for Experimental Psychology in Leipzig (1879).
5. The phrase "soul theory without soul" was coined by F. A. Lange (1828–1875) in his *History of Materialism* (1866).

physical body depends upon what is seen outwardly by the eyes and perceived through the senses, and needs nourishment, and discovers clouds, mountains, and so forth, in its surroundings in the physical realm—that is, if we tried to discover the essential context for the I in the same sense as we know the context for the physical body, then we would come to a cosmic portrait or tableau that invisibly permeates our surroundings even today and is identical to the cosmic tableau of ancient Saturn. In other words, whoever wishes to come to know the I in its world must be able to imagine a world like that of ancient Saturn. This world is hidden; it is a world that is, for human beings, beyond sense perception. Indeed, at our present level of development, we cannot bear the perception of it. The Guardian of the Threshold veils it from us.[6] It thus remains concealed—for a certain level of spiritual development is required to withstand the sight of such a tableau.

In fact, the sight of such a tableau as ancient Saturn presents is one to which a person must first become accustomed. Before anything else, you must form an imagination of how one could ever experience such a cosmic tableau as something real. All that you perceive with the senses must be removed from your thinking. Also, insofar as it consists of the usual ebb and flow within the soul, you must abandon your inner world. You must erase thinking about what is in the world—and even dissolve all ideas themselves. You must remove from the outer world everything perceived through the senses; you must extinguish the activity of the soul and of ideas within your inner world. Having done this, if you wish to form an idea of the soul condition that must be reached if a human being is really to grasp this thought—remember, absolutely everything is removed, only the human being remains—then one can only say that you must be able to bear the terror, the fear of the fathomless void, the endless emptiness, that yawns around us. One must be capable of experiencing an environment completely saturated with fear and terror and yet, at one and the same

6. The expression "The Guardian of the Threshold" comes from Bulwer Lytton's *Zanoni* (Blauvelt, NY: Garber Communications, 1989). For Rudolf Steiner's description, see *How To Know Higher Worlds* (Hudson, NY: Anthroposophic Press, 1994).

time, be able to overcome these feelings through the inner firmness and certainty of one's own being. Without these two dispositions in the soul—the terror of an infinite void of existence and the overcoming of this fear—you cannot possibly experience any inkling of how ancient Saturn existence underlies our cosmic existence.

People, on their own, seldom cultivate the two experiences that I have just characterized. One also finds very little that has been written about this condition. Of course, those who, over the course of time, have tried to explore it with clairvoyant forces know of it. Yet, there are very few indications in written or published sources, that people have experienced either this terror before an infinite abyss or the overcoming of this fear.

In order to gain some insight into this matter, I investigated recent literature in which something like this terror in the face of an immeasurable void appeared. Philosophers are usually very clever, speaking knowledgeably about concepts, but completely avoid mentioning awe-inspiring impressions. So one does not easily find something recorded in philosophical literature about this matter. I will not speak now of sources where I found nothing. But once I did find an echo of these experiences in the journal of the Hegelian philosopher, Karl Rosenkranz.[7] In this journal, Rosenkranz described very intimate feelings that he had experienced while immersing himself in Hegelian philosophy. I came across a remarkable passage that he recorded quite innocently in his journal. It was clear to Rosenkranz that Hegelian philosophy is based on Hegel's understanding of "pure being." In the philosophical literature of the nineteenth century there has been a great deal of superficial talk about Hegel's principle of "pure being"—but, in fact, it is very poorly understood. One can almost say that philosophy in the second half of the nineteenth century understands about as much about Hegel's "pure being" as an ox understands about Sunday when he has been munching fodder the whole week through! Hegel's concept of "pure

---

7. Karl Rosenkranz (1805–1879), German Hegelian philosopher. See his *Aus einem Tagebuch* (Leipzig, 1854), p. 24ff.

being"—not the process of being, but the state of being as such—is not quite what I characterized as the dreaded emptiness into which fear flows, but all of space in Hegel's "being" is tinged with a quality that cannot be experienced by humankind: the Infinite filled with Being. And Karl Rosenkranz once experienced this as the dreadful, shattering state of the coldness of the cosmic expanse of space devoid of content other than sheer being.

To grasp what lies at the basis of the cosmos, it is not enough to speak about it merely in concepts or to make up ideas about it. It is much more important to call up an Imagination of what one experiences facing the infinite void that characterizes ancient Saturn existence. Then the soul grasps the feeling of horror, even if only an inkling of it. One can prepare oneself to behold this Saturn condition clairvoyantly by replicating the feeling of vertigo in mountain heights, of standing at the edge of an abyss without a secure footing, of being driven from one place to the next, overwhelmed by forces over which one no longer has any influence. That is the first step, the initial feeling. Then one loses not just the ground under one's feet, but what the eyes see, the ears hear, the hands can grasp—absolutely everything that exists in the surrounding space. And, inevitably, one loses every thought, plunging into a kind of twilight or sleep state in which one cannot grasp anything cognitively. Or else—one immerses oneself into every feeling, and then nothing else is possible but to slip into a condition of dread, often gripped by a state of dizziness that cannot be overcome.

There are two possibilities for human beings today to overcome the grip of fear at the abyss. One established way is through an understanding of the Gospels, through an understanding of the Mystery of Golgotha. A person who truly understands the Gospels—not in the way modern theologians speak about them, but who absorbs the very deepest of what can be experienced inwardly of the Gospels—takes something with him or her into the abyss that expands as if from a single point and completely fills the void with a feeling of courage, of being protected through a union with the being who consummated the sacrifice at Golgotha. That is one way. The other way is to penetrate the spiritual worlds without the Gospels but with true, authentic anthroposophy. That, too, is possible. As you know, I always emphasize that, when we consider the Mystery of Golgotha, we do not begin with the Gospels—for we would discover the Mystery of Golgotha even if there were no Gospels. This is something that was not possible *before* the Mystery of Golgotha occurred, but it is so today, because through the Mystery of Golgotha something came into the world that allows human beings to grasp the spiritual world directly out of impressions from the spiritual world. We may call this the presence of the Holy Spirit in the world, the rule of cosmic thoughts in the world. But one must be prepared.

If, when we must face the terrifying void, we take either the Gospels or anthroposophy with us, then we cannot get lost nor plunge into the infinite abyss. If we approach this ghastly void with the preparation set forth in *How to Know Higher Worlds* (and the other works following it),[8] and penetrate the spiritual world—where everything that arises convulses our feelings and seizes our thoughts—we will meet beings who are not at all like those in the realms of animal, plant, or mineral. As we become familiar with and adjusted to Saturn existence, a world in which there are no clouds, no light, no sound, we will come to know beings. Indeed, we will come to know the beings who, in our terminology, are called the Spirits of Will or the Thrones. These Spirits of Will whom we come to know as an objective reality, comprise, so to speak, a surging sea of courage.

What human beings at first can only imagine becomes objective *presence* through clairvoyance. Think of yourself immersed in the sea, and yet immersed in it as a spiritual being who feels united with the Christ being, upheld by the Christ being, swimming, but now not in a sea of water but in a sea that completely fills an infinite expanse and consists of flowing courage, surging energy! This is not simply an indifferent, undifferentiated sea. All possibilities and varieties of what

---

8. *How To Know Higher Worlds* (1904), *Theosophy* (1904), *Stages of Higher Knowledge* (1905-1908), *An Outline of Occult Science* (1910), *A Road to Self-Knowledge* (1912) and *The Threshold of the Spiritual World* (1913).

we may describe as the feeling of courage come to meet us there. There we become acquainted with beings who consist of courage, yet are also quite individualized. Although they are made up entirely of courage, we encounter them also as concrete beings. Naturally it seems very strange to say that one meets beings who are as real as human beings composed of flesh, but who consist of courage not flesh. But this is so. We encounter the Spirits of Will who are beings of just this sort, and, meeting them, we thereby describe Saturn existence—for that is precisely what the Spirits of Will, composed of courage, represent. This is Saturn. It is a world that is not shaped like a sphere; it does not have six corners or four corners. Aspects of space do not apply. Thus there is no possibility of finding an "end" to Saturn existence. If we wanted to use the image of swimming again, we could say that Saturn is a sea that has no surface. Instead, everywhere, in every direction, Spirits of Courage or Spirits of Will are to be found.

I will characterize in later lectures how it is that one does not come to this insight immediately. For now I am going to use the sequence I used before: Saturn, Sun, Moon. It is actually better to go in the opposite direction—in the way that it is actually perceived clairvoyantly, namely, from Earth to Saturn. But for now I shall characterize it as: Saturn, Sun, Moon. The sequence in itself makes no difference.

The unique thing about it is that when one lifts oneself to this vision, something arises that is extremely difficult to imagine if one has not taken care to arrive at the ideas slowly and deliberately. For something ceases to exist that is more intimately tied to the ordinary capacity of imagination than anything else: *space ceases to exist.* There is no longer any meaning to expressions such as: one swims "on top of," or "underneath," "in front of," or "behind," "to the right" or "to the left"—or indeed any other similar reference to spatial relationships. In ancient Saturn, spatial relationships make no sense at all. "Everywhere" is the "same." But the most important thing is that when one enters the first periods of Saturn existence, time also ceases. There is simply no earlier or later. That is naturally very difficult for human beings today to imagine, because today a person's ideas themselves flow within time: one thought appears before or after another one.

The absence of time, however, may be approximated through a feeling. But this feeling is not a pleasant one.

Imagine that your capacity for forming ideas is paralyzed so that everything that enables you to remember, everything you plan to do, becomes paralyzed like a rigid rod. Thus you feel as if your ideas are held fast and you can no longer touch them. In this condition you cannot say that something you experienced "before" happened at an "earlier" point in time. You are connected to it, it is there, but it is absolutely fixed. Time has ceased to have any meaning. It absolutely does not exist. Therefore, it is meaningless to ask: "Now that you have described the Saturn and Sun existences and so forth, can you tell me what was there before the Saturn existence?" "Before" has no meaning in that context. Time did not exist then, and we must do without any designations relating to time. Saturn existence is similar to a situation in which the world has been boarded up. Thoughts have come to a standstill. This is the case for clairvoyance, too. Normal thoughts have been left behind; they do not reach that far. Expressed pictorially: your brain is frozen. To the extent that you can perceive this state of paralysis, you can approximate the image of a consciousness that no longer encompasses time.

Having come this far, one notices a remarkable change occurring in the whole picture. Beings of other hierarchies penetrate and become active within the paralysis that is the timelessness of the infinite ocean of courage with its Spirits of Will. At the very moment when the absence of time is evident, one notices the activity of other beings. One notices the presence of something within the infinite ocean of courage, but with unspecified awareness. It is as if one did not experience it. Something lights up this expanse—but it is more like a glow than a quick flash of lightning. It is the first differentiation—a glow, but not a glow that gives the impression of a glowing light.

You must try to comprehend these things in different ways. For example, you might imagine something like the following: You meet someone who speaks to you, and you have the feeling, "How intelligent this person is!" And as the person continues to speak, this feeling intensifies, and you recognize, "This person is wise, has experienced the infinite, and thus is able to recount wise things." Furthermore, this person makes you feel as if he or she exuded an aura of enchantment. Imagine, then, this element of enchantment infinitely intensified. Imagine that in the ocean of courage, clouds appear in which there are not exactly flashes of lightning but shimmering radiance. When you take all of this together, you have an imagination of the beings now active within the Spirits of Will, beings who are not merely wisdom, but radiant streams of wisdom. You have here an idea of what, by means of clairvoyant perception, the Cherubim are. The Cherubim are the beings who stream into the ocean of courage.

Now imagine that nothing else surrounds you except what I have described. Actually, as I emphasized earlier, you cannot say that you have something "around" you. You can only say it is "there." You have to think your way into it. Now the image of something lighting up is not quite accurate. For this reason I said that it is not like a flash but more like a glowing—for everything occurs at the same time. It is not something that comes into being at one moment and disappears at another. Everything is simultaneous. Nevertheless, one has a feeling of a connection between the Spirits of Will and the Cherubim. One has the feeling that they established a relationship one to another. This becomes a conscious awareness. And one also becomes conscious that the Spirits of Will, the Thrones, sacrifice their own beings to the Cherubim. That is the final image one receives moving backward toward Saturn. One receives the image of the Spirits of Will directing this sacrifice to the Cherubim. Beyond this point it is as if the cosmos were "boarded up."

But to the extent that we experiences this sacrifice of the Spirits of Will to the Cherubim, something is pressed out of—separated—from our being. We can express this with the words: From the sacrifice brought by the Spirits of Will to the Cherubim, *time is born*. But this time is not abstract time, as we usually speak of it; it is an independent being. Only at this point can we speak of something beginning. Time initially is a time being, a being made up entirely of time. Beings are born, who consist only of time. These are the Spirits of Personality, whom we know as Archai in the hierarchy of spiritual beings. In

Saturn existence, the Archai are entirely time. We have also described them as "Time Spirits"—as spirits who order time. They are born as spirits, but they are actually beings who consist entirely of time.

It is extraordinarily important to participate in the sacrifice of the Spirits of Will to the Cherubim and in the birth of the Spirits of Time. Only after time is born does something else emerge that allows us to speak about the Saturn condition as if it were something similar to what now surrounds us. What we call the element of warmth in Saturn is the sacrificial smoke of the Thrones, which generates time. I have always said that Saturn exists as a state of warmth. In doing so, I have described what exists there. For, among all of the elements we have around us at present, we can identify only warmth as an element that also existed in ancient Saturn. Warmth was generated out of the sacrifice that the Spirits of Will presented to the Cherubim. This also shows us how we should think about fire. Where we see fire, where we feel warmth, we should not think about it materialistically, as human beings today naturally and customarily do. Rather, wherever we see warmth, wherever we feel warmth, that is still today the sacrifice of the Spirits of Will to the Cherubim. Even though the spiritual foundation of warmth is invisible in our surroundings, it nonetheless exists. Through this insight the world arrives at the truth that, behind each manifestation of warmth, stands a sacrifice.

In *Occult Science—An Outline* mostly only the outer condition of ancient Saturn was described, to avoid offending people too much. Even that caused offense. Those who can think only in current scientific terms regard the book as pure nonsense. But think what it means, if a person could actually say:

• Ancient Saturn had at its innermost being, at its very foundation, beings belonging to the Spirits of Will who sacrificed themselves to the Cherubim.
• Out of the smoke generated by the sacrifice of the Spirits of Will to the Cherubim, time was born.
• Out of the birth of time, the Archai or the Time Spirits were sent forth.

• Warmth, as we know it, is the outer semblance, the reflection, of the sacrifice of the Spirits of Will.

• Now, outer warmth is an illusion (*maya*). If we wish to speak the truth, it is: wherever warmth is manifest, we have, in truth, sacrifice—the sacrifice of the Thrones before the Cherubim.

Cultivating the capacity of imagination is the second stage of Rosicrucian initiation. (This is mentioned often in *How To Know Higher Worlds* and elsewhere.) Anthroposophists must form imaginations out of sound representations of the world. In this way we can transform thinking into fantasy-imbued imagination. We can take, for example, what we have spoken of today. The Thrones or Spirits of Will kneel before the Cherubim with complete devotion that arises not out of a feeling of insignificance but out of the consciousness that they have something that they can sacrifice. The Thrones in this willingness to sacrifice, which is based upon strength and courage, kneel before the Cherubim and offer up their sacrifice to them. The Thrones send the sacrifice forth as effervescent warmth, flaming warmth, so that the smoke from the fire of sacrifice blazes upward to the winged Cherubim! So may we picture this reality. And now, arising from this sacrifice, as if we were speaking a word into the air and this word were time, but time as *beings*—from the totality of these occurrences—the Spirits of Time or the Archai emerge. This sending forth of the Archai is a powerful image. And this image, placed before our soul, is extremely potent for certain imaginations that can bring us ever deeper into the realms of hidden knowledge.

This transformation of the ideas we receive into imaginations, pictures, is what we must accomplish. Even if the pictures we make are primitive, even if they are anthropomorphic, even if these beings we try to portray look like winged persons—that is beside the point. It doesn't matter. Whatever needs to be added to our efforts will eventually be given to us. What our imaginations should not have will disappear. If we simply allow ourselves to be immersed in such pictures, that activity itself will actually guide us to such beings.

If you can accept this attempt to characterize courage-filled beings, overflowing with wisdom, you will see that the soul must soon turn to all manner of pictures that are remote from concepts formed by reason. Intellectual concepts came into existence much later. We ought not to approach the Saturn existence, in any case, in a purely intellectual way. You must come to understand what it means for clairvoyance to unfold in a person's mind: someone who describes something out of naive clairvoyance portrays it differently than a person who is intellectually oriented. An intellectual for his or her part never properly understands such minds. I want to give you an example of this. Take Albert Schwegler's (1819–1857) *History of Philosophy* (Stuttgart, 1848), a book that students used to like to study before taking their examinations but which, since the soul has been removed from philosophy, is no longer useful.[9] Even though the book has suffered from revisions in later editions, what was important in the original has not been entirely lost. This book is a history of philosophy from the Hegelian perspective. Thus you can take Schwegler's *History of Philosophy*, and you will have a good picture of philosophy in general at the time it was written and an excellent source on Hegelian philosophy. But now read the short chapter on Jacob Boehme, and you can discover how helpless a person writing an intellectual philosophy is, confronted with a spirit like Jacob Boehme.[10] Fortunately he left out Paracelsus, otherwise he would have written quite terrible things about him. But read

9. Albert Schwegler (1819–1857), philosopher and classicist. His *Geschichte der Philosophie im Umriss* was first published in Stuttgart in 1848.
10. Jacob Boehme (1575–1624) settled in Görlitz as a shoemaker in 1594. In 1600, he was granted a profound mystical experience while polishing a pewter mug. For the remainder of his life, he sought to put what he had learned into language. A great mystic, philosopher, Sophiologist, and theosophist, Boehme drew deeply on Paracelsian alchemy, Kabbala, as well Christian esoteric tradition, to create a body of work which was to influence diverse strands of the Western tradition, including the theology of the Pietists and Quakers, Romanticism, German idealism (particularly Schelling), Russian philosophy, and contemporary thinkers such as Paul Tillich and Nikolai Berdyaev. Theophrastus Bombastus Paracelsus von Hohenheim (1493–1541). See Rudolf Steiner, *Die Mystik im Aufgang des neuzeitlichen Geisteslebens und ihr Verhaeltnis zur modernen Weltanschauung* (1901, GA 7).

what Schwegler wrote about Boehme. He found in Boehme a mind in which not the picture of ancient Saturn but a repetition of the Saturn picture had dawned in a naive way. This repetition of the Saturn picture is something that is repeated in the Earth period. In Boehme, Schwegler came upon a spirit who could do no more than try to describe with words and pictures something that could not be understood through the intellect. Every purely intellectual means of grasping the repetition of the Saturn picture fails. It is not as if a person cannot understand these things at all, but one cannot grasp them if one only maintains the standpoint of ordinary, dry, philosophic reasoning.

You see, the important point is to lift ourselves beyond the sufficiency of ordinary intellect. Something as excellent as Schwegler's *History of Philosophy* is still produced by means of ordinary intellectual capacities and thus remains an example of how an extraordinary intellect is absolutely brought to a standstill by a spirit like Jacob Boehme.

Today, in our consideration of ancient Saturn, we have tried to penetrate the inner aspect of this ancient planetary embodiment of our Earth. In the lectures to come we will do the same with Sun and Moon existences in order to arrive at concepts that will be no less impressive than those we achieved when we looked back to ancient Saturn and allowed an imagination to arise in us of the Thrones as they sacrificed themselves to the Cherubim and thereby created the beings of time. For time is the result of sacrifice and consists of living Time. We shall see how all of these things will be transformed during the Sun existence and how other mighty processes in cosmic existence occur as we move from Saturn existence to Sun existence and then to Moon existence.

2. The Inner Aspect of the Sun Embodiment of the Earth

BERLIN, NOVEMBER 7, 1911

YOU WILL HAVE GATHERED from the previous lecture that to describe each of the three stages of development preceding the creation of our own Earth is extremely difficult. We have seen that to do so we must first build up the concepts and ideas needed to reach such strange and distant states of our cosmic development. I have already pointed out that no description of the ancient Saturn period and the planetary embodiments of our Earth following it—such as, for example, the description given in *An Outline of Occult Science*—is exhaustive. In that book I had to be content to clothe the subject in pictures drawn from what is familiar and close at hand, for the book was meant to be accessible to the public and not too shocking. The description given in *An Outline of Occult Science* is not exactly inaccurate, but, pictorially, it is dipped in illusion or *maya*. One must work through the illusion to penetrate to the truth.

For example, ancient Saturn may be described as a heavenly body that did not consist of those components we know as earth, water, or air, but was made up entirely of warmth—and this is correct within certain limits. Likewise, any reference to space is only a pictorial description for, as we saw in the last lecture, not even time existed on ancient Saturn. There was no space on ancient Saturn, at least not in our sense of that term; while time first came into being then. When we put ourselves in the context of ancient Saturn, then, we are in a realm of spaceless eternity. Thus, if we attempt to picture this, we must be clear that it is only a picture.

Were we then to have entered ancient Saturn's "space," we would have found no substance there dense enough to be described as gas. There would have been only warmth and coldness. In reality, we could not speak of coming out of one part of space and entering another. There was only the feeling of moving between warmer and colder conditions. Even clairvoyants who imagine themselves within the time period of ancient Saturn experience only the impression of the ebb and flow of spaceless warmth. But this impression is only the outer veil of the Saturn state. For this warmth or fire, as we call it in occultism, reveals itself to us in its spiritual substrata; and, as we have seen, spiritual actions, spiritual accomplishments, were in fact occurring on ancient Saturn.

We have tried to make a picture of what kind of spiritual activity was occurring on ancient Saturn. We said that the Spirits of Will, the Thrones, performed deeds of sacrifice. This means that, if we look back upon what took place on Saturn, we see the Cherubim and the sacrifice that flowed from the Thrones. Sacrifice flowed from the Thrones to the Cherubim, and these acts of sacrifice appear, when viewed from the outside, as warmth. Conditions of warmth are thus the outer, physical expression of sacrifice. Indeed, wherever we perceive warmth in the entire cosmos, this warmth is the outward expression of what stands behind it. Warmth is an illusion. Acts of sacrifice by spiritual beings are the reality behind the warmth. If we wish to characterize warmth accurately, therefore, we must say: *Cosmic warmth is the revelation of cosmic sacrifice or cosmic acts of sacrifice.*

Then we have seen, too, that as the Thrones present their sacrificial deed to the Cherubim, what we call time is simultaneously born. I have already mentioned that "time" is a modern word that does not quite fit what I am trying to describe. Time here does not yet encompass the abstractions "earlier" and "later" as we perceive them today. Time began as a configuration of spiritual beings, the Spirits of Personality also identified as "Time Spirits." These Time Spirits are really the ancient manifestation of time, the offspring of the Thrones and Cherubim. But the circumstances under which the beings of the time-aspect originated in ancient Saturn are deeds of sacrifice.

If we wish to reach a true understanding of what stands behind the warmth—when it is said that ancient Saturn consists of warmth—we must not adopt merely outwardly physical concepts. Remember that warmth as we use the term is a physical concept. Instead, we must adopt concepts derived from the life of the *soul*—the moral, wisdom-filled life of the soul. No one can know what warmth is who cannot imagine what it means to sacrifice willingly what one possesses, what one has, even what one is. One must come to understand what it means, from the perspective of the soul, to offer up one's own being, to renounce oneself consciously. In other words, one must imagine giving one's best for the healing of the world, not holding one's best for the sake of self, but wanting to sacrifice one's best at the altar of cosmic all. If we grasp all this as living concept and as a feeling permeating our soul, it can lead us gradually to understand what stands behind the appearance of warmth.

Try to imagine what is connected with the concept of sacrifice in modern life—namely, that it is inconceivable that a person who sacrifices with understanding does so against his or her will. If someone sacrifices against his or her will, the person must have felt pressed to do so. There must have been coercion. But that is not at all what is meant by sacrifice here. Here sacrifice flows as a matter of course from the being who offers it. If someone sacrifices without external coercion or the expectation of achieving something—if someone sacrifices out of an inner sense of urgency—then that person will experience inner warmth and bliss. When we feel aglow with inner warmth and happiness, this expresses something we can only describe by saying that *a person who offers a sacrifice and feels permeated with warmth glows with happiness.* We ourselves can experience how the glow of sacrifice approaches us in the illusion of external warmth in the world. Only a person who can grasp that, where there is warmth in the world there is an underlying soul-spiritual reality, truly understands what warmth is. Warmth exists and becomes active through the joy of sacrifice. Whoever can experience warmth in this way gradually arrives at the reality that exists or lies hidden behind the phenomenon, the illusion, of physical warmth.

If now we wish to press forward from ancient Saturn existence to ancient Sun existence, we must lay the basis for concepts with which to create an image of the substance of *ancient* Sun, not our present Sun. Once again, in *An Outline of Occult Science* I presented only the outward appearance. Ancient Sun enhanced warmth by adding air and light to it. Just as we had to search beyond warmth to perceive the glow of sacrifice brought about by the Spirits of Will, so too now—if we wish to understand the air and light that were added to warmth on ancient Sun—we must look for something *moral* as the essence of air and light. Only if we look for what we can experience within ourselves in a soul-spiritual way can we arrive at an idea, a representation, a feeling, of the air and light on ancient Sun.

We can describe this feeling as a soul experience in the following way. Imagine that you observed a genuine deed of sacrifice or imagined the Thrones presenting their sacrifice to the Cherubim, as we described it in the last lecture, and that you were so moved by this picture of sacrifice that it enlivened your soul with bliss. What would your soul feel if you were to observe such sacrificing beings or if you were to imagine a picture of this kind that awakened and enlivened your soul? If you have feelings full of life—if you cannot stand unfeelingly before the delight one feels in a deed of sacrifice—you would have to experience a profound awakening at the sight of this act of sacrifice. You would have to feel in your soul that to gaze upon the supreme happiness that arises from sacrifice is the most beautiful deed, the most beautiful experience that could ever arise in the soul!

Another feeling that would arise is an attitude of complete surrender. Indeed, you would have to be a block of wood if sacrifice did not create a longing in the soul to gaze upon it with absolute devotion and convey a mood of self-surrender. Consider such selfless giving over of oneself! A deed of sacrifice is active. It is self-surrender transformed in activity. And contemplation of active, concerned self-surrender can create an affinity for the giving over of oneself, for losing oneself—for forgetting about self. If we cannot create such a mood, or at least an inkling or an echo of it, we can never truly come to a closer understanding of sacrifice.

Indeed, if we pour this mood of disinterested giving up of self into the soul, we may reach what a higher form of knowledge can give us. A person who is unable to create a spirit of self-surrender cannot achieve higher knowledge. What is the opposite of this attitude of self-surrender? It is self-will, the assertion of one's own will. These are two poles in the soul's life: loss of self in what one is contemplating and self-willed assertion of what lies within the self. These are two great opposites. If you wish to attain real knowledge and permeate yourself with wisdom, self-will is lethal. In ordinary life, we know self-will only as prejudice—and prejudices always destroy higher insight.

In fact, one must intensify in one's thinking what I am describing here as capacity for self-surrender, for only through an intensified sense of self-surrender can a human being work toward the higher worlds. In the higher worlds, one must be able to experience the capacity to lose oneself—at least as a mood of soul. Let me emphasize here that we can never attain higher knowledge if we work only with ordinary scientific knowledge or everyday thinking. We must be clear that ordinary science and everyday thinking work out of ordinary human will, through all that self-will has created in the experiences, feelings, and ideas we have inherited or cultivated. We can be misled here—indeed, delusions are very common in this area. People come, for example, and say: We are supposed to accept this or that aspect of knowledge presented by spiritual science, but I will not accept anything that is not consistent with what I already think: I won't accept anything without proof. Certainly, one should accept nothing without evidence. But if we take from what is presented to us only what we already know, we cannot advance a step! Anyone wishing to become clairvoyant will never say that he or she will accept only what he or she has already proved. Those who wish to become clairvoyant must be absolutely free from all self-seeking and know in advance that all that comes to them from the cosmos can only be described by the word *grace*. Such people anticipate everything and anything from illuminating grace. For how does one achieve clairvoyant knowledge? Only by setting aside everything we have already learned. Ordinarily, we think: I have my own judgment. But we must remember that ordinary judgment only comes out of renewing what your ancestors once thought, or what stimulates your desires, and so on. It is never a question of making one's own judgments. Those who most insist that they are exercising their own judgment are the least aware how slavishly they are tied to their own prejudices. All of this must be eliminated if we wish to attain higher knowledge. The soul must be empty and quietly able to wait for what it can receive out of the space-less, timeless, objectless, eventless, secret, hidden world. On no account should we believe that we can acquire higher knowledge unless we allow to ripen within us a mood out of which we meet all that is offered to us as revelation or enlightenment—illumination. Only in this mood can we await whatever approaches us and gives us something as nothing other than grace, as what *should* come to us.

How does such knowledge reveal itself? How is what comes to us revealed when we have sufficiently prepared ourselves? It reveals itself as a feeling of being blessed by a gift from the spiritual world that comes to meet us. If we wished to describe what stands before us in life in this way, full of blessing and filling us with this recognition—be it a being or anything else—we could express it only as follows. We experience what comes to us as bestowing a blessing, as granting a gift, as giving us something. To grasp the nature of a being, whose main characteristic consists of the capacity for granting, giving, offer-ing—for showering and pouring forth blessings—to grasp such a nature we would need to grasp the image of the sacrifice of the Thrones to the Cherubim! Imagine that a being came to someone who understood the meaning of the Thrones' sacrifice to the Cheru-bim—a being who would transform the capacity to understand the Thrones' sacrifice into a capacity to give—to pour one's gifts around oneself in blessing. Imagine that we are looking at a rose and are delighted by it, thus experiencing the feeling of being blessed by something we see as "beautiful." Then imagine another being who, by comprehending the significance of the Thrones' sacrifice to the Cherubim, could confer all that it had on its surroundings, pouring everything available into the world, in the spirit of giving—if we imagine such beings, then we have those Spirits of Wisdom described in *An Outline of Occult Science* who, during Sun existence, were added to those we came to know during Saturn existence.

Now, if I were to ask what is the character of these Spirits of Wisdom who appeared during Sun existence and were added to the spirits already present during the Saturn existence, I would have to answer as follows. These spirits have as their defining characteristic the virtue of giving, of bestowing, of effecting blessings. If I wanted to find a designation for these beings, I would have to say: They are the Spirits of Wisdom, the mighty Grantors, the great Givers of the Cosmos! Just as we have called the Thrones the great Sacrificers, so we have to say of the Spirits of Wisdom that they are the great Givers, who grant their gift which is the same gift as that out of which the cosmos is woven and lives, for they themselves streamed out into the cosmos and first created order.

That is the effect of the Spirits of Wisdom on the Sun: they give their own beings into their surroundings. But what, we may ask, happens on the Sun, if we want to see with higher sense perception what is represented to outer observation?

When we look at the Sun, we observe what is described in *An Outline of Occult Science*. In addition to warmth, the Sun also consists of air and light. But to say simply that the Sun consists of air and light as well as of warmth is the same as saying, for example, of landscape: In the distance I see a gray cloud. If one were a painter and had this impression, one would paint a gray cloud. But if one were to approach it more closely, one would perhaps find something like a swarm of insects rather than a gray cloud. Actually, what seemed like a gray cloud was a number of living beings. We are in a similar situation when we consider ancient Sun existence from a distance. From afar, ancient Sun appears to be a body consisting of air and light. But, if we look at it more closely, we no longer see a body of air and light. Instead, there appears the great virtue of bestowing by the Spirits of Wisdom. No one discovers the true nature of air who merely describes air according to outward, physical properties. These properties are only illusion (*maya*), external manifestations. Wherever there is air in the universe, the actions of the gift-granting

Spirits of Wisdom lie behind it. Weaving, working air reveals the virtue of bestowing by the Spirits of the Macrocosm. Only the person who sees the true nature of air, says: I perceive here the element of air, but, in reality, the Spirits of Wisdom are placing their gifts into their surroundings; something streams into the environment from the Spirits of Wisdom.

Thus we know now what we have really said about ancient Sun when we say that it consists of air. We know now that what appears outwardly as air is actually the activity of the Spirits of Wisdom allowing their own being to flow forth into their surroundings. But at this point something remarkable presents itself to clairvoyant vision on the ancient Sun. To understand this we must become clear how, out of the life of the soul, we can create an even more accurate idea of the virtue of bestowing. Let us recreate a feeling such as we can have when we are able to permeate ourselves with a perception or an idea in the mood of sacrifice that we have described here. An idea so permeated always gives us a particular feeling. It is not like a scientific idea. The most similar experience may be found in the artistic realm where, in order to give the world an independent entity, an idea must master the way in which color or form streams out into the world.

To characterize a being who has the capacity to give such a gift, one may say that productivity, creativity is bound up with this gift, for the act itself of giving is a creative activity. Whoever has an idea and feels that the idea can bring healing into the world, and then presents it in works of art, has rightly understood the fruits of the virtue of bestowing. Think of a creative idea in the mind of the artist, and how it then becomes manifest in matter: this idea is actually a spiritual being of air. Where air exists, we face creative activity. And because this living creativity existed on the Sun, the association of air with creative ability is identifiable as fact.

If we recall that the Spirits of Time were born on ancient Saturn, we also know that time existed on the Sun—for time came over to the Sun from Saturn. Time existed there. Because the archetypal bestowing arose, a possibility existed on ancient Sun that could not have occurred on ancient Saturn. Consider what would have become of giving if time had not existed: there would be no bestowing, for giving consists both of giving and receiving. Without receiving, giving is inconceivable. Thus giving consists of two acts: giving and receiving. Otherwise giving has no purpose. On the Sun, giving stands in a most unusual relation to receiving. Because time already exists on the Sun, the gift, sent into the surroundings of the ancient Sun, is preserved in time. When the Spirits of Wisdom pour out their gifts, they remain present in time. Something must then enter that is capable of receiving. In relationship to the activity of the Spirits of Wisdom receiving occurs at a later point in time. The Spirits of Wisdom give at an earlier moment, and what is necessarily bound up with their giving as receiving occurs at a later point in time.

To gain an accurate picture of this, once again we must take the experience of our own soul into account. Imagine that you have tried very hard to understand something or to formulate some thought. Now you have created this thought. The next day you clear your mind, so that everything that you created in your thoughts on the previous day can be brought back to mind. Thus, you receive today what was formulated yesterday. So it was on the ancient Sun: what was given at an earlier point in time remained preserved and then was received at a later moment. But what was the significance of this receiving?

Like the archetypal giving, receiving, too, is a deed or event on the ancient Sun. Receiving differentiates itself from giving only in terms of time. Receiving occurs later. The giving comes from the Spirits of Wisdom. But who receives? Before someone can receive, there first must be a recipient. In the same way that the sacrifice of the Thrones to the Cherubim brought about the birth of the Spirits of Time on Saturn, the birth of bestowing in the universe by the Spirits of Wisdom on the Sun created those spirits we call Archangels or Archangeloi. The Archangels are the ones who receive on the ancient Sun. But they receive in a very special manner, for what the Archangels receive from the Spirits of Wisdom, they do not keep for themselves. Rather they reflect it back, just as a mirror reflects back the image it receives. Thus the Archangels on the Sun have the task of receiving what was given at an earlier point in time, so that it is preserved and reflected again by the Archangels into a later time. Therefore, on the Sun, we have an earlier act of giving and a later act of receiving, but a receiving in the form of a streaming or reflecting back of what was given at the earlier point in time.

Imagine that the earth were not as it currently is, but that what had happened during an earlier time could stream once again into the present. We know that something like that actually occurs. We live in the fifth post-Atlantean cultural epoch and the events of the third post-Atlantean cultural period, the ancient Egypto-Chaldean era, stream into this period. What occurred during the third epoch will reemerge and be reflected back again. That is a recapitulation of the giving and receiving that occurred during the ancient Sun development. Thus we may think of the Spirits of Wisdom as the bestowers in ancient Sun times and the Archangels as the receivers. Something quite remarkable arises from this, which you can represent accurately only by imagining an inwardly enclosed globe from whose center radiates something to be given away. Something radiates out from the center to the periphery and from there reflects back to the middle point. From within the outer surface of the globe the Archangels radiate back what they have received. From the outside you need not imagine anything. We must imagine something moving out from the center that comes from the Spirits of Wisdom. It radiates in all directions and is received by the Archangels who reflect it back again. What is it that reflects back into space? What is this gift of the Spirits of Wisdom that radiates back again? What is the radiating wisdom that is directed back to its source? It is *light*. The Archangels are also the creators of light. Light is not at all what it appears to be in outward illusion. Where light occurs, the gifts of the Spirits of Wisdom are radiating back to us. And the beings whose existence we must presume wherever there is light are the Archangels. Thus we must say: the Archangels are hidden within the flooding rays of light. Behind the flooding rays of light that come to us the Archangels are hidden. The Archangels' capacity to stream forth light arises out of the virtue of bestowing that is radiated to them by the Spirits of Wisdom.

We thus arrive at a picture of the old Sun. Imagine a center where the Spirits of Wisdom are immersed in their contemplation of the legacy from ancient Saturn—the deed of sacrifice of the Thrones to the Cherubim. Contemplating this deed of sacrifice causes the Spirits of Wisdom to radiate the substance of their own being—to radiate streaming, flowing wisdom in the form of the virtue of bestowing. Because this virtue is permeated by time, it is sent forth and then reflected back again, so that we have before us a globe, illumined *within* by virtue reflected back to its source and center. For we must imagine that the ancient Sun illuminates in an inward, not an outward direction. And this creates something new that we can describe in the following way. Imagine these Spirits of Wisdom, seated at the center of the Sun, contemplating the sacrificing Thrones and radiating their own being far out into their surroundings. Then, from the surface of the globe, they receive back what they radiated forth in the form of light. Everything is illuminated through and through. But what do they receive from what radiates back to them? Their own being, their innermost being, has been surrendered as a gift to the macrocosm. Now it radiates back—their own being returns to them from the outside. They see their own inner being distributed throughout the cosmos and radiated back as light, as the reflection of their own being.

Inner and outer are the two opposites that now come before us. The earlier and the later transform themselves and become the inner and the outer. Space is born! Out of the gift of the virtue of bestowing given by the Spirits of Wisdom space arises on the old Sun. Before this, space could have only allegorical meaning. Now, however, on the old Sun, we actually have space, but only in two dimensions: there are no above and below, no right and left, only outer and inner. Actually these two opposites already emerge at the end of ancient Saturn, but they recapitulate the process in the creation of space on ancient Sun.

And if we want to imagine all of these occurrences again—just as previously we brought before our soul the sacrificing Thrones giving birth to the Time Spirits—we would not portray a body consisting of light, for light does not yet radiate outward but exists only as reflection radiating inward. Rather, we must imagine a globe as inner space. At its center, a recapitulation of the picture of Saturn occurs: the Thrones present as spirits kneeling before the Cherubim—those winged beings who offer their own being—and, in addition to these, the Spirits of Wisdom immersed in contemplation of the sacrifice. Now one can imagine that the glow lying within the sacrifice (the sacrificial fire of the Thrones), transforms itself into the sacrifice of the Spirits of Wisdom: their sacrifice is represented materially as air that rises during the act of sacrifice as sacrificial smoke. Thus we have a complete picture if we imagine:

- the sacrificing Thrones kneeling before the Cherubim,
- the choirs of Spirits of Wisdom surrendering in devotion to the vision of the sacrifice of the Thrones at the center of the Sun,
- their devotion growing into an image of sacrificial smoke, which spreads out in all directions, streams outward, condenses into clouds at the periphery,
- the Archangels being created out of the clouds of smoke,
- the gift of the sacrificial smoke radiating back from the periphery in the form of light,
- the light illuminating the interior of the Sun,
- the gift of the Spirits of Wisdom being given back, thereby creating the sphere of the Sun.

This sphere consists of the outpoured gifts of glowing warmth and sacrificial smoke. At the outer periphery sit the Archangels, the creators of light, who reflect what earlier came into being on the Sun. It took time, but eventually sacrificial smoke could return as light. What were the Archangels preserving? They preserved what arose earlier, the gifts of the Spirits of Wisdom that the Archangels received and then radiated back. But what previously existed as time they gave back as space, and, by radiating back time as space, the Archangels gave back what they themselves had received from the Archai. Thus they become the Angels of Beginning, because they brought what existed earlier into a later time. Archangels—Messengers of Beginning![1]

---

1. *Archangeloi* in Greek: *archai* = beginning, origin; *angeloi* = messengers.

It is remarkable when, out of true occult knowledge, a "Word" such as this re-emerges, and when we recall how this "Word," arising in the most ancient traditions, has been passed on to us through the school of Dionysius the Areopagite,[2] the pupil of Paul. It is remarkable to see that this word is so deeply imprinted that, when we discover it again, independently of what was written, what originally arose—the original meaning—arises again. That fills us with the greatest respect. We feel linked to the ancient, holy Mystery schools of initiation wisdom. It is as if this ancient tradition were streaming into us, for we grasp it with understanding, even though we ourselves are responsible for acquiring this knowledge independently of the old tradition. Those who can experience something of the mood of the ancient forms of expression that have been handed down to us, even though they may be unaware of these traditions, feel themselves placed under the influence of the Time Spirits within the human spirit. A wonderful feeling of being linked with the whole of human evolution arises from this: a feeling of certainty in these matters.

The Archangels preserve the recollection of the archetypal beginnings. Whatever existed on one or another of the planets is recapitulated at a later time, but something else is always added to the later manifestation. Thus, in a certain way, we also meet the being of the Sun in what we find on our own Earth.

This entire imagination, this whole feeling that we can develop, gives us an image of the sacrificing Thrones, of the Cherubim receiving their offering, of the glow radiating from the sacrifice, of the sacrificial smoke spreading out like air, of the light radiating back from the Archangels who preserve what occurred in the beginning for a later time. This feeling can awaken in us an understanding of everything related to these creations.

---

2. Dionysius the Areopagite, a member of the Athenian Areopagus, who was converted to Christianity by Paul (Acts 17:34). The text referred to here, *On the Heavenly Hierarchies,* was published under his name in Syria. See *Dionysios Areopagita, Die Hierarchie der Engel und der Kirche* (Munich, 1955). Regarding the authenticity of this work, see Steiner, *Christianity as Mystical Fact and the Mysteries of Antiquity.*

This milieu, which I have portrayed here as a milieu of the soul, presents from a more spiritual perspective what we earlier attained through a physical representation. And we shall now see that it is out of this milieu that the Being is born who appeared on the Earth as the Christ Being. We can understand what the Christ Being brought to the Earth only if we assimilate the concept of the grace-engendering virtue of bestowing as it reflects in the light of the cosmos into the inner substance of the Sun body—which is permeated and illuminated by this light. If we hold up this image, which we have just described, transform it into an Imagination and consider that this is what this Being brought to and embodied on Earth, then we will be able to experience more deeply the spiritual Being of the Christ impulse. We will be able to understand the dim inkling that can live in the human soul when it senses that what has just been described by this representation can live again on Earth.

Let us imagine that what we have just described of the Sun was gathered up and concentrated completely in the soul of a Being and then, at a later time, brought forward again. Imagine that this Being appeared on Earth and worked in such a way that out of what the archetypal deed and smoke of sacrifice created—that is, the light-engendering time and the bestowing virtue—an extract of activating grace would be carried over and reflect soul warmth and glorious light out of the cosmos. Imagine all of this concentrated in a single Soul, who in turn gives this to the Earth-existence, and that assembled around this Soul are those who are intended to radiate this back and preserve it for the remainder of Earth-existence. In the center is the One who bestows out of the sacrifice and through sacrifice; around this Being are those who are intended to receive it. Here we have linked together, on the one hand, what the sacrifice is and what belongs to it, translated into earthly existence, and, on the other hand, the possibility of destroying this sacrifice, for everything that can be given to the human being to bring about grace may be either rejected or accepted. Imagine that all of this were embodied in an intuition—then one would have what one experiences standing before Leonardo da Vinci's *Last Supper:* here we have the entire Sun together with the Beings of sacrifice, the Beings of bestowing virtue, the Beings of soul-warming bliss and light-filled splendor—as grasped by the soul—radiated back from the Ones who have been chosen to preserve what arises in earlier times for later times. All this has been set out especially for the Earth, together with the possibility that it can also be rejected by the betrayer.

The Being of the Earth, insofar as the Sun Being reappears on the Earth, can be experienced in this way. If this is felt not in an outward, intellectual manner, but in a truly artistic way, one can experience the real driving force in such a great work of art that reflects an extract of Earth existence. And if next time we see this picture we notice how the Christ grows out of the Sun milieu, then we will understand more fully what we have often said: that if a spirit came down from Mars to the Earth and could not understand everything he saw, that spirit would still be able to understand the mission of the Earth if he allowed Leonardo's *Last Supper* to work upon him. An inhabitant of Mars would be able to see that Sun-existence must be concealed within Earth-existence, and everything that we could say about the significance of this for the Earth would be clear to him. That inhabitant of Mars would understand that the Earth has meaning, and know what was significant for the Earth. He would say to himself: "This could occur somewhere on Earth and have meaning only for a corner of the Earth's existence. But if this deed could really be represented, the deed that streams toward me out of the colors of the central figure in relation to the surrounding figures, then I would feel what the Spirits of Wisdom experienced on the Sun echoing again here in the words: Do this in remembrance of me! Here is the preservation of the earlier in the later. We will only understand these words when we grasp them in the context of the entire cosmos, as we have just learned to do. Here I just wanted to point out how an artistic deed of the first rank stands in relationship to the entire development of the cosmos.

In the next lecture it will be our task to understand the Christ Being from the perspective of the spiritual Being of the Sun in order to go on to the perspective of the spiritual Being of the Moon.

3. The Inner Aspect of the Sun Embodiment of the Earth and the Transition to the Moon Embodiment

BERLIN, NOVEMBER 14, 1911

IN THE LAST TWO LECTURES I TRIED to point out that something spiritual lies behind all that is material in the phenomena in our universe. I tried to characterize the spiritual reality to be found behind the phenomena of warmth and streaming air. To describe such characteristics for you, I had to reach back into the most distant past of our evolutionary development. We also looked into our own soul life to describe the spiritual context that forms the basis of the material universe. After all, when we characterize something we must take the ideas we use from somewhere else. Words alone are not enough: one must have very definite ideas.

We have seen that the spiritual context which we must refer to lies far from anything human beings experience at the present time, far from what human beings today are able to know. Thus, to understand this context, we have to call upon conditions seldom found and contexts not generally understood in our own life of soul and spirit. We have seen that we have had to search for the deepest nature of the conditions of warmth and fire far from the manifestation of outward, physical fire or warmth. Certainly, when we identify sacrifice—indeed, the sacrifice of specific beings, the Thrones, whom we met during the ancient Saturn state of the Earth's development, and who at that time presented their sacrifice to the Cherubim—as the essence of all conditions of fire and warmth in the cosmos, this must seem fantastic to a person today. And yet, to speak truly, we must say that as it occurred at that point in the development of the cosmos, everything that appears to us outwardly, illusorily, in the condition of warmth or fire actually consists of sacrifice.

Similarly, we pointed out last time that behind everything that we call streaming air or gas lies something very distant—namely, what we have called the virtue of bestowing, the devoted pouring forth of their own being by spiritual beings. That is what exists in every breath of wind, in every stream of air. What is perceived as outwardly phys-ical is really only an illusion, maya. Only when we have progressed from the illusion to the spiritual reality, will we have a correct idea. Fire or warmth or air are no more present as realities in the world than the human being is present in the image a person sees in a mir-ror. For, as a mirror image is essentially an illusion in relation to the human being, so fire or warmth or air are illusions, and the truths behind them are the reality—just as the real human being stands in relation to his or her image in the mirror. It is not fire or air that we seek in the realm of the true, but sacrifice and the virtue of bestowing.

When we saw the virtue of bestowing added to sacrifice, we ascended from the ancient life of Saturn to that of the Sun. Within the second embodiment of our Earth, we find something that leads us a step nearer to the true circumstances of our development. And here we must once again introduce a concept that belongs to the realm of true reality as opposed to the world of illusion. That is, before we take up the actual circumstances of our evolutionary devel-opment, we must acquire a particular concept.

Let us approach this concept as follows. When a human being in his or her outward life does something or accomplishes something, this generally results from his or her will impulse. Whatever a human being does, whether it is just a hand movement or a mighty deed, a will impulse stands behind the activity. Everything that leads a person to carry out a deed or to achieve something emanates from this. And it will probably be said that a strong, forceful deed, for example, one that brings healing and blessing, proceeds from a strong will impulse, and a less important act proceeds from a weaker impulse. In general, we are inclined to assume that the magnitude of the deed depends on the strength of the impulse of will.

Only to a certain degree, however, is it correct to say that if we strengthen our will, we shall accomplish something significant in the world. Beyond a certain point, that is no longer the case. Surprisingly, certain deeds that a human being can carry out—above all, deeds connected with the spiritual world—are not dependent upon the strengthening of our will impulse. Of course, in the physical world in which we live, the magnitude of the deed does depend on the strength of the will impulse: we have to make a greater effort if we want to accomplish more. But in the spiritual world this is not the case, rather the opposite applies. To accomplish the greatest deeds, to achieve the greatest results in the spiritual world, a strengthening of the positive will impulse is not what is necessary, rather a certain resignation, a renunciation is needed. We can proceed on that assumption even in the smallest, purely spiritual matters. We achieve a certain spiritual result not by bringing our earnest desires into play or being occupied with them, but by subduing our wishes, restraining our desires, and forgoing their satisfaction.

Let us suppose that a person intended to accomplish something in the world through inner spiritual means. The individual has to prepare himself or herself by learning above all to suppress his or her wishes or desires. And while one becomes stronger in the physical world if one eats well and is well nourished and thus has more energy, one will achieve something significant in the spiritual world—this is a description, not advice—when one fasts or does something to suppress or renounce wishes and desires. Preparation that involves relinquishing the wishes, desires, and will impulses arising in us is always part of the greatest spiritual endeavors. The less we will, the more we can say that we let life stream over us and do not desire this or that, but rather take things as karma casts them before us; the more we accept karma and its consequences; the more we behave calmly, renouncing all that we otherwise would have wanted to achieve in life—the stronger we become. This is true, for example, in respect to the activity of thinking.

In the instance of a teacher or educator who is filled with longings and above all is fond of good food and drink, it will become evident that the words he or she directs at pupils do not accomplish very much: what the teacher says to the students goes right in one ear and out the other. Such a teacher will believe that the students are to blame for this, but that is not always the case. An educator who sees a higher meaning in life, lives in moderation, eats only as much as is necessary in order to sustain life, and above all accepts by choice the things that destiny bestows, will gradually notice that his or her words have great power. Even the glance of such a teacher can have a great effect. Indeed, it may not even be necessary for the teacher to look at a pupil. Such a teacher need only be near the student, need only have an encouraging thought. Even if the thought is not expressed verbally, it is nonetheless conveyed to the student. All of this depends upon the degree of renunciation and resignation a person exercises with regard to what is otherwise strongly desired.

The path of renunciation is the right means of spiritual activity and leads to spiritual results in higher worlds. In this respect we can encounter many illusions—and even though an illusion of renunciation seems outwardly similar to true renunciation, illusions do not lead to the right results. You are all acquainted with what is called, in ordinary life, asceticism: self-inflicted suffering. In many cases such self-torment can be self-indulgence, something a person chooses from a desire to accomplish something greater or out of some other source of desire for self-satisfaction. In such cases, self-denial is not effective, for self-denial has meaning only when it accompanies renunciation that is rooted in the spirit. We must understand the concept of creative renunciation, creative resignation. It is extremely important that we recognize renunciation or creative resignation—which we can actually experience in the soul—as an idea that is far removed from everyday life. Only then will we be able to take a step further in human evolution. For something like this occurred in the course of evolution in the transition from the development of the Sun condition to that of the Moon condition. Something like resignation occurred then in the realm of the beings of the higher worlds who, as we know, are linked to the course of the Earth's development. To understand this we shall need to consider the ancient Sun development once again. But, first, we will draw attention to something we already know, but which may have seemed puzzling in some respects up until now.

We have pointed repeatedly to precedents in development that we can trace back to beings who remained behind in the course of development.[1] We know, indeed, that luciferic beings intrude upon humankind on earth. And we have frequently pointed out that these luciferic beings, because they did not reach the stage of development that they could have achieved during the development of the ancient Moon, are able to invade our astral body during earthly evolution. In this context, we have often used the trivial comparison that it is not only students who repeat a grade at school, but cosmic beings in the great course of cosmic evolution may also fail to complete a stage of development and later interfere in the stages of development of other beings. Thus luciferic beings, who stayed behind during the ancient Moon development, interfere with human beings on the Earth.

Superficially, one could easily think that these beings must be flawed beings, weaklings in world evolution—otherwise why did they fail to achieve what they could have achieved? That thought could occur to us. But another thought we could also formulate is that human beings would never have come into their freedom, would never have developed an independent capacity to make decisions, had luciferic beings not been held back on the Moon. On the one hand, it is due to luciferic beings that we have desires, drives, and passions in our astral body that continually drive us from a certain height and pull us toward the lower regions of our being. On the other hand, however, were it not for our capacity to become evil and stray from the good through the power of the luciferic beings in our astral body, we could not act freely or have what we call free will or freedom of choice. It must be said, therefore, that we owe our freedom to the luciferic beings. The one-sided perspective that luciferic beings exist only to lead humanity astray is insufficient. Rather, we must regard the remaining behind of the luciferic beings as some-

---

1. See, for instance, *The Spiritual Guidance of the Individual and of Humanity.*

thing good, and as something without which we would not be able to achieve our worth as human beings in the true sense of the word.

Yet something much deeper lies at the basis of what we call the remaining behind of the luciferic and ahrimanic beings. We have already encountered it on ancient Saturn, but it is so difficult to recognize that we can hardly find words in any language to characterize it. Yet, we can characterize it very clearly if we move forward to the reality of the ancient Sun by taking into account the concept of resignation or renunciation we described today. For the basis of the remaining behind of beings and the influence stemming from it lies in resignation or renunciation on the part of higher beings.

We can see, then, that the following occurred on the Sun. We have said that the Thrones—the Spirits of Will—offer sacrifice to the Cherubim. They present this sacrifice, as we saw last time, not only during the Saturn era; they continue to do so during the Sun era. The Thrones, the Spirits of Will, sacrifice to the Cherubim in the Sun era also. We saw, too, that the real essence of all that existed in the world as conditions of warmth or fire lies in this sacrifice. Now, if we look back into the Akashic record, we can notice something else occurring during the Sun period. The Thrones sacrifice, and maintain their activity of sacrifice. We see the sacrificing Thrones. We also see a number of Cherubim—to whom the sacrifice ascends—receiving the warmth that flows from the sacrifice into themselves. But at the same time a number of Cherubim do something else: they renounce the sacrifice; they do not participate in it. Recognizing this, we complete the image that we allowed to enter our soul the last time.

In this picture, we have the Thrones who sacrifice and those Cherubim who accept the sacrifice; and we also have the Cherubim who do not accept the sacrifice but give back what presses toward them as sacrifice. It is extraordinarily interesting to trace this in the Akashic Chronicle. For, because the virtue of bestowing flows from the Spirits of Wisdom into the sacrificial warmth, we see how during the ancient Sun the smoke of sacrifice, which is reflected back in the form of light by the Archangels from the outermost periphery of the

Sun, ascends. But we see something else as well. It is as if, within the expanse of the ancient Sun, something entirely different is also present, namely, sacrificial smoke that is neither reflected by the Archangels as light nor accepted by the Cherubim and therefore flows back—so that we have clouds of sacrifice in the Sun expanse: sacrifice which ascends and sacrifice that descends; sacrifice that is accepted and sacrifice that is renounced and returned. We also find this self-encountering of the actual spiritual cloud image in the expanse of ancient Sun between what we called last time the outer and the inner. We find it as a separate layer between these two dimensions on the Sun. Thus, in the middle, we have the sacrificing Thrones, in the heights the Cherubim who accept the sacrifice, and then those Cherubim who do not accept the sacrifice but divert it back again. Through this "diverting back" a ring of clouds comes into being, and around this we have the reflected mass of light.

Imagine this picture in a living way. We have this ancient Sun expanse, this ancient Sun mass, like a cosmic globe, beyond which nothing is imaginable, so that we think of space extending only as far as the Archangels. Imagine that at the center we have a ring formation made out of the meeting between the accepted and rejected sacrifices. Out of these accepted and returned sacrifices arises something in the ancient Sun that we can call a division of the entire Sun substance, a divergence. If we wish to compare the ancient Sun to an outward image, we can compare it only to our present Saturn: a globe surrounded by a ring. The accumulating mass of the sacrifice is drawn inward into the center, and what remains outside is ordered into the form of a ring. Thus, we have the Sun substance divided into two parts, separated through the force of the arrested powers of sacrifice.

What do the Cherubim who renounce the sacrifice bring about? Here we approach an extraordinarily difficult subject. You will be able to grasp the concepts we will now consider only after a long process of meditation. Only after long reflection on the concepts to be given here will you discover the realities underlying them. The resignation we spoke of must be brought into relationship with the creation of time we learned occurred on ancient Saturn. We have seen that time first arose on ancient Saturn with the Spirits of Time, the Archai, and that it makes no sense to speak of time before ancient Saturn. Now a recapitulation occurs within this process, but, even so, it is still possible to say that time continues from that point on. Continuation, duration is a concept encompassed by the term "time." When we say, "Time is continuous," this means that when we investigate what is said about Saturn and Sun in the Akashic Chronicle, we discover that time is created during the Saturn epoch and is also present on the Sun. Now if all conditions continue in the way we characterized them with regard to Saturn and the Sun in the last two lectures, then Time would form an element in everything that happened in the course of evolution. We could not eliminate the element of time from any event in evolution. We have seen that the Spirits of Time were created on ancient Saturn, and that time is implanted in everything. And everything we have pictured or imagined about evolution since then must be conceived in the context of time. If what occurred consisted only of what we have presented—offering sacrifice and the virtue of bestowing—all of this would then have to be subject to time. Nothing would exist without being subject to time. Everything that comes into being and everything that passes away—and therefore pertains to time—everything would be subject to time.

Those Cherubim who renounced the sacrifice and at the same time what existed in the sacrificial smoke, renounced these things because they thereby deprived themselves of the properties of this sacrificial smoke. Now, among the properties of the sacrificial smoke was, above all, time, and with it, the processes of coming into being and passing away. In the whole renunciation of the sacrifice, therefore, lies a capacity of the Cherubim to grow beyond the conditions of time. These Cherubim move beyond time—they are no longer subject to time. Thus the conditions of ancient Sun's development are divided so that certain conditions, continuing in a direct line from Saturn as sacrifice and the virtue of bestowing, remain subject to time; whereas other conditions, under the direction of the Cherubim who renounced the sacrifice, wrest themselves out of time so that eternity, permanence, not being subject to the processes of coming into being and passing away may also exist. This is most remarkable: we come to the point in the development of the ancient Sun when time and eternity become separated. By means of the resignation of the Cherubim during the Sun development, eternity came about as a consequence of certain conditions that occurred during that development.

Just as, gazing into our own soul, we saw certain effects arising in the soul as the human being takes up renunciation and resignation, so we now see also eternity and immortality occur on ancient Sun because certain divine-spiritual beings have renounced sacrifice and the legacy of the virtue of bestowing. Just as we saw that time came into being on Saturn, so we see now that through certain circumstances time was wrested out of the Sun phase of development. I have said—of course, please note this— that this was already being prepared during the Saturn epoch, so that eternity does not actually begin during the Sun period. But it is only in the Sun epoch that this can be seen clearly enough to express it in concepts. The separation of eternity from time is so barely perceptible on Saturn that our concepts and words are not precise enough to characterize how something like this existed for ancient Saturn and its development.

We have now become acquainted with the meaning both of resignation—the renunciation of the gods during the time of the ancient Sun—and of the achievement of immortality. What were the further consequences of this?

From *An Outline of Occult Science* (although the description remains in a certain respect veiled in maya) we know that the Moon period of development followed the Sun period—that at the end of the Sun period, all existing conditions were immersed in a kind of twilight, a cosmic chaos, and that these then emerged again as Moon. We can see the emergence of sacrifice as warmth again. But what remains as warmth on the Sun emerges on the Moon as heat. What was previously the virtue of bestowing reappears as gas or air. Resignation, the renunciation of the sacrifice, also continues. What we called resignation is present in everything that occurs on the ancient Moon. This is really so: what we were able to experience as resignation on the Sun we must also think of as a force in all that exists on ancient Moon, having come over from the Sun, and as something different from what we think of as existing in the external world. What existed as sacrifice appears in maya as warmth; what was the virtue of bestowing appears as gas or air; what existed as resignation appears as liquid, as water. Outwardly, water is maya, and it would not exist in the world were it not for its spiritual foundation in renunciation or resignation. Wherever there is water in the world, there is divine renunciation!

Just as warmth is an illusion, and behind it exists sacrifice; just as gas or air is an illusion behind which stands the virtue of bestowing; so water as substance, as external reality, is only a material illusion, a reflection of what truly exists: the resignation by certain beings of what they could have received from other beings. One could say, it is only possible for water to flow in the world when resignation underlies the phenomenon. Now, we know that, during the transition from the Sun to the Moon, conditions of air densified into conditions of water. Water first came into being on the Moon; during the Sun period, there was no water. What we saw during the ancient Sun development in the gathering mass of clouds became water as it pressed together, and emerged as the Moon's ocean during the Moon period.

When we take this into account, it is possible to understand a question that can now be raised. Water arises out of resignation; in fact, water actually *is* resignation. Thus, we acquire a very unusual type of spiritual concept for what water really is. But we can also ask the question: Is there not a difference between the condition that would have arisen had the Cherubim not accomplished this resignation and the condition that arose when they deprived themselves of what was offered? Isn't this difference expressed in some way? Yes, it is expressed. It is expressed by the fact that the consequences of that resignation arose during the Moon conditions.

If this resignation had not occurred, if the renouncing Cherubim had accepted the sacrifice brought to them, they would have had—pictorially speaking—the sacrificial smoke within their own substance: acceptance of the sacrifice would have been expressed in the sacrificial smoke. Let us assume these Cherubim would have carried out this or that action. Then that action would appear, expressed outwardly, through self-transforming clouds of air. What the Cherubim would have done by accepting the sacrificial substance would have been expressed in the outward form of air. But they rejected the substance of sacrifice and thereby withdrew from mortality and entered immortality, withdrew from the transitory and entered the enduring. The substance of the sacrifice is still there, but is, so to speak, released from the forces that would otherwise have absorbed it. The sacrificial substance no longer needs to follow the inclinations and impulses of the Cherubim, for these Cherubim have released it, have turned it back.

What happens then with this substance of sacrifice? Other beings are able to become independent. These beings are found near the Cherubim and would have been under their direction if the latter had accepted the substance of sacrifice. But the substance is no longer within these Cherubim and is independent of them. Because of this, the possibility arises for the opposite of resignation to occur: other beings draw the poured-out substance of sacrifice to themselves and become active within it. These are the beings who remained behind, and so the presence of beings who stayed behind is a consequence of the Cherubim's act of renunciation. The Cherubim themselves produced the beings who stayed behind. Thus, they created the possibility of "remaining behind." Through the Cherubim's rejection of a sacrifice, other beings who do not renounce it, but surrender to their own wishes and desires, and bring them to expression, are able to take possession of the sacrifice and its substance, and to gain the possibility of becoming independent beings alongside the other beings.

Thus, with the transition from the development of the Sun to the Moon and with the Cherubim becoming immortal, the possibility arises for other beings to separate themselves in their own substance from the continuing development of the Cherubim, indeed, to separate themselves altogether from immortal beings. We also see, by discovering the deeper reason for remaining behind, that the responsibility—if we wish to speak about the ultimate factor of causation—for holding back these beings does not rest with the beings themselves. That is the most important point that we must grasp. If the Cherubim had accepted the sacrifice, the luciferic beings could not have remained behind, for they would not have had the opportunity to become embodied in this sacrificial substance. Renunciation was the prerequisite for beings to become independent in this way. Wise cosmic guidance orders things so that the gods themselves called their opponents into being. If the gods had not deprived themselves, it would have been impossible for beings to oppose them. Or, to express it simply, we could say that the gods were able to foresee that if they continued to create only as they had done since the transition from Saturn to the Sun, then free beings who acted out of their own initiative would never come into being. The gods recognized that in order for free beings to be created, the possibility had to be given for opponents to arise against them in the cosmic all so that they could meet resistance in whatever was subject to time. They knew that if they themselves were the only ones to order everything, they would never be able to find such opposition. We can imagine the gods acknowledging that they could make it very easy for themselves if they were to accept all of the sacrifice—for then all evolution would be subject to them. But they decided not to do that. They wanted beings who were free from them, who were capable of opposing them. Therefore the gods determined not to accept all of the sacrifice in order that beings, through the gods own resignation and the fact that the others themselves accept the sacrifice—might become their opponents!

We see, therefore, that we must not look for the origin of evil in so-called evil beings—but in so-called good beings, who by their renunciation first made it possible for evil to arise through beings capable of bringing evil into the world. Now, someone could very easily object—and I ask that you allow this thought to work very precisely within your soul—someone could object: "Until now I had a much better opinion of the gods! I used to think that the gods were capable of setting the stage for human freedom without necessarily creating evil. How is it that all of these good gods were not able to bring human freedom into the world without evil?" I would like to remind you of the Spanish king who found the world terribly complicated and commented that, if God had left the creation of the world to him, he would have made it much simpler. Human beings may think, in their weakness, that the world could have been made simpler, but the gods knew better, and, therefore, did not leave the creation of the world up to human beings.

From the point of view of spiritual science, we can characterize these conditions even more exactly. Let us assume that something needs a support, and someone suggests that the necessary support could be provided by erecting a column upon which the object could then be placed. The person to whom this suggestion was addressed could then say, "But there must be another way of doing this! Yes, why shouldn't it be done in another manner?" Or someone could say, when using a triangle during construction, "Why should this triangle have only three angles? Perhaps a god could have made a triangle that did not have three angles!" But it makes as much sense to say that a triangle should not have three angles as it does to say that the gods should have created freedom without the possibility of evil and suffering. Just as three corners belong to a triangle, so to freedom belongs the possibility of evil brought about through resignation on the part of spiritual beings. All that I have been speaking of belongs to the resignation of the gods. For, in order to guide evil back to the good, after they had risen to the level of immortality by renouncing the sacrifice, the gods created evolution out of immortality. They did so by means of this very resignation. The gods did not avoid evil, which alone could grant the possibility of freedom. If the gods had suppressed evil, the world would be poor and unvaried. The gods had to allow evil to come into the world for the sake of freedom, and therefore they also had to acquire the strength necessary to lead evil back to the good. And this capacity is something that can come only as a consequence of renunciation and resignation.

Religions always exist to portray the great cosmic mysteries in pictures and imaginations. We have referred to the ancient phases of development today, and by adding the concept of resignation to those of sacrifice and the virtue of bestowing, we have taken another step into true reality in contrast to maya and illusion. Religion gives us such pictures and concepts. Therefore in biblical religion, too, we can gain access to the concepts of sacrifice and the resignation or rejection of the sacrifice. For instance, there is the story of Abraham, who was going to present his own son as a sacrifice to God, and of God's forgoing the patriarch's sacrifice. If we take this concept of "forgoing" into our soul, then meditative images such as we have already formulated also come to us. Once I suggested that we assume the sacrifice of Abraham had been accepted and that Isaac was sacrificed. If God had accepted this sacrifice, the entire ancient Hebrew people, who stem from Isaac, would have been taken from the earth. By renouncing the sphere of the Hebrew people, withdrawing it from his circle of influence, so that it came to be outside him, God granted as a gift all who derive from Abraham. If God had accepted Abraham's sacrifice, God would have taken into himself the whole sphere where the ancient Hebrew people were active, for the sacrificed Isaac would have been together with God. God relinquished this course, however, and thereby allowed this entire line of evolution to transpire on earth. All concepts of resignation, of sacrifice, can be awakened in us through the deeply meaningful picture of sacrifice presented by the ancient patriarch.

We can find another instance of resignation or sacrifice by higher beings in earthly history, and here, too, we may refer to something that we already mentioned last time—namely, Leonardo da Vinci's painting, *The Last Supper*. Imagine that scene in which we have before us at the same time the essential meaning of both the Earth and the Christ. Let us penetrate the full meaning of the picture, and so let us recall the words we find in the Gospel: "Could I not summon a whole choir of angels, if I wanted to avoid the sacrifice of death?"[2]

2. Matt. 26:53.

With resignation and renunciation Christ refused this obvious and easy solution he could have invoked. The greatest example of renunciation that Christ Jesus brings before us occurred when he allowed his betrayer, Judas Iscariot, to enter his sphere. If we are to see in Christ Jesus what we should be able to see in him, we must see in him a reflection of those beings who had to renounce sacrifice and whose very nature is that of resignation. The Christ renounced what would have occurred if he had not allowed Judas to act as his opponent, just as the gods themselves during the time of the ancient Sun called forth their own opponents through their deed of renunciation. So we see this event—the coming forth of the opponents to cosmic powers—repeated pictorially on Earth. We see Christ in the midst of the twelve, together with Judas, who stood there as the betrayer. In order that what is of incomparable worth to humankind could enter the course of development, Christ himself had to place his opponent in opposition to himself.

This picture makes a profound impression upon us, because gazing at *The Last Supper* reminds us of a powerful, cosmic moment. Holding before us the words of Christ, "He who dipped his hand with me in the dish will betray me,"[3] we see the earthly reflection of the opponents of the gods set in opposition to the gods by the gods themselves. I often say that everything that inhabitants of Mars would see, were they to descend to Earth, would be more or less interesting, even if they were not able to understand it fully. But by looking at this picture by Leonardo da Vinci, such Martians would discover something from a cosmic perspective that would be relevant not only to the Earth but to Mars as well and, indeed, to the entire solar system. And thereby the significance of the Earth would be recognized. What is portrayed in *The Last Supper* in an earthly picture has meaning for the whole cosmos: the setting into opposition of certain powers over against the immortal, divine powers. And Christ, who overcame death and demonstrated the triumph of immortality on Earth—and appears in the midst of his apostles—

---

3. John 13:26; Matt. 26:33.

gives evidence of a significant, cosmic moment that arose as the gods differentiated themselves from time-bound beings and achieved a victory over time, that is, became immortal. All this may be felt in our hearts when we look at *The Last Supper* by Leonardo da Vinci.

Please do not say that one who views *The Last Supper* with simple, naive sensitivity does not understand what we have said today. Such a person does not need to know these things. For the mysterious depth of the human soul is such that one does not need to know intellectually what is felt in the human soul. Does the flower know the laws by which it grows? No, but it grows in spite of that. What need has a flower for natural law? What need then has a human soul for reason—for intellect— if we are to feel the incomparable magnitude of what is there before us, when spread out before our eyes we see a god and that god's opponent, when the loftiest that is capable of being expressed, the distinction between immortality and mortality, is brought before us? One does not need to know that, intellectually. Rather, when a human being stands before this picture that mirrors the very meaning of the world, the experience penetrates the soul with magical force. Nor did the painter need to be an occultist in order to paint it. Nevertheless, powers existed in Leonardo's soul that could bring to expression precisely this highest, most significant meaning. That is why the greatest works of art have such a powerful effect; they are deeply linked with the meaning of the cosmic order. In earlier times, artists were connected to the significance of the cosmic order in dim consciousness without knowing it. But art would perish, it would not be able to continue, were it not that, in the future, spiritual science as a new form of knowledge will bring a new foundation to the arts.

Unconscious art has become a thing of the past. Art that allows itself to be inspired by spiritual science stands at the beginning of its development. Although artists in the past did not need to know what stood at the basis of their art works, artists in the future will have to know, but they will have to know by means of powers that can once again portray immortality—powers that can present something out of the full content of the soul. For whoever tries to make spiritual science an intellectual science expressed in schemes and paradigms does not understand it. But whoever with all the concepts we have developed here—such as sacrifice, bestowing virtue and renunciation—experiences with every word what seeks to spring forth from the word, the idea, itself—experiencing what flows out of the many-sided nature of the pictures—that individual understands spiritual science.

One can present schemes if one believes that the development of the world fulfills itself in abstract concepts. But, if one wishes to present such living concepts as sacrifice, bestowing virtue and resignation, schemes no longer suffice. These three words can be presented schematically—if only one does not think much beyond a few letters. But if we wish to consider these concepts—sacrifice, the virtue of bestowing, and renunciation—then we must paint pictures for ourselves such as those we described the last time: the sacrificing Thrones, who sent their sacrifice up to the Cherubim, who spread out the smoke of sacrifice, who received the light back from the Archangels, and so forth.

And when, in the next lecture, we move forward to consider the Moon existence, we shall see how the picture becomes richer. We shall see how the liquefying of the gathering cloud masses— which ripple as Moon mass—and the enchanting lightning of the Seraphim have to be added to it. Then we shall have to try to reach a fuller understanding. About this, let me say: In the future, humankind will find how to create the possibility, the artistic material, the artistic means, to bring to expression in and for the outer world what otherwise may be read in the Akashic Chronicle.

4. The Inner Aspect of the Moon Embodiment of the Earth

BERLIN, NOVEMBER 21, 1911[1]

WE HAVE PURSUED A DIFFICULT ASPECT of our world-view to the point where, to some extent, we have learned to see the spiritual reality that lies behind appearances in the outer, sensible world. Outwardly, however, appearances only very slightly betray the real fact that the characteristic form of the spiritual—as we experience it in our soul life—actually stands behind what we see in the sensible world. Yet we have come to recognize that spiritual activity, spiritual qualities and characteristics do indeed stand behind such appearances. For example, we now recognize that what appears to us in ordinary life as the quality of warmth, heat, or fire, is the spiritual expression of sacrifice. And in what we encounter as air—which, in our concepts, reveals so little that it is spiritual—we recognize what we call the bestowing virtue of particular cosmic beings. In water, we recognize what can be called resignation, renunciation.

In earlier world-views—I mention this briefly—the existence of the spiritual within the outwardly material was, of course, more quickly intuited and recognized. Evidence of this may be seen in our habitual use today of the word *spirit*—which today we use in a particular way concerning what is spiritual—to refer to especially vol-

1. This lecture, as will become evident, was given on the hundredth anniversary of the death by his own hand of the great German dramatist, poet, and prose writer—the "genius's genius"—Heinrich von Kleist (1777–1811). See Joachim Maas, *Kleist, A Biography* (New York: Farrar, Strauss, and Giroux, 1983) and Philip B. Miller, ed. and trans., *An Abyss Deep Enough, Letters of Heinrich von Kleist, with a Selection of Essays and Anecdotes* (New York: Dutton, 1982).

atile substances. I say "spiritual" rather than "spirit." In the outer world, however, people do not necessarily apply the term *spiritual* to true spiritual reality or what is beyond the senses. As some of you know, a letter was once addressed to a Munich society of spiritualists and no one knew what a society of spiritualists was, so it was delivered to the main office of the merchants of "spirits," that is, alcoholic beverages.

To return to our theme: today we will look at the significant transition that occurred in the development of the planet Earth as evolution progressed from ancient Sun to ancient Moon. Thus, we will have to consider another kind of spiritual development.

We must begin with the point we took up in the last lecture—the act of renunciation. We saw last time that, in this renunciation or "forgoing," spiritual beings give up the opportunity to receive a sacrifice—a sacrifice that we recognized as the sacrifice of will or the will substance. When we imagine that certain beings wished to sacrifice their will substance and that higher beings declined to accept this will by their act of forgoing, then we will easily rise to the concept that this will substance—which these beings wished to sacrifice to higher spiritual beings—had to remain with the beings who wished to sacrifice it but were not allowed to do so. Thus, within the context of the cosmos, there are beings who were ready to present their sacrifice, that is, were prepared devoutly to surrender what reposes in their innermost being, but were not permitted to do so and therefore had to keep it within themselves. Or, to put it another way: because the sacrifice was rejected, these beings could not establish a certain bond with higher beings that would have come about had they been allowed to sacrifice.

Cain's confrontation with Abel in the Bible personifies and historically symbolizes some of the meaning of this "rejected sacrifice," albeit in an intensified way. [2] Cain also wanted to offer his sacrifice to his God. But his sacrifice was not found pleasing, and God would

---

2. For other aspects of the deep significance of the story of Cain and Abel, see Rudolf Steiner, *The Temple Legend* (London: Rudolf Steiner Press, 1985) and *The Effects of Spiritual Development on the Human Sheaths* (London: Rudolf Steiner Press, 1978).

not accept it. Abel's sacrifice, on the other hand, was accepted by God. What we want to pay attention to here is Cain's inner experience when he discovered that his sacrifice was rejected. To reach the greatest possible degree of understanding in this matter, we must be clear that we should not introduce into the higher regions, of which we are speaking of here, ideas that have meaning only in ordinary life. It would be false to say that the rejection of the sacrifice came about through fault or wrongdoing. In these regions we cannot yet refer to sin and atonement as we are familiar with them in ordinary life. Rather, we have to view these beings from the perspective of the higher beings who refused the sacrifice. In other words, the higher beings were simply relinquishing or withdrawing their acceptance of the sacrifice. There is nothing that indicates any fault or failure in the mood of soul that we characterized last week. Rather, the act of surrender and resignation encompasses all that is great and meaningful. Yet, we can sense that, within those beings who wanted to offer the sacrifice, there did arise a mood that initiated something like opposition—even if it was extremely faint opposition—toward those beings who refused their sacrifice. Therefore, when this mood of opposition presents itself to us at a later time, as in the case of Cain, it is presented in a magnified manner. We will not find the same mood that we find in Cain also in those beings who developed during the transition from the Sun to the Moon. Among these beings, the mood of opposition occurs in a different degree. Again, we can come to know this mood in an authentic way only if we look into our own soul, as we did during the last lecture, and ask ourselves, where we can find such a mood in our own soul, and what soul conditions can make us aware of the mood that must have developed in the individuals whose gift of sacrifice had been rejected.

This mood in us—and here we come closer and closer to earthly human life—is actually familiar to every soul in its uncertainty, and at the same time in its torment or pain, in a way that I will address more fully in next Thursday's public lecture: "The Hidden Depths of Soul Life."[3] This mood or attitude, familiar to every soul, reigns in the secret depths of soul life and presses toward its surface where the mood—perhaps—creates the least torment. But we human beings often go around in this mood. Without being aware of it in our higher consciousness, we carry it within us. We may recall the words of the poet: "Only one who knows longing knows what I suffer."[4] These words capture the vague yet persistent torment of the soul that also carries a nuance of pain with it. What is meant here is longing as a mood of soul. This is longing as it lives continuously in the human soul—as a soul mood—and not just when the soul aspires to or strives for this or that.

In order to transport ourselves into what occurred spiritually in the evolutionary phases of ancient Saturn and the Sun, we had to raise our gaze to special conditions of the soul that start to appear when the human soul begins to strive and orient itself toward a higher striving. In the second lecture we tried to clarify the nature of surrender or sacrifice by drawing it out of our own soul life. We saw what a human being can achieve of the wisdom that we see trickling into and created out of what one could call: the "willingness to give" or the "readiness to surrender one's own self." The closer we approach the earthly circumstances that have developed out of earlier conditions, the more we encounter a mood of soul that is similar to what human beings today can still experience. But we must be clear that our whole soul life, insofar as our soul is inserted into an earthly body, lies like a top layer over a hidden soul life that flows in depths beneath its surface. Who could fail to know that there is a hidden life of soul? Life teaches us well enough that such a soul life exists.

In order to clarify something about this hidden life of the soul, let us assume that a child—let us say in the seventh or eighth year or at another time of life—experiences this or that. For example, having been blamed for doing something which, in fact, he or she did not

---

3. Lecture of November 23, 1911. In *Menschengeschichte im Lichte des Geistesforschung* (GA 61), untranslated.
4. Line from Mignon's song in Goethe's *Wilhelm Meister*.

do, a child may have experienced an injustice—children are often especially sensitive to this. Nevertheless, it was convenient for those around the child to settle the matter by blaming the child for doing this or that. Children, indeed, are acutely sensitive to suffering an injustice in this way. But life is such that, after this experience has eaten deeply into this young life, the following years added other layers to the soul's existence, and the child, at least in terms of everyday life, forgot the matter. Perhaps such a matter never again arises. But let us assume that at the age of fifteen or sixteen the young person, let us say at school, experiences a new injustice. And now, what otherwise lay at rest deep within the surging soul, begins to stir. The young person in question doesn't even need to know that a recollection of what he or she experienced in earlier years is at work, and may actually form completely different ideas and concepts. If what had occurred earlier had not taken place, however, then—for example, if it were a young man—he would simply go home, shed a few tears, and perhaps also complain a bit, but he would get over it. But since the earlier event did occur—here I emphasize very pointedly that the young person does not need to know what is happening—the earlier event works beneath the surface of the life of soul, just as beneath the smooth appearance of the ocean's surface waves may be surging. And what otherwise would have resulted only in tears, complaints, and insults, now becomes a student's suicide! Thus, from the deepest levels, the hidden depths of the soul life rise to the surface to play their role. And the most important force that rules in these depths— becoming most significant as it presses upward in its original form— and about which we nevertheless remain unconscious—is longing. We know the names that this force has in the outer world, but these are only vague, metaphoric names, because they express relationships that are complex and do not at all rise into consciousness.

Let us take a familiar phenomenon—those who live in the city may be less affected by it but even they nonetheless will have observed it in others—I mean, the feeling one describes as "homesickness." If you were to explore what homesickness really is, you would see that basically homesickness is something different for every human being.

For one person it is this, for another person, something else. One person longs for the familiar tales he or she listened to at home, never realizing that he or she is really yearning for home—what lives within the individual is an unfocused longing, an undirected wishing. Another longs for his or her mountain, or—when watching rippling water—for the river where he or she often used to play. All these different qualities that are often unconsciously at work in the soul may be included in the term "homesickness" which expresses something that can be played out in thousands of different ways and yet is best described as a kind of longing. Even more indefinite are the yearnings that arise as perhaps the most tormenting ones in life. The human being is not aware longing is involved, but nevertheless that is what it is. But what is this longing? By bringing it into connection with the mood of the beings who wished to offer sacrifice but had to renounce their sacrifice, we have suggested that it is a kind of will and wherever we examine this longing, we can see that it is a type of will. But what kind of will is it? It is a will or intent that cannot be fulfilled, for, if it could be satisfied, the longing would cease. It is a will that cannot be realized—that is how we must define longing.

Thus, we would have to characterize the mood of those beings whose sacrifice was rejected somewhat as follows. What we can perceive in the depths of our soul life as longing is what remains in us as an inheritance from those ancient times we are now speaking of. Just as we receive other qualities as legacies from other ancient stages of development, so we receive from the Moon phase of evolution all forms of longing to be found in the depths of the soul, all forms of will that cannot be fulfilled, of will that is held in check. By turning back the sacrifice offered during this phase of development, beings with restrained, held-back wills were created. Because they had to restrain and keep this will within themselves, they were in a very special situation. And here, again, if one wishes to feel and experience these matters, one must transpose them into one's own condition of soul—for mere thoughts will scarcely suffice to penetrate these conditions.

A being who can sacrifice the will becomes, in a certain sense, united with the other being in relation to whom the sacrifice occurs. That, too, we can feel in human life—how we live and weave ourselves into a being to whom we bring a sacrifice; how fulfilled and happy we feel in the presence of that being. Here we are speaking of sacrifice to higher beings—encompassing, universal beings—to whom the sacrificing beings glance upward in utter delight. And for this reason, what is held back by the beings as restrained will, as longing, can never be the same as it would have been in inner mood—in inner soul content—as it would have been had they been allowed to complete their sacrifice. For if the sacrificing beings had been permitted to make their sacrifice, it would have become part of the other beings. We may say then, by way of comparison, that, if the Earth and the other planetary beings had been allowed to sacrifice to the Sun, then they would have been united with the Sun. But, if they were not permitted to sacrifice to the Sun and had to withhold what they would have sacrificed, then they would remain separate and draw their sacrifice back into themselves.

If we grasp what is now expressed in a single word, then we notice that something new has entered into the cosmic all. Understand clearly that it cannot be expressed in any other way: beings who would sacrifice to another all that lives within them, who would surrender themselves to a universal being—such beings, when the sacrifice is not accepted, are instructed to carry the sacrifice within themselves. Don't you feel that something flashes up here that we may call "ego" or "egoity," which later emerges as *egoism* in all of its forms? In this way we can feel that what flowed into evolution continued to live on as a legacy within those beings. Within longing we see egoism flashing like lightning, albeit in its weakest form; and we also see longing slipping into cosmic development. And thus we see how beings who surrender to longing, that is, surrender themselves to their egoism, are—if something else does not intervene—condemned in a certain way to one-sidedness, to living merely in themselves.

Let us imagine a being who has been permitted to sacrifice. This being lives in the other being—and forever lives in the other. A being who has not been permitted to sacrifice can live only within its own being. Thus such a being is excluded from all that he or she would have experienced in the other being—in this instance, in higher beings. In this case, in fact, the beings in question would have been taken out of the course of evolution, condemned. and banished to one-sidedness—had something not occurred that sought to enter the course of development to eliminate the one-sidedness. This "something" is the entry of new beings who prevent the condemnation and exile into one-sidedness. Just as in the instance of the Beings of Will on Saturn and the Beings of Wisdom on the Sun, so on the Moon we see the Spirits of Movement step forth. By this we are not imagining movement in space. Rather, by the term "movement" we refer to something that is more related to the process of thinking. Everyone knows the expression "movement of thought," although this refers just to the flow and the fluidity of one's own thinking. But even from this expression we can see that if we wish to gain a comprehensive grasp of movement, we must understand that movement is something other than merely changing position in space—that is just one aspect of movement. If a number of human beings are devoted to a higher being who expresses all that is in them because the higher being accepted all that was offered in sacrifice, then these human beings live and are fulfilled in that one being. If their sacrifices are rejected, however, these human beings must live within themselves and can never be fulfilled. Thus the Spirits of Movement enter and lead the beings who would otherwise have had to depend upon themselves into relationship with all of the other beings. The Spirits of Movement must not be thought of as beings who just bring about changes in location. Rather, they are beings who bring forth something whereby one being continuously comes into new relation to others.

We can form an idea of what is attained at this stage of the cosmos if we again reflect on the corresponding mood of soul. Who does not know what torment it is when longing comes to a halt, a standstill, and cannot experience change of any kind. It forces a person into the unbearable state we call boredom. But this boredom, which we usually attribute only to superficial people, has all manner of levels. This boredom even has levels that affect great and noble natures, in whom there lives what their own nature expresses as a longing that cannot be satisfied in the outer world. And what better way is there to satisfy this longing than through change? The evidence for this is that beings who feel this longing search continuously for relations with new beings. The anguish of the longing is often overcome through what is brought about by changed relations with constantly new sets of beings.

Thus, we see that while the Earth went through its Moon phase, the Spirits of Movement brought change, movement, and ever-renewing connections to new beings and situations into the lives of the yearning-filled beings who otherwise would have become desolate, for boredom is a kind of desolation. Movement in space from one place to another is only one aspect of this broad spectrum of movement of which we are speaking. We experience another kind of movement when, in the morning, we have a specific thought content in our soul that we do not have to keep to ourselves but can give to someone else. In this way, we overcome one-sidedness in our longing through variety, change, and movement in what we experience. What we have in external space is just a special kind of capacity for change.

Consider a planet facing the Sun. If the planet were always in the same position in relationship to the Sun, if it never moved, it would remain fixed in its one-sidedness. The planet would always turn just one side to the Sun. But then, to bring about a change in its position, the Spirits of Movement come and lead the planet around the Sun. A change in location is just one kind of change. And when the Spirits of Movement bring about change of location in the cosmos, they bring about a specific instance of the general phenomenon of movement.

Because the Spirits of Movement have introduced movement and change into the cosmos, something else has to come with it. We have seen in evolution—that is, in the whole cosmic multiplicity evolving in the form of the Spirits of Movement, Spirits of Personality, Spirits of Wisdom, Spirits of Will, and so forth—that substantiality is also present in the form of the bestowing virtue that streams toward radiating wisdom to form the spiritual basis of air and gas.

This now flows together with the will that has been transformed into longing and, in these beings, becomes what human beings know—not yet as thought, but as *picture*. We can visualize this best with the image we have when dreaming. The fleeting, fluid dream picture can call forth an image of what occurs in a being in whom will lives as longing and who is led into relation with other beings by the Spirits of Movement. As a being is brought before another, the first being cannot entirely surrender itself to the other, for its own egoity lives within it. But the being in question can receive a fleeting picture of the other being—a picture that lives like a dream picture within it. In this way, what we may call the rising tide of images in the soul arises. In other words, picture consciousness came into being during this phase of development. And since we human beings ourselves went through this phase of development without our current earthly I-consciousness, we must imagine ourselves without what we attain today through our I. In that period, we existed and wove within the cosmic all, while something lived within us that we can compare with our experience of longing.

In a certain way—if one forgot the conditions of suffering manifest on earth—one could imagine that suffering could not be other than the poet describes: "Only one who knows longing knows what I suffer." It was during the Moon phase that suffering and pain as manifestations of the soul came into our nature and into the nature of other beings who are bound up with our evolution. Thereafter the otherwise empty inner self—the inner self that suffers from longing—was filled with a healing balm in the form of picture consciousness poured into these natures through the activity of the Spirits of Movement. If this had not happened these Moon beings—Moon natures—would have been empty in their soul, empty of everything other than longing. But the balm of the pictures trickles in, fills the solitude and emptiness with manifoldness, and thus leads beings out of the state of exile and condemnation.

When we take such words seriously, we have both what lies spiritually at the foundation of what developed during the Moon phase of our Earth, and what now lies layered beneath the Earth phase in the deep recesses of our consciousness. But this lies so deep within the recesses of our soul—and I shall show this the day after tomorrow in a popular form in a public lecture[5]—that it can become active in these recesses without our being aware of it and then emerge into consciousness, just as surging waters in the ocean depths create waves on its surface. Beneath the surface of our ordinary I-consciousness we have a deep-seated soul life that can surge to the surface. And what does this soul life say when it comes to the surface? Once we understand the cosmic foundation of this unconscious life of the soul, we could say that our soul life, which we can feel rising out of the recesses of the soul, is a breaking-through of what was set in motion during the Moon phase of development, but first penetrated us during the Earth phase itself. And when we grasp the interplay of the Moon nature with our Earth nature, then we have the real explanation of what was brought over spiritually to Earth existence from the ancient Moon.

Keep in mind, as I have just described, that it was necessary for pictures to surface continuously in order to alleviate the desolation. If you do so, then a concept of great import and significance will come to you: namely, that the longing human soul in its yearning, tormented emptiness, satisfies and keeps this longing in harmony through the constant succession of pictures arising one after the other. And, after the images arise and remain a while, then the old longing dawns again in the recesses of the soul, and the Spirits of Movement call up new pictures. Then fresh images are present again for a while, until the longing for new pictures is once again renewed. The important statement we must make about this aspect of the life of the soul is that, if the longing is satisfied only through images that in turn constantly seek out new images, then there is no end to this infinite flow. The only way to intervene in this process is if something enters the unending flow of images that can redeem the longing with something other than pictures, that is, with realities. In other words, the phase of the planetary embodiment of our Earth in

---

5. See note 3.

which images guided by the activity of the Spirits of Movement satisfy the longing must be replaced by the planetary phase of the Earth embodiment that we must call the phase of *redemption*. Indeed, as we shall see, the Earth may be called the "Planet of Redemption," just as the earlier embodiment of the Earth, Moon existence, may be called the "Planet of Longing," a longing that could be appeased, but only through a never-ending process stretching to infinity. Throughout this life, while we live in earthly consciousness—which, as we have seen, brings before us the act of redemption through the Mystery of Golgotha—there arises out of the recesses of our soul that which continuously creates a longing for redemption. It is as if we had waves of ordinary consciousness at the surface of consciousness; and, beneath this, in the depths of the ocean of our soul life, the bedrock of our soul lived in the form of a longing; and this longing aspired ceaselessly to carry out the sacrifice to the universal being who can satisfy it—not just appease it with an infinite sequence of pictures, but fulfill it once and for all.

As earthly human beings, we can actually feel these moods. They are the best a person can experience. Indeed, those earthly human beings who today—in our time, above all—feel this longing are those who are coming toward our spiritual-scientific movement. In external life we learn to recognize everything that satisfies our ordinary, surface consciousness. Out of our unconsciousness, however, there pulses something that can never be satisfied by external particulars and longs for the central foundation of life. But we can attain this central basis only once we have a universal science that concerns itself with the totality of life, not just with particulars. What arises in the depths of the soul today—seeking to be brought into higher consciousness—must be brought into contact with universal existence that lives in the world. If this contact is not made then the longing for something unachievable arises out of the recesses of the soul.

Spiritual science, in this sense, is a response to the longings that live in the recesses of the soul. And, since everything that occurs in the world has its prelude in an earlier time, we should not be surprised that a person living today would want to subdue the power of the longing in his or her soul through spiritual science—especially when such soul forces lie beyond conscious awareness and threaten to consume a person, as these longings do. Had such a person lived earlier, when this spiritual wisdom did not exist and so was unobtainable, he or she would have wasted away with ever-present longing for spiritual wisdom and been denied the possibility of grasping the meaning of life—precisely because he or she was a "great spirit." Today, on the other hand, something can trickle into the soul that would ease the longing for images and drown out and silence the desolation. Earlier, a person could only long for a cessation of this march of images, and long for it all the more as the throng of images became increasingly persistent!

When we hear Heinrich von Kleist writing to a friend in the following way we can hear this expressed in the voice of someone who lived in an era when one could not yet attain this spiritual wisdom that pours itself out like balm into the longing of the soul:

Who desires to be happy on this Earth? I would almost like to say, shame on you, if you want to be happy! What shortsightedness it is, O noble human being, to strive for such a goal here, where all ends in death. We meet, we love each other for three springs, and then, for an eternity, flee from each other. And yet what is the striving worth, when there is no love! Ah, there has to be something more than love, happiness, fame and x, y, z; something our souls do not even dream about.

It cannot be an evil spirit who stands at the pinnacle of the world. It is just something incomprehensible. Don't we, too, smile when children cry? Just think of this unending vastness! Myriad realms of time, each one a life, and each one a manifested existence such as this world of ours! What is the name of the little star we see when the heavens are clear and we gaze at Sirius? And this gigantic firmament is only a speck of dust in relation to infinity! O moment of stillness, tell me, is this a dream? Between two linden leaves, which we watch as we lie on our backs in the evening, lies a perspective, richer in intuitions

than our thoughts can grasp and words can express. Come, let
us do something good and die doing so! One of the millions of
deaths we have already died and must yet die in the future. It is
as if we go from one room into another. Look, the world appears to me as if it were all boxed up together, the small is just
like the great! [6]

The longing expressed in these words drove this individuality to
write to his friend in this way. But this spirit—Kleist—could not yet
find a satisfaction for his longing in the way that modern souls can
today when they approach spiritual science with energetic understanding. For this spirit is one who ended his life one hundred years
ago when he shot, first his friend, Henriette Vogel, and then himself, and who now rests on the banks of the Wannsee, in the lonely
grave that first enclosed his remains a century ago.[7]

It is a remarkable act of Providence—one would like to say, of
karma—that we can speak here of what Kleist expresses, which best
describes what we tried to say about the transformation of the
withheld sacrifice of will into longing—the easing of which can
occur through the Spirits of Movement and the impulse toward
final satisfaction of longing, which may be attained on the "Planet
of Redemption." It is a remarkable karmic resolution that, precisely
on this day, we speak about what reminds us of a soul who brought

---

6. Letter of August 31, 1806.
7. Heinrich von Kleist (1777–1811). The citation is taken from a letter dated August
31, 1806. See Erich Schmidt, ed., *Kleists Saemtliche Werke* (Leipzig and Vienna,
1905), vol. 5, p. 326ff, *Penthesilea* (Tuebingen, 1808); *Das Kaethchen von Heilbronn
oder Feuerprobe* (Berlin, 1810); *Prinz Friedrich von Homburg* (Berlin, 1821).
   On November 21, at 4 P.M. in the Stimmings Inn in Potsdam Kleist shot Henriette Vogel and then shot himself. On the morning of his death he wrote to his
friend and cousin (by marriage), Marie von Kleist: "My dear Marie, if you knew
how death and love took turns crowning these last moments of my life with blos-
soms, those of heaven, and those of earth, surely you would be willing to let me die.
I assure you, I am wholly joyous. Mornings and evenings I kneel down, something
I could never do before, and I pray to God. For this my life, the most tormented of
any that anyone has ever lived, I can now at last thank Him, since he makes it good
through the most glorious and sensual of deaths."

this unfocused longing to expression in the most elevated language, and then poured this yearning into the most tragic deed in which the longing can be embodied. How can we fail to recognize that this man's spirit in its totality, as he stands before us, is actually a living embodiment of what lives deep within the soul and leads us back to an existence other than an earthly existence—if only we want to recognize it? Does not Kleist describe for us in the most meaningful way what a person can experience of what impels human beings to seek what lies beyond them— which, later, he would have comprehended if he had not prematurely severed the thread of his own life? Did he not experience just what you may find described in the first pages of *The Spiritual Guidance of the Individual and Humanity?*[8]

Think of von Kleist's *Penthesilea.*[9] How much more there is in Penthesilea than she can fathom with her own earthly consciousness![10] We could not understand her in her particularity at all if we could not presume that her soul is infinitely more expansive than the narrow little soul that she—a great soul—encompasses with her earthly consciousness. Therefore, in the play, a situation must arise that artistically draws the unconscious into the drama. Thus, the possibility that the series of events—as Kleist sets them before Achilles— would be surveyed with higher consciousness must be prevented. Otherwise, we would not be able to experience the magnitude of the tragedy. Penthesilea is led captive to Achilles, but she is deluded into

---

8. Steiner, *The Spiritual Guidance of the Individual and Humanity*.
9. Kleist wrote his ferocious tragedy *Penthesilea*, based on the late Greek legend of the bloody battle between Achilles and Penthesilea, the Queen of the Amazons, in 1806, offering it to Goethe "on the knees of my heart." Kleist called it his most personal work: "My innermost nature is contained in it."
10. Cf. Joachim Maass, *Kleist, A Biography*, p. 142: "Kleist, a psychological visionary of the first rank, possessed a knowledge which his contemporaries had no suspicion of and which, when it was brought to their attention in *Penthesilea*, they did not understand. He had insights which today are the concern of depth psychology and which have been expressed most uncannily by Rilke in his *Duino Elegies*. In a very strange way, Kleist had followed Rousseau "back to nature" and with clairvoyant eye looked into the darkness of the human soul. But people of his time did not understand him."

believing that Achilles is her prisoner. That is why reference is made to "her" Achilles. What lives in the aware consciousness must be plunged into nonconsciousness.

And what role does this lower consciousness play in a situation like the one portrayed in *Katie of Heilbronn*,[11] especially with respect to the remarkable relationship between Katie and Wetter of Strahl, which is not carried out in full consciousness but in the deeper levels of the soul where powers reside that move from one person to another unbeknown to human beings. With this situation before us, we feel the spiritual nature of what lies within the ordinary forces of gravitation and attraction in the world. We feel what lies within the forces of the world. For example, in the scene where Katie stands facing her beloved, we see what lives beneath consciousness and how it is related to what lives externally in the world and to what one refers to dryly as the attracting powers of the planets. A century ago not even a penetrating, striving soul could plunge into this deeper level of consciousness. Today, it is possible to do so.

The tragedy of the *Prince of Homburg* also strikes us in a completely different way today than it did a century ago.[12] I would like to know how an abstract thinker who wishes to attribute everything a human being accomplishes to reason would explain a figure like the Prince of Homburg, who carried out all of his great deeds in a kind of dream state, even those deeds that finally led to victory. Indeed, Kleist clearly shows that the Prince could not have achieved his victory out of his aware consciousness and that, with regard to higher consciousness, he was not a particularly distinguished person—for afterward he whimpered in the face of death. Only when what lived deep within his soul was drawn out by an extraordinary effort of will—only

---

11. "No sooner had *Penthesilea* seen the light of day than a counterfigure in , *Kätie von Heilbruonn [or The Ordeal by Fire: A Great Historical Chivalry Play]*, made her appearance" (ibid., 134).

12. Kleist's last and greater play, written 1810, "a work that Nietzsche described as approaching closest among the moderns to that 'almost mystical idea,' a rebirth of tragedy" (Miller, *An Abyss Deep Enough*).

then—was the Prince able to pull himself together.

What remains as a legacy for the human being out of the Moon consciousness is something that cannot be brought out by abstract science. It is something that must be derived from concepts that are many-sided, subtle, and capable of grasping spiritual matters with soft contours—that is, concepts such as are brought by spiritual science. The greatest concepts connect themselves to the intermediary and the ordinary ones.

Thus we see that spiritual science shows how conditions we experience in our soul today are connected to the cosmos and cosmic totality. We also understand how only what we experience in the soul can generate a concept of the spiritual foundation of things. Furthermore, we begin to comprehend that in our age it becomes possible to satisfy what the age preceding our own longed for, but which could only be given in our time. Thus, a kind of admiration arises for those human beings in a previous age who could not find their way to what their hearts longed for—the world could not give it to them. Truly, when we remind ourselves that all human life is a whole and that a person today can devote his or her life to spiritual movements that human beings long ago already had need of—as indeed their destinies show us—then a certain admiration for such individuals can arise.

And so we may point to spiritual science as a bearer of the redemption of human longing. Above all we may do so on a day that, since it is the centenary of the tragic death of one of these yearning individuals, is well suited to remind us that spiritual science now provides what tempestuous but also woeful human beings have sought for a long time. This is the thought—perhaps also the anthroposophical thought—that we can lay hold of on this hundredth anniversary of the death of one of the greatest German poets.

5. The Inner Aspect of the Earth Embodiment of the Earth

BERLIN, DECEMBER 5, 1911

SO FAR IN THESE LECTURES we have placed before our souls a series of observations showing that the spiritual stands behind everything that we call maya, or the great illusion. Today, let us ask ourselves once more: How do we come to know that behind all that surrounds us—from the perspective of our senses and our understanding of the cosmos as it is conveyed through our physical bodies—the spiritual is discernible?

We were able to characterize the spiritual in the course of our previous explorations because we insisted on putting aside the immediate, outward appearances of the world and penetrating the qualities of true reality, which we identified as the willingness to sacrifice, the virtue of bestowing, and resignation or renunciation—qualities we could come to know only if we looked into our own souls—qualities, in fact, that we could comprehend and receive *only* in the context of our own souls. In other words, if we want to understand those qualities that we presume embody what is real and true behind the world of illusion—and if we wish to understand them in their true nature—we must say: This world of true being or existence, this world of reality contains real, live qualities or characteristics that we may compare only with qualities we can perceive within our own soul. If, for example, we wish to characterize what expresses itself outwardly in the appearance of warmth—characterizing it in relationship to its true nature as sacrificial service, as sacrifice streaming into the world—we must lead the element of warmth back to the spiritual, at the same time eliminating the external veil of existence, thereby demonstrating that this quality in the outer world is recognizable as the same as our own spiritual nature.

Before continuing our observations we must consider another idea. Does everything that we find in the world of maya really disappear into a kind of nothingness? Is there really nothing in the world of sense perception and outward understanding that corresponds, as it were, to what is true or real?

The following would be a good comparison. We may say that, just as the inner powers of a stream—or, indeed, of the ocean itself—lie concealed within the watery mass, the world of truth or reality lies initially hidden. Therefore we may say that the world of maya may be compared with the rippling play of waves on the water's surface. The comparison is good because it shows us that something does indeed flow upward out of the depths of the ocean, causing the rippling waves on the surface. It shows us, too, that this something is the substantiality of the water and a certain configuration of its forces. But whether we use this or that comparison is unimportant. We still must pose the question: Is there something in the broad realm of maya that "really" exists?

Today, I want to proceed as we did in the previous lectures. We will gradually approach what we wish to place before our soul, taking soul experiences as our starting point. Having progressed spiritually through the Saturn, Sun, and Moon existences, we have now reached the Earth existence. Thus we shall begin with even more familiar—one could even say, more common—experiences of the soul than we did last time. Last time, we worked out of the hidden depths of soul life, out of what arises in what spiritual science calls our astral body. There, we felt longing stirring, and we saw how longing worked within a being—in this case, the human being. We saw, too, how such longing in soul life could be alleviated only in a world of pictures. We came to understand the world of pictures as the inner movement in soul life. And thereby we found our way from the microcosm of the individual soul to the macrocosm of world creation, which we attributed to the Spirits of Movement.

Today, then, I want to take as our starting point a familiar soul experience that was already known and alluded to ancient Greece, and is today still very meaningful in its truthfulness. This experience is hinted at in the words: All philosophy, that is, all striving toward a certain human knowledge, arises out of wonder.[1] This formulation is, in fact, correct. Whoever reflects a little and pays attention to the process one experiences in one's soul as one approaches some kind of learning will already have discovered that a healthy path to knowledge always has its origin in wonder or in wondering about something. Amazement and wonder—out of which all learning processes arise—belong precisely among those soul experiences that elevate and bring life to all that is dull, empty, and dry. For what sort of knowledge would it be that took a place in our soul, yet did not arise from wonder? It would certainly be a kind of knowledge that was immersed in emptiness and pedantry. Only that soul process leading from wonder to the bliss we experience in solving a riddle—thus raising itself beyond wonder—only that soul process beginning in wonder ennobles and gives inner liveliness to learning. You should actually try to feel the dryness of knowledge that is not saturated with these inner feelings. The context of true, healthy knowledge is the wonder and delight that solving a riddle engenders. Other kinds of knowledge can be acquired from outside and can be applied on some basis or other. Nevertheless, in all seriousness, any knowledge that is not embraced by these two feelings does not really spring from the human soul. All the "aroma" of knowledge that the atmosphere of the living element in knowledge creates arises out of these two things—wonder, and delight over gratified wonder.

But what kind of origin does wonder itself have? Why does wonder, that is, amazement about something external, arise in the soul? Wonder and astonishment arise because we stand before some being or thing or fact and feel strangely delighted by it. This strangeness is the first element that leads to wonder and surprise. But we do not feel wonder or amazement about everything that is strange to us. We

---

1. See Plato, *Theaetetus*, 155c and Aristotle, *Metaphysics*, 982b.

experience wonder toward something strange only if, at the same time, we also feel related to it. We could describe this feeling as follows: There is something in this thing or being that is not yet a part of me, but which could become a part of me. When we perceive something with wonder and astonishment we feel that it is strange, and at the same time related to us.

This word *wonder* is connected with the word *astonishment*. Something is added to the phenomenon of wonder to which one can find no cognitive relationship. But that can only be the fault of the individual—at least the responsibility ought to rest with the person. And a person would not approach that something "wondrous" in a spirit of rejection or denial unless he or she had concluded that the thing or event *ought* to be related to him or her. For why do those who operate out of materialistic or purely intellectual concepts deny, for example, what others recognize as a wonder, if they do not have direct evidence that it is a lie or an untruth? Even philosophers today have to admit that one can never prove on the basis of phenomena spread out before humanity in the world that the Christ who incarnated in Jesus of Nazareth was not resurrected from the dead. Arguments can be made against this assertion. But what are these arguments? In terms of logic they are untenable. Enlightened philosophers today already admit that. For the arguments that can be brought forward on the materialistic side—for example, that no one until now has seen anyone arise from the dead as Christ arose from the dead—these arguments are logically at the same level as the argument that someone who had only seen fish must conclude that there are no birds. One can never derive in a logically consistent way, on the basis of the existence of one class of beings, that other beings do not exist. Likewise, one cannot derive anything about the event at Golgotha—which must be described as a "wonder"—on the basis of human experiences on the physical plane. However, if you tell someone about something that one would have to call a "miracle" (even though it were true), and the person says, "I cannot understand it," then that person is not opposing what we have said about the concept of astonishment, because this person is, in fact, showing that this same starting point for all knowledge also holds true for him- or herself. That person is demanding that your statement find an echo within him- or herself. In a certain sense, this individual wants to own, spiritually or cognitively, what is being communicated, and, since that person does not believe this is possible, and that it has no relationship to him or her, such a person declines to accept it. Although we can arrive at the concept of "wonder" on our own, we should also acknowledge that amazement and astonishment—from the perspective of all ancient Greek philosophy—arise when human beings come face to face with something strange and yet must time recognize at the same something related or familiar there.

Let us now try to build a bridge between these concepts and those that we brought before our souls last time.

We demonstrated last time how a certain advance in evolution was brought about by beings who were ready to offer sacrifices, and by other beings' refusal to receive these offerings, and the return of the sacrifices to the beings who offered them. We recognized in the returned sacrifices one of the main factors in ancient Moon development. Indeed, one of the most significant aspects of ancient Moon development is that certain beings brought sacrifices to higher beings, who then returned the sacrifices; because of this, as the smoke from the offering of the Moon beings pressed upward toward the higher beings who would not accept the sacrifices, the smoke was guided back as substance into the beings who had wanted to offer the sacrifice. We have seen, too, that the beings of the ancient Moon are most distinctive in that they felt pressing back into themselves what they had wished to send up to higher beings as the substance of sacrifice.

Yes, truly, we have seen that the substance that sought to become part of the higher beings but was not able to do so remained behind in the very beings who sent it forth; and that thereby the capacity for longing arose in these beings who had offered a sacrifice that was rejected. Indeed, we have even now, in all that we experience as longing in our own soul, a legacy of the event on the ancient

Moon—a legacy from beings who discovered that their sacrifice had not been accepted. The whole character of ancient Moon development, its spiritual atmosphere, when understood from a spiritual perspective, may be characterized by the fact that beings existed then who wished to present their sacrifice, but found that their offering was not accepted because the higher beings waived any claim to the sacrifice. Such is the peculiarly melancholic cause behind the characteristic atmosphere of the ancient Moon: rejected sacrifice. And Cain's rejected sacrifice, which points symbolically to the starting point for the evolution of earthly humankind, appears as a kind of recapitulation of this fundamental principle in ancient Moon development that took hold of Cain's soul—Cain, who also saw that his sacrifice was not accepted. Just as in the case of the beings of ancient Moon existence, such a rejection is something that can create a sorrow, a pain, in us that gives birth to longing.

We saw last time that the entry of the Spirits of Movement on the ancient Moon created a balance or redress between this rejected sacrifice and the longing that arose in the beings when the sacrifice was not accepted. At least the possibility was created whereby the longing that arose in the beings whose sacrifice was rejected could be satisfied to some extent. Imagine, in the most lively way, the following:

You have the higher beings to whom sacrifice should be given but who sent back the substance of the sacrifice. Longing arises in those beings who wanted to make the sacrifice and now feel: "If I had been able to give my sacrifice to the higher beings, the best of my own being would be living in those beings. Indeed, I myself would be living within those higher beings. But because I have been excluded from these beings, I stand here, and the higher beings stand over there!" The Spirits of Movement, however (and we should understand this almost literally) now bring these beings—in whom longing from the rejected sacrifice gleams toward the higher beings—into positions from which they can approach the higher beings from many different sides. And what rests in these beings as rejected offering is balanced, compensated for, by the wealth of impressions received from the higher beings encircling those who offered the rejected sacrifice. Thus a relationship is created between the beings who wished to offer the sacrifice and the higher beings who rejected it. And what remained unsatisfied because of the return of the offering can be compensated for in their new relation—so that it is as if the sacrifice had been accepted.

We can clarify what is meant here if we visualize the higher beings symbolically as the Sun and then, in a single position, the lesser beings gathered together as a planet. Let us suppose that the beings of the lesser planet wished to present their sacrifice to the higher planet, that is, to the Sun. But the Sun returned it, and the substance of the sacrifice must remain with the beings who offered the sacrifice. In their solitude and separation, these beings are filled with longing. Then the Spirits of Movement bring them into a circuit moving around the higher beings. Instead of sending forth a flow of the substance of sacrifice directly to the higher beings, it is possible for the beings who now contain the sacrifice within themselves to bring the substance into movement *around* the higher beings, thereby bringing the sacrifice into relation with the beings of a higher nature. It is just as if a person cannot appease a profound longing through one great fulfillment, but experiences instead a series of partial gratifications. That person's whole soul is brought into motion by such a series of partial gratifications. We described this very precisely the last time. We saw that because a being cannot feel inwardly united with the higher beings in sacrifice, impressions coming from without arise as a substitute. These substitute gratifications show us how such beings are able to achieve partial satisfaction.

Yet it is undeniable that the intended sacrifice would have had a different form in the higher beings than it had when it remained within the lower beings. For the actual conditions necessary for that intended form of existence lay in the higher beings. The conditions of existence in the lower beings are different from those within the higher beings. Once again, we can imagine this pictorially. If the entire substance of a planet flowed into the Sun, and the Sun did not reject it, the beings of this planet, as Sun beings, would discover different conditions of existence than they would if the

Sun had returned the substance back to the planet. An alienation of what we must call the content of the sacrifice takes place through its rejection—an alienation of this substance of the sacrifice from its origin.

Consider this thought. Beings are forced to retain something within themselves that they would gladly present as a sacrifice and that they feel could fulfill its true purpose only if it could be presented as an offering. If you could recreate the experience of such beings you would have what one may call "the exclusion of a certain portion of cosmic beings from their own essential meaning and great cosmic purpose." Beings have something within themselves that would actually—if we may speak pictorially—only fulfill its purpose in another place. Consequently, this displacement of the rejected sacrifice's smoke—this displacement of the rejected substance of sacrifice—removes this sacrificial substance from the course of the rest of the cosmic processes.

If you grasp this thought not just with your intellect—for the intellect does not work in such matters—but if you grasp what is being expressed with your feeling, you will experience something like being torn out of the universal cosmic process. For the beings who rejected the sacrifice, it is just something they have pushed away from themselves. But for the other beings, those in whom the substance of the sacrifice remains, it is something that bears the imprint of alienation from one's own origin. Here, then, we have beings whose substantiality expresses alienation from one's origins. If one understands this sensitively—if one places sensitively before one's soul this idea of something in which alienation from its origins dwells—then one has the idea of death. Death in the universe is nothing other than what had to occur within the beings whose sacrifice was rejected and who had to retain that sacrifice within themselves. Thus we advance from resignation and renunciation, which we found in the third stage of evolution, to what was refused by the higher beings: death. And the true meaning of death is nothing other than the state of not being in one's true place, of being excluded from one's true place.

Even when death occurs concretely in human life, the same principle holds true. For when we look at a corpse left in the world of maya, it consists only of a substantiality that has been separated at the moment of death from the I, the astral body, and the etheric body and has thereby been alienated from what gave it, as physical body, its only real significance. For the physical body of a human being has no meaning without the etheric body, the astral body, and the I. At the moment of death, the physical body becomes meaningless; it is excluded from its source of meaning. When a person dies, what is no longer sense-perceptible presents itself to us in the macrocosm. Because cosmic beings in higher spheres gave back what was intended to be brought to them as sacrifice, this rejected substance of sacrifice became subject to death—for death is the exclusion of cosmic substance or a cosmic being from its true purpose.

With this, we come to the spiritual nature of what we call the fourth element in the universe. If fire is in the purest sense sacrifice—and wherever fire or warmth occurs sacrifice lies spiritually behind it; if, behind everything that is spread out around our Earth as air, we discover gift-granting or bestowing virtue; if we can characterize flowing water, that is, the fluid element, as spiritual resignation or renunciation; then we must characterize the element of earth as the only bearer of death, as that which has been alienated from its meaning through rejection. Death would not exist if there were no element of earth. Here you have in concrete form something that shows how the solid arises out of the fluid. And this, too, in a certain way, reflects a spiritual process. Imagine, for instance, that ice forms in a pond, thus making the water become solid. What causes the water to turn to ice in fact cuts the water off from what gives it meaning as water. In this process you have the spiritual manifestation of becoming solid—the spiritual manifestation of becoming earth. For, with regard to the characteristics of the four elements, ice is, actually, earth; only what is fluid is water. Being separated from one's purpose and meaning is what we call death, and death presents and fulfills itself in the element of earth.

We began by posing the question whether anything real could be found in our world of illusion (or maya), whether anything within it corresponds to reality. Consider very carefully the concept we have now placed before our soul. I told you at the beginning that the concepts in these lectures are rather complicated. Therefore, we must not just accept them intellectually. We must meditate upon them. Only then will they become clear to us. Let us take this concept of death, that is, the concept of what is Earth-related—for it presents a truly remarkable aspect. Of all the other concepts that we dealt with we had to say that there is no reality in what we find around us in the world of maya, that what is true is only to be found in the fundamentally spiritual. But here we have ascertained that something in the sphere of maya characterizes itself as death—precisely because it is separated from its purpose and because it actually ought to be in the spiritual realm. In other words: something is cut off and confined within this maya. It actually should not be there. Throughout the entire vast realm of maya or illusion we have only deceptions and illusions. Nevertheless, we do find something in maya that corresponds to what is true: namely, that in the moment something true is cut off from what gives it meaning in the spiritual it becomes subject to destruction and death. Here we have nothing less than the great truth that, *within the world of maya the only thing that shows itself in its reality is death!* All other appearances we must trace back to their reality; what is true lies behind all other appearances that arise in maya. Only death is to be found in maya in its reality, for it consists of what is separated from the real and taken into maya. Thus, in the whole sphere of maya, death is the only reality.

And so, if we turn from what spreads out everywhere in universal maya to the great principles of the cosmos, a most important, most pertinent consequence presents itself for spiritual science in the following proposition: In our world of maya only death actually exists as something real.

We can also approach what I want to say here from another side. We can, for example, consider the beings of other realms that are here around us. We can ask: Do minerals, for example, die? For the occultist it is meaningless to say that minerals die. For that would be similar to saying that a fingernail that has been cut has died. The fingernail is not something that in and of itself has a right to its own existence. It is a part of us, and when we cut the nail, we separate it from us and tear it away from the life it shared with us. It dies only when we ourselves die. In the same sense, for spiritual science, minerals do not die. For minerals are only members of a great organism, just as the fingernail is a member of our organism; and when a mineral seems to be destroyed, it is merely torn from the greater organism, as the piece of fingernail is separated from our organism when we cut it. The destruction of minerals is not death, for a mineral does not live in and of itself, rather it lives within the greater organism of which it is a member.

If you recall my lecture on the nature of plants,[2] you will know that the plant as such is not independent, either. The plant, too, is a member of the entire Earth-organism, but not quite in the way that minerals are part of a larger organism. From a spiritual-scientific point of view it is meaningless to speak of the life of an individual plant; one must rather speak of the Earth-organism, for plants are everywhere parts of this organism. When we come to the death of plants, the situation is similar to cutting a fingernail. We cannot say that the fingernail has died. The same is true of plants, for they belong to the greater organism, which is identical with the entire Earth. The Earth is an organism. It goes to sleep in spring, sending the plants, as its organs, out toward the Sun. In fall, the Earth reawakens and spiritually receives the plants back into itself by accepting their seeds into its being. It is meaningless to view the plants individually, for the Earth-organism as a whole does not die, even though individual plants wilt. Similarly, when our hair turns gray, we do not die, even though we cannot turn our gray hair black again—at least, not by any natural means. Of course, we are in a different position than the plants. But

2. Lecture given by Rudolf Steiner in Berlin, December 8, 1910, entitled "*Der Geist im Pflanzenreich*." Published in Rudolf Steiner, *Antworten der Geisteswissenschaft auf die grossen Fragen des Daseins* (Berlin, 1910–1911, GA 60).

the Earth may be compared to a human being who can turn gray hair back into black hair. The Earth itself does not die. What we see in wilting plants is a process that takes place on the Earth's surface. Although they wilt, however, we can never say that plants truly die.

Neither can we say of the animals that they die as we do. For the individual animal does not truly exist—only the group soul of the animal exists within the supersensible. What the animal really is, its true existence, exists only on the astral plane as the group soul: the individual animal is densified out of the group soul. And when the animal dies, it is set aside as a member of the group soul and is then replaced by another.

What we encounter as death in the mineral, plant, and animal realms is therefore only the semblance, the illusion of death. In reality, only the human being dies, for the human being has developed individuality so far that it descends into the physical body, in which a person must carry out an earthly existence in order to be real. Death has meaning only for the human being during earthly existence.

To grasp this, we must say: *Only human beings can actually experience death.* Moreover, as we learn from spiritual-scientific research, only human beings can really overcome death. Only for us is true victory over death possible. For all other beings, death is only apparent—it does not really exist. If we were to ascend beyond humanity to beings of the higher hierarchies, we would discover that the higher beings do not know death in the human sense. True death, that is, death in the physical realm, is only experienced by those beings who have to draw something out of existence in the physical plane. Human beings must achieve I-consciousness in the physical context. And that cannot be found without death. Neither for beings who stand in rank below the human being, nor for beings who stand above the human being, is it meaningful to speak of death. On the other hand, there is no undoing the most significant earthly deed of the Being whom we call the Christ Being. Indeed, with regard to the Christ Being, we have seen that the Mystery of Golgotha—the victory of life over death—becomes the most important event of all. And where can this victory over death be carried out? Can it occur in higher worlds? No! For among the lower beings to whom we referred in the mineral, plant, and animal realms, we cannot speak of death because these beings actually have their true being in the higher world beyond the senses. And with regard to higher beings one cannot speak of death, but only of transformation, metamorphosis, and reordering. The incision into life that we call death occurs only with the human state. And human beings can experience death only in the physical context. If human beings had never entered the physical plane, they would never have known death, for a being who has not entered the physical plane knows nothing of death. There is nothing in other worlds that may be called death—in other worlds there is only transformation and metamorphosis. If the Christ had to go through death, then he had to descend to the physical realm! For he could experience death only in the physical realm.

Thus we see that the reality of higher worlds works in maya in a remarkable way in the historical development of the human being. If we are thinking of historical events in the right way, we must realize that although an event occurs in the physical realm, its source lies in the spiritual world. This is true of all historical events—*except one!* For we cannot say of the event at Golgotha that it occurred on the physical plane and something corresponding to it exists in a higher world. True, Christ Himself belongs to the higher world and descended to the physical plane. But an archetype, such as we have for all other historical events, does not exist for what was accomplished at Golgotha. The Mystery of Golgotha could occur only in the physical realm.

Evidence for this will be provided out of spiritual science. For instance, in the course of the next three thousand years, there will be many new examples of the event at Damascus. We have often spoken of this. Human beings will develop capacities so that they will be able to perceive the Christ on the astral plane as an etheric figure, as Paul did at Damascus.[3] This experience of perceiving Christ

---

3. Acts 9. See Rudolf Steiner, *Das Ereignis der Christus-Erscheinung in der aetherischen Welt*, (1910, GA 118).

through higher capacities—which will develop more and more among human beings in the course of the next three millennia, will begin in our twentieth century. From this time onward these capacities will gradually emerge, and over the next millennia they will be cultivated by a great number of human beings. That is, many people will come to know that Christ is a reality—that he lives—*by looking into higher worlds*. They will become acquainted with him, *as he lives now*. Nor will they become acquainted only with how he now lives, rather they will become convinced—precisely as Paul was—that he died and rose again. The basis for this, however, cannot be found in higher worlds, it must be found on the physical plane.

If a person today comes to understand and grasp how Christ's own development progresses and how, with it, certain human capacities also develop—if a person understands this through spiritual science—then there is nothing to prevent this person, when they pass through the portal of death, from participating in the Damascus event—for death now actually manifests as an initial shining forth of Christ into the world of humanity. Those who prepares themselves today for this event while in the physical body can also experience it in the life between death and new birth. Those, however, who do not prepare themselves for it—who gain no understanding of it in this incarnation—can know nothing, during the life between death and a new birth, of what is already happening now and, for the next three thousand years, will continue to happen in relation to Christ. They will have to wait until they are incarnated again. Then, when they are on Earth again, they will have to make further preparation for it. The death on Golgotha and what was created out of that death—which was needed to bring about the whole of Christ's subsequent development on Earth—can be grasped only in the physical body. It is the only important fact for our higher life that must be grasped in the physical body. Once understood in the physical body, it will be worked on further, cultivated more, in the higher worlds. But first it must be understood in the physical body. The Mystery of Golgotha could never have occurred in the higher worlds and has no archetype in the higher worlds. It is an event that encompasses a death confined entirely within the physical realm. Therefore, it can only be understood within the context of the physical plane. Yes, it is one of the tasks of the human being on Earth to achieve this understanding in one of his or her incarnations.

Here we must say, therefore, that we have found something significant on the physical plane that demonstrates an immediate reality, an immediate truth. What is it that is real on the physical plane? What on the physical plane is so real that we stop short and say: "Here we have something that is true!" It is death in the world of humankind; but not death in the other realms of nature. To understand the historical events that occur in the course of earthly evolution, we must rise from the historical event to the spiritual archetype. But this is not the case with the Mystery of Golgotha. In the Mystery of Golgotha we have something that belongs immediately and directly to the world of reality.

The other side of what has just been said also manifests itself. This is extraordinarily interesting. It is most significant that we find that the event at Golgotha is denied nowadays to be a real event and that, if we are talking of outward history, people say that it is impossible to prove this event as historical fact. Among momentous historical facts, there is rarely one that is so difficult to prove through external, historically verifiable, means as the Mystery of Golgotha. Compared to this, think how easy it is to work with the historical arguments for the existence of a Socrates or a Plato or some other Greek figure who is important for the progress of humanity in the outer world. Still, many people—up to a certain point, justifiably— say: You cannot claim on the basis of history that Jesus of Nazareth actually lived! And yet, contrary historical evidence does not exist. Nevertheless, it is true, one cannot deal with the fact of the Mystery of Golgotha in the way that one deals with other historical facts.

It is most remarkable that this event, which occurred on the outer physical plane, shares a common characteristic with all facts of the supersensible realm: namely, that it does not allow itself to be proven in any outward way. And many of those people who deny the supersensible world are the same ones who lack the capacity to grasp this event—which is not at all a supersensible one. In fact, the reality of the event is supported by the effects it produces. Yet people suppose that these effects can occur without the real event itself actually having occurred historically. They explain that the effects are a consequence of sociological circumstances. But for someone who is familiar with the course of cosmic creation, the idea that the effects of Christianity could have occurred without a force standing behind them is about as clever as saying that cabbages can grow in a field without planting seeds.

We can go even further and say that for the individuals who participated in the compilation of the Gospels there was likewise no possibility of proving the historical event of the Mystery of Golgotha as a historical fact based on historical evidence—for it took place without leaving traces perceivable by outward observation. Do you know how the compilers of the Gospels, with the exception of the author of the Gospel of St. John—who was a direct witness of these events—became convinced of the truth of these events? They were not persuaded by historical sources, for they had nothing more than the oral tradition and the books of the Mysteries. These circumstances are outlined in my *Christianity as Mystical Fact.* They convinced themselves of the actual existence of Christ Jesus through the constellations of the stars, for they were still very learned about the relationship of the macrocosm to the microcosm. They had the knowledge—one can also have it today—with which one can calculate a significant point in world history through the constellations of the stars. They could say: "When the constellations are thus and so, then that Being who is described as the Christ must have lived on Earth." In this way the authors of the Gospels of St. Matthew, St. Mark, and St. Luke were persuaded about the historical events. They gained the substance of the Gospels through clairvoyance, but the conviction that this or that could have occurred on Earth was drawn out of the constellations in the macrocosm. Anyone who knows this must believe the authors of the Gospels. Proving the inaccuracy of objections to the historicity of the Gospels is a thankless task. As anthroposophists, we must be clear that we place ourselves on an entirely different basis—the basis obtainable through insight into spiritual science.

In this regard, I would also like to draw attention to something that I have tried to establish during these lectures. The realities of which anthroposophy speaks cannot be undermined or struck down by objections that are in and of themselves correct. Human beings can say a great deal that is correct according to their knowledge; that does not disprove spiritual science. In the lecture, *How Does One Find a Basis For Theosophy?*[4] I drew a comparison and said: A little boy used to go into the village to get rolls for his family for breakfast. Now, in that village a roll cost two kreuzers and the boy was always given ten kreuzers. The boy brought home a number of rolls from the baker— one should note here that he was not a great arithmetician—and thought nothing more about it. Then a foster son was taken into the family, and he was sent to get the rolls from the baker instead of the other boy. The foster son was a good arithmetician, and so he said to himself: "You go to buy rolls and take ten kreuzers with you. A roll costs two kreuzers, and since ten divided by two equals five, you should bring home five rolls." But upon returning home, the boy discovered that he had brought six rolls. He said to himself: "That's wrong! You can't buy that many rolls for ten kreuzers, and since the addition is correct, tomorrow I expect to bring back five rolls." On the next day he received again ten kreuzers and again brought back six rolls. The addition was correct, but it did not correspond to the reality, for in fact the reality was different. It was the custom in that village, that whoever bought ten kreuzers' worth of rolls received an extra roll, that is, one received six rolls instead of five. The boy's calculation was correct, but still it did not correspond to the reality.

---

4. Lecture by Rudolf Steiner in Stuttgart, November 29, 1911: *"Wie begruendet man Theosophie?"* Only an incomplete transcript of the lecture exists, thus the lecture has not been published. See the lectures given in Berlin on October 31 and November 7, 1912, published in *Ergebnisse der Geistesforschung* (1912–1913, GA 62). The story of the little boy and the purchase of the rolls was used as a starting point in a lecture cycle given in Hanover: *Die Welt der Sinne und die Welt des Geistes* (1911–1912, GA 134).

Thus, the most critically thought-through objections to spiritual science can be "correct," but they may not have anything to do with the reality, which may stand on quite different principles. This is a wonderful example with which to demonstrate, even theoretically, the difference between what is arithmetically correct and what is actually true.

Thus, our efforts have shown that the world of maya leads back to reality. This process has shown us that fire is sacrifice, that the airy element is flowing, giving, bestowing virtue, that everything fluid is the result of renunciation, resignation. Today, we have added to these three truths a fourth: that the true nature of the earth or solid element is death, the separation of a substance from its cosmic purpose. When this state of separation was initiated, death itself entered as a reality into the world of maya or illusion. The gods themselves could never know death unless they descended in some way into the physical world, so as to understand death in its true nature in the physical world, the world of maya or illusion.

This is what I wanted to add to the concepts that we have discussed. Again, note that we can gain clarity about these concepts—so necessary, as we shall see, for a fundamental understanding of what is in the Gospel of Saint Mark—only through disciplined meditation, and by allowing them repeatedly to influence our soul.[5] For the Gospel of Mark can be understood only if one lays a foundation in the most significant cosmic concepts.

5. Lectures by Rudolf Steiner given in Basel, September 15–24, 1912. See Rudolf Steiner, *The Gospel of Saint Mark* (Hudson, NY: Anthroposophic Press, 1986).

Appendix

In lecture six of part one, in the general context of his exposition of the realities of heliocentricity and geocentricity in cosmic evolution, Rudolf Steiner refers to an exchange or "mix-up" that occurred between ancient and modern times with regard to the planets Mercury and Venus. Speaking of what was taught in the Mystery Schools of Zoroaster, he gives a surprising sequence of planets— Earth, Moon, Mercury, Venus, Sun—adding:

> You might think that if the Earth is here, and here the Sun, I should draw Mercury here, near the Sun, and here Venus. This is, however, not right, because both planets were, with regard to their names, mixed up by later astronomy. What is called "Mercury" today, was called in ancient teachings "Venus"; and the planet referred to as "Venus" today was, in all the old teachings, called "Mercury." Mark this well: *One does not understand the old writings and teachings if one applies what is said there about Venus and Mercury to what is meant today by the same names.* What is said about Venus has to be applied to present-day Mercury, and what is said about Mercury to Venus, because both of these designations were mixed up later. At the time when the world system was turned around, when the Earth was stripped of her central position, one not only changed the perspective, but allowed Mercury and Venus to roll around each other in relation to the old designations. (See page 98.)

This statement, and others like it—mostly in lectures around the same time—have caused confusion and perplexity in many of those trying to understand it, especially since, in some cases, Steiner frames the statement in mystery, saying, "This happened in order to conceal certain things"[1] or "Here I come to a point where a little secret, so to speak, must be unveiled, one that may only be divulged at this point. . . ."[2]

Elisabeth Vreede gives some historical perspective in the Seventh Letter of *Anthroposophy and Astronomy*:

> Without now going into the very complicated question of the "transposition of Mercury and Venus" in detail, it can be shown here how it happens that both Ptolemy and Copernicus call the same star "Venus" while giving it a different place in the sequence. We must also remember that the Ptolemaic system did not actually take the *spatial* relationships into consideration, but rather the *temporal* relationships and similarity of rhythms that arise from them. Thus Mercury is found to revolve in its epicycle in less time than Venus does, and from this point of view is therefore the nearest to the stationary Earth. Ptolemy was far from considering the relative distances of the planets from the Earth or the Sun, establishing instead *merely the order of the spheres*. Thus it was clear to him that the spheres of Saturn, Jupiter, and Mars are farther away from the Earth than the sphere of the Sun; and that Venus and Mercury lie below the Sun, although, as he says, other and more ancient astronomers were even doubtful about this, and from the point of view of the observations of that time, it could not be decisively known: "Thus a greater amount of belief seems to be due to the older astronomers' methods of arrangements, which separate the planets that are in opposition from those that do not come into opposition, but which remain near the Sun."[3] That Mercury must be the planet nearest the Earth, and then Venus, is borrowed from tradition, and this tradition is one that originated in the Mysteries. For in the Mysteries it was known that human beings in the life after death pass first through the Moon-sphere, then through

---

1. *Egyptian Myths and Mysteries*, lecture 4.
2. *The Apocalypse of St. John*, (Hudson, NY: Anthroposophic Press, 1993), lecture 3. See, too, Douglas Caughill, "The Mystery of Mercury and Venus: A Case of Mistaken Identity," *Anthroposophy Today*, Autumn 1994.
3. Ptolemy, *Handbook of Astronomy*, vol. 2, book 9, chapter 1.

that of Mercury, and then through that of Venus. But insofar as external observation is concerned, and the observations and calculations that became possible later—for example, the passage of Mercury and Venus across the Sun—it became equally clear that the little reddish-colored and scarcely visible Mercury stands nearest to the Sun, while the brilliantly shining Venus, being further from the Sun, stands nearest to the Earth. Therefore what is presented to us is a non-agreement—a transposition of the *spheres* with respect to their corresponding *planets*. That is as far as we can deal with the subject at present.[4]

The historical transposition involved in moving from the Ptolemaic to the Copernican systems is clear—but only if one does not look too closely, for there are other implications, as Rudolf Steiner suggests in a 1912 lecture:

The intrinsic nature of spiritual life as it is in the present age developed for the first time when modern natural science came upon the scene with men like Copernicus, Giordano Bruno, Galileo, and others. Nowadays people are taught about Copernicus in their early school days, and the impressions thus received remain with them all their life. In earlier times the soul experienced something different. Try to picture to yourselves what a contrast there is between a person of the modern age and one who lived centuries ago. Before the days of Copernicus everyone believed that the Earth remains at rest in cosmic space with the Sun and the stars revolving around it. The very ground slipped from under humanity's feet when Copernicus came forward with the doctrine that the Earth is moving with tremendous speed through the universe. We should not underestimate the effects of such a revolution in thinking, accompanied as it was by a corresponding change in the life of feeling. All the thoughts and ideas of people were suddenly different from what they had

4. Elizabeth Vreede, *Anthroposophie und Astronomie* (Dornach: Philosophisch-Anthroposophicher Verlag, 1980) pp. 73–75. An English edition is in process of publication by Anthroposophic Press, Hudson, NY.

been before the days of Copernicus. And now let us ask: What does occultism have to say about this revolution in thinking?

Anyone who asks from the standpoint of occultism what kind of world-view can be derived from the Copernican tenets will have to acknowledge that, although these ideas can lead to great achievements in the realm of natural science and in external life, they are incapable of promoting any understanding of the spiritual foundations of the world and the things of the world, for there has never been a worse instrument for understanding the spiritual foundations of the world than the ideas of Copernicus—never in the whole of human evolution.... In earlier, pre-Copernican thought, the external world was indeed maya, but much traditional wisdom, much truth concerning the world and the things of the world still survived. Since Copernicus, however, human beings have maya around them, not only in their material perceptions, but their concepts and ideas themselves are maya. People assume nowadays that the Sun is firmly fixed in the middle, and that the planets revolve around it in ellipses. In the near future, however, it will be realized that the view of the stars held by Copernicus is much less correct than the earlier Ptolemaic view. The view of the world held by the school of Copernicus and Kepler is very convenient, but, as an explanation of the macrocosm, it is not the truth.[5]

Thus there is much at stake behind this question of the transposition of Mercury and Venus. Above all, what is at issue is the true relation between the Earth and the Sun—heliocentricity and geocentricity. Phenomenology, medieval alchemy, spiritual vision all point to the spiritual reality of geocentricity, but, as the lecture printed as the second part of this Appendix shows, "geocentricity" itself is not a simple thing.

To cast further light on this question, a short essay (conflated from two earlier essays) follows, by Dr. Georg Unger, retired director of the Mathematical-Physics Institute in Dornach, Switzerland.

---

5. *Esoteric Christianity and the Mission of Christian Rosenkreutz*, lecture of December 18, 1912.

A. Concerning the So-called Interchange of Mercury and Venus

by Georg Unger

Widespread misunderstanding exists concerning Rudolf Steiner's remarks about the interchange of Mercury and Venus. Students of Steiner's work are often confused whenever—primarily, in lectures—he refers to this interchange.

One hears all sorts of curious statements. For instance, it is said that, during the transition from the Ptolemaic to the Copernican systems, the two planets changed places; or it is said that, in ancient times, the two planets were named differently—that their names were subsequently changed—so that a colleague, looking at Venus shining in the evening sky might remark that we are really looking at Mercury (or the other way round). In other words, it is thought that when we look at Venus radiant in the evening twilight, we ought to say to ourselves that it is "really" Mercury we are looking at.

These statements are variations on a theme, mostly based on something Rudolf Steiner referred to in lectures, especially in 1908/9.[2]

To understand what kind of interchange is meant in each case, we must look first at the context in which Steiner spoke. In fact, a *change of place* did occur in our model of the planetary system when the move from the Ptolemaic system to the ideas of Copernicus, Tycho Brahe, and Kepler was made (see figure on page 99). Let us begin with this well-known fact.

According to ancient traditions, including Aristotle, the sequence of the *spheres* surrounding the Earth begins with the *Moon Sphere*, followed by the spheres of *Mercury, Venus*, the *Sun, Mars, Jupiter*, and *Saturn*. Ptolemy used this sequence in his "Almagest,"[3] his study of the movement of each planet against the background of the fixed stars. Ptolemy's study, however, was not intended to show the *size* of the spheres in relation to each other.

Later, when the shift occurred to the Copernican system, all the planets were shown to circle the Sun. The popularity of this view was increased by Copernicus' contemporary, Rheticus, who suggested putting the Earth and the Moon where the Sun had been in the Ptolemaic model, while moving the Sun to where the Earth had been. This journalistic simplification contributed greatly to the rapid acceptance of the Copernican system long before Galileo had found serious proof of it. A consequence of this exchange, however, is that in this model Venus is closer to the Earth than Mercury is. This is part of what Rudolf Steiner meant when in his lecture of April 15, 1909, he said that when "...the solar system was changed around, when the Earth was relieved of its central position—then not only the perspective was changed—Mercury and Venus were also tumbled around each other in relation to their ancient designations." (See page 98.)

Here Steiner mentions a *change of names* in one breath with the *place change* of the exoteric solar systems. We must keep these two— change of name and change of place—clearly distinct, for Rudolf Steiner continues: "You will be able to relate this drawing to the physical planetary system very easily." But his drawing during the lecture already reversed the names Venus and Mercury.

What is the reason for this exchange of names? In his 1908 cycle, *The Apocalypse of Saint John*, speaking of the "Morning Star," Rudolf Steiner mentions that, after the Mystery of Golgotha, the decision was made in the Mysteries to veil a certain occult truth, making use of a "mask." In this case, the simplified instruction was given "to exchange the names of Mercury and Venus." In mentioning this, Rudolf Steiner said, he was exposing a "minor occult secret."[4]

Here Steiner's words can be understood only if we take into account that the exchange of names was already known in theosophical literature. (A. P. Sinnett, for example, in his continuation of *Esoteric Buddhism*, mentioned exoteric names used by astronomers in comparison to the exchanged esoteric terms.)

Thus Rudolf Steiner was speaking to people who were familiar with the literature and who would have known about the exchange of names. This is not to say that he simply passed on Sinnett's ideas. Knowing Rudolf Steiner's method of portraying only what he had himself researched supersensibly, we can assume that he had checked the facts, even if not necessarily in every detail. But this Sinnett connection sheds a different light on Steiner's earlier remarks; for in contrast to Sinnett, Rudolf Steiner considers early Christian literature. What Steiner says about a "mask" refers only to such literature. This resolves the problem posed by his earliest remarks, which differ from one another. If, as he says in 1909, the secret was known already in all the ancient Mysteries, why did the names get changed at the approach of the Copernican system? Evidently, he was referring to something that he explained in more detail only much later, in 1924, in his lecture cycle *Rosicrucianism and Modern Initiation*, where he explains that, with the "Fall" of humanity (into luciferic temptation) in early Lemurian times, the Earth lost its dignity as center of the solar system.[5]

Here we learn that, in a certain sense, the physical order of the planets, which approached humanity through Copernicus, is a "false" fact. It is as if we would say of someone who has been killed, "He is dead—that is a fact," and ignore the fact that he had been alive previously. This is the secret of the ancient Mysteries: that the physical order no longer corresponds to the spiritual spheres. Awareness of the order of the planets was about to become widely known during the period following Christ. That is why a "mask" was chosen in early alchemical literature after the time of Christ: the alchemists spoke of "Venus" when they meant occult "Mercury" (and vice versa). We can imagine that certain alchemical experiments develop differently when physical Venus, which comes closer to the Earth than Mercury does, enters the spiritual sphere of Mercury. By "masking" the true identity of the planets, they hoped to prevent misuse.

Clearly, this is an important issue. That is why, in the lecture cycle *Rosicrucianism and Modern Initiation* (January 1924), Steiner returns to this theme, showing how in early and true Rosicrucianism the spread of Copernicanism was seen to be fraught with the danger of misinterpreting the central position of the Sun, always known in occult circles. This is now presented in the following mood: the great Sun-Spirit has come to Earth through the Christ event. The outer Sun has become "the wrongful prince of the world." It is then described how in the divine plan the Earth was to be the center of the solar system; however, due to an aberration in the human race, a certain "false fact" had to be established: the Sun as center of the planetary system. This dangerous truth was known in the Mysteries and well guarded there. When the time came for science to discover this aspect of things, the spiritual connection was hidden as a kind of protection in certain writings.

So much for these sources. All other citations known to me point out, in more or less abbreviated form, these facts:

1. The older Mysteries knew of the central position of the physical Sun.
2. Shortly before or following the Mystery of Golgotha an
   interchange in nomenclature took place.
3. Apart from that, the planets have changed places in the
   notional world system.

I begin with the third point. As I already mentioned, the Ptole-maic universe was in fact arranged so that the sequence of the traditional planets from Earth outward was: Moon, Mercury, Venus, Sun, Mars, Jupiter, Saturn. The known exoteric basis for this is that it is the order of the *velocities* with which these heavenly bodies move across the background of fixed stars. Its spiritual basis lies in the fact that it is experienced spiritually as *the sequence of spheres inhabited by the hierarchies or gods*. There was still a faint memory at the time that the soul after death expands, or passes, through the planetary spheres in this order.

Assuming the reader's knowledge of the Ptolemaic system of epicycles, we can make the transition to the Copernican system as follows. First, draw a model of the Ptolemaic system of spheres. Then take the Earth plus Moon out of their central position and place them where Ptolemy has the Sun, while moving the Sun in turn to the center. Now Mercury and Venus are circling the Sun, disposing of the Ptolemaic epicycles. Similarly, the Earth-orbit now makes redundant the epicycles of Mars, Jupiter, and Saturn (which according to Ptolemy are all rotating at the same speed); looked at critically, the whole matter is a simple artifice, anticipating a result that can be demonstrated by careful geometric reflection, insofar as the two world systems are geometrically equivalent.

When Steiner says at one point that Venus and Mercury have been allowed to spin around each other, he may have had this artifice (perhaps attributable to Rheticus) in mind. As we have noted, this is a matter of a change of place relative to the Sun *in a conceptual model.*

Now the second point: if an exchange of names took place in certain writings as a protection or mask, this can of course have no retrospective effect on earlier times. Thus there can be no contradiction between such an occult shift in names and the exoterically-assured, continuous identity of today's Venus, say, with the planet of Ishtar, the goddess of the Babylonians. The outer documents, in the form of clay tablets with the name attached to the orbital periods (of the present Venus), leave no room for doubt. The same holds true for Mercury. In short, the actual change of names can only apply to later writings—we may assume, of the Rosicrucians and alchemists. What has been said so far is in harmony with the fact that the older Mysteries were aware of the "two kinds of space"—the one that today we call physical space, the other that we would call nowadays the home of the spiritual spheres. A modern physicist has no difficulty in conceiving of different spaces simultaneously or, loosely spoken, in the same place.

This also explains why the central position of the Sun in physical space was an occult secret and "dangerous." Not simply that one could misinterpret this placement at the center as being of true spiritual significance (we recall the phrase "false fact"), but it could have consequences. If we clarify for ourselves that the physical planet Venus (as we name it today), or at least its mark on the heliocentric

Venus sphere, describes a path that passes through a part of the spiritual spheres of Venus, Sun, and Mercury, such knowledge could be important in determining the most effective constellations (for example, for a medical application of copper). However, in the wrong hands, this could easily lead to misuse.

Thus, each and every aspect of Steiner's indications, given at widely separated times, are found to be in full agreement. Yet passages we have not mentioned in detail, from lectures shortly after 1908, speak of this interchange being known in all the Mysteries; this is used as the basis for claims that the present names of the planets are "false." I believe, on the contrary, that these references relate only to the fact that one knew in the pre-Christian Mysteries of the "wrongful or false" position of the Sun as physical center. If there is still doubt as to the exact meaning of these passages, then one might reflect that between 1908 and 1924 Steiner's own spiritual research had progressed, and that the later indications could be taken as a more precise statement of what he had said previously. With this I believe the puzzling aspects of the question of an "interchange" have been largely clarified.

NOTES

1. Conflated from two articles that previously appeared in English, reprinted with kind permission of Dr. Unger.

2. E.g., *Egyptian Myths and Mysteries* (lecture 4, September 5, 1908): "Here I would like to add one thing, because misunderstandings have crept into the naming of the planets. In all occult nomenclature, what astronomy today calls "Venus" is called "Mercury" and vice versa. Purely exoteric astronomers know nothing of the Mysteries behind all this, because in the past it was not desired that the esoteric names should be revealed. This happened in order to conceal certain things."

3. *Almagest*, from the Arabic "the greatest," to distinguish it from another work called "The Little Astronomer."

4. "What does 'Morning Star' mean? We know that the Earth passes through the conditions of Saturn, Sun, Moon, Earth, Jupiter, Venus, and Vulcan. This is the way it is usually expressed, and it is quite correct. But I have already pointed out that the Earth-evolution is divided into the Mars period and the Mercury period

because of the mysterious connection existing in the first half of the Earth-evolution between the Earth and Mars, and in the second half between the Earth and Mercury. Thus in the place of Earth we sometimes put Mars and Mercury. We say that the Earth in its evolution passes through Saturn, Sun, Moon, Mars, Mercury, Jupiter, and Venus. Thus the most potent stellar force in the second half of the Earth-evolution is seen in Mercury. Mercury is the star representing the directional force, the upward journey on which man must embark.

"Here I come to a point where a little secret, so to say, must be unveiled, one which may only be divulged at this point. The teachers of spiritual wisdom have always had what might be called a mask against those who would only have misused Spiritual Science, especially in bygone times. They did not express themselves directly, but presented something that was intended to conceal the true state of affairs. Now the esotericism of the Middle Ages knew only rather rough and ready measures and called Mercury 'Venus' and Venus 'Mercury.' In truth if we wish to speak esoterically, as the writer of the Apocalypse has done, we must speak of Mercury as the 'Morning Star.' By 'Morning Star' he meant 'Mercury': *I have given the direction upward to your I, to the Morning Star, to Mercury.*[*] You may still find in certain books of the Middle Ages, which describe the true state of affairs, that the stars of our planetary system are enumerated thus: Saturn, Jupiter, Mars, and then Earth is followed not as it is now by Venus, Mercury, but by the reverse, Mercury, Venus" (*The Apocalypse of Saint John*, Nuremberg, June 20, 1908, p. 71).

5. For the full text of the relevant lecture, see the next section of this Appendix..

---

[*] Compare with Rev. 22:16: "I, Jesus, have sent my angel to you. He shall confirm these words to you in the congregations. I am the root and the stem of David. I am the radiant Morning Star."

from:

B. Humanity's Relation to the Sun[1]

DORNACH, *January 11, 1924*

What I have been telling you in recent lectures needs to be carried a little further. I have tried to give you a picture of how spiritual knowledge took its course through the centuries and of the form it has assumed in recent times. I have shown you how, from the fifteenth century until the end of the eighteenth, and even on into the beginning of the nineteenth century, the spiritual knowledge that existed in humanity before then as clear and concrete—albeit instinctive—knowledge now manifested more in a devotion of heart and soul to the spiritual in the world.

We have seen how a direct knowledge of nature—and how the spiritual world works in nature—remains unmistakably present in the eleventh, twelfth, and thirteenth centuries. In Agrippa of Nettesheim, for example, whom I have described in my book *Mysticism at the Dawn of the Modern Age,*[2] we have a personality who still knew quite well that in the several planets of our system are spiritual beings of specific character and kind.[3]

In his writings, Agrippa assigns to each planet what he calls the *Intelligence* of the planet. This points to traditions that had existed from ancient times and were, even in his day, something more than

---

1. Adapted from Rudolf Steiner, *Rosicrucianism and Modern Initiation: Mystery Centers of the Middle Ages*, lecture 4, Mary Adams, trans., (London: Rudolf Steiner Press, 1982).
2. Blauvelt, NY: Steinerbooks, 1980.
3. Heinrich Cornelius Agrippa von Nettesheim (1486–1535), German physician, theologian, and philosopher. He wrote on occult philosophy, Kabbala, and Pythagorean analyses and magic, which helped to link him with the legend of Faust (Source, *Webster's New Biographical Dictionary*).

mere traditions. It would have been impossible for someone like Agrippa of Nettesheim to look up to a planet in the way that became customary in later astronomy and which is still customary today. For Agrippa, the external planet—no, every single star—was no more than a sign, an announcement, so to speak, of the presence of spiritual beings to whom people, when they turned their gaze toward the star, could look up to with the eye of the soul. Agrippa of Nettesheim knew that the beings united with individual stars rule both the inner existence of that star or planet and also its movements in the universe—indeed, that they hold sway over its whole activity. Such beings Agrippa called the *Intelligence* of the star.

At the same time, Agrippa also knew that hindering beings work there and undermine the good deeds of the star, working both from the star as well as into it. He called these beings the *Demon* of the star. And with this knowledge went an understanding of Earth, which also saw the Earth as a heavenly body, having its Intelligence and its Demon. This understanding of *Star Intelligence* and *Star Demonology*—with all its implications—has been completely lost.

Let us consider for a moment at what this understanding implied.

Earth was looked on as ruled in her inner activity and movement in the cosmos by a group of Intelligences whom one could group together under the name *Intelligence of the Earth star*. But what *was* the Intelligence of the Earth-star for those of Agrippa's time? It is exceedingly difficult today even to speak of these things, for humankind's ideas have traveled very far from what was accepted then as a matter of course by people of insight and understanding. *The Intelligence of the Earth-star was humanity*. People of those times saw in humanity—in the human being—a being who had received from cosmic spirituality the task or mission not merely—as modern humanity imagines—to walk about on Earth and travel over it by train, buy and sell, write books, and so on—no, people in those days saw themselves as beings to whom the world-spirit had given the task of ruling and regulating Earth *and* bringing, as it were, law and order into all that has to do with the place of the Earth in the cosmos. They expressed their view of humanity by saying: Because of what humankind is, through the forces and powers it bears within, humanity gives to Earth the impulse for her movement around the Sun, for her movement in cosmic space.

In those days, there was still a feeling for this. It was known that such a task had once been allotted to humanity. World spirituality had really made humanity the Lord of the Earth, but in the course of their evolution, human beings had not shown themselves equal to the task; they had fallen from their high estate. When people speak of knowledge today, one can seldom catch even a last echo of this view. However, what we find in religious belief regarding the Fall goes back ultimately to this view. There the point is that humanity originally had a very different status on Earth and in the universe—that it has in fact fallen from a high estate. However, apart from this religious view, wherever human beings think they have attained knowledge by correct methods of thought, it is only here and there today that we still find an echo of the ancient knowledge that once proceeded from instinctive clairvoyance, which was well aware of humanity's true calling and of its Fall into present narrow limitations.

It might happen, for example, that one has a conversation with a person—this is a fact—who has thought very deeply and has also acquired a deep knowledge of spiritual matters. The conversation turns on whether human beings, as they exist on Earth today, are really self-contained creatures who carry their whole being within them. Such a person will say to you that it cannot be. Human beings must really be far more comprehensive beings, otherwise they could not have the striving they have now, they could not develop the great idealism of which we can see such fine and high examples. In their true nature human beings must be great and comprehensive beings, who have somehow or another committed a cosmic sin and, as a result, have been banished to the limits of present earthly existence, so that today human beings are really imprisoned in a cage, as it were. Here and there, you may still meet a stray survivor, so to speak, of this view. But, generally speaking, where can we find people who consider themselves qualified scientists who give serious attention to these great and far-reaching questions? And yet, people can only find the way to an existence worthy of being human by facing such questions.

Thus it was really true that humanity was considered the bearer of the Intelligence of the Earth. But now, a person such as Agrippa of Nettesheim also ascribed a demon to the Earth. When we go back to the twelfth or thirteenth century, we find this Demon of the Earth whose eventual development on Earth was inevitable because he found in humanity a ready tool for his activity.

To understand this we must become familiar with how people in those days thought of Earth's relationship to the Sun, or rather of earthly humanity to the Sun. In order to describe for you how they understood this relationship, I must again speak in imaginations; for these things will not allow themselves to be limited to abstract concepts. Abstract concepts came later and are very far from being able to span the truth; we must therefore begin here to speak in pictures, in imaginations.

In *An Outline of Occult Science* I described how the Sun separated from the Earth or, we could say, separated the Earth from itself. The Sun, you must remember, is the original home of the human race; ever since the Saturn period humanity has been united with the whole planetary system, including the Sun. Humankind's home is not on Earth, but has only a temporary resting place on Earth. In reality, according to the prevailing view of those times, human beings are *solar beings*. In their whole nature and existence, they are united with the Sun. And so we should, as human beings, as Sun-beings, have a completely different relationship to the Earth than we do. What should happen, first of all, is that the Earth should conform to her impulse to bring forth the human seed in etheric form out of the mineral and plant kingdoms, and the Sun should then fructify the seed. Then the etheric human form should arise, and, by establishing its own relationship to the physical substances of the Earth, this should then take on earthly substantiality.

The contemporaries of Agrippa of Nettesheim knew—while Agrippa's own knowledge was, unfortunately, somewhat clouded, his better contemporaries actually did hold this view—that human beings should not be born as they are now in the earthly way, but should come into being in the etheric body through the interaction of Sun and Earth; and then, going about the Earth as an etheric being, they should *give themselves* Earthly form. Human seeds should grow up out of the Earth with the purity of plant life, appearing here and there as ethereal fruits of the Earth, darkly gleaming. Then in a certain season of the year these beings should be overshone by the light of the Sun and thereby assume human form, though still etheric; then human beings should draw physical substance to themselves—not from the body of the mother, but from the Earth and all that is thereon—and incorporate physical substance into themselves from the earthly kingdoms. That, in their view, should have been the manner of a human being's appearance on Earth, according to the purposes of the cosmic spirituality.

The development that occurred later was attributed to the fact that humanity had allowed an urge that was too deep, a desire too intense for the earthly and material, to awaken within. Its connection with the Sun and the cosmos was thus forfeited and could find existence on Earth only in the form of the stream of inheritance, which allowed the opportunity for the Demon of the Earth to begin his work. The Demon of the Earth could not have done anything with human beings who were Sun-born. Sun-born humans on Earth would have actually been the fourth hierarchy. Indeed, if one wanted to place humanity, one would have had to say:

First Hierarchy:	Seraphim, Cherubim, Thrones;
Second Hierarchy:	Exusiai, Dynamis, Kyriotetes;
Third Hierarchy:	Angels, Archangels, Archai;
Fourth Hierarchy:	Humanity—three different stages or gradations of humanity.

Because it gave rein to strong impulses toward the physical, however, humanity did not become the being of the lowest branch of the hierarchies, as it were, but became the being at the summit—the topmost branch—of the earthly kingdoms. *Mineral* kingdom, *plant* kingdom, *animal* kingdom, *human* kingdom; this became the picture of how humanity exists in the world.

Furthermore, because humanity has not found its proper task on the Earth, the Earth herself does not have her proper and worthy position in the cosmos; for since humanity has fallen, the true Lord of the Earth is not there. What has happened? The true Lord of the Earth is absent, and so it has become necessary that her place and course in the cosmos, which cannot be regulated from the Earth herself, be regulated from the Sun. Therefore, the tasks that should really be accomplished on Earth have been given to the Sun. The person of medieval times looked up to the Sun and said: In the Sun are certain Intelligences; they determine the movement of the Earth in the cosmos; they govern what happens on the Earth. This should, in reality, be the task of *human beings*; the Sun-forces should work on Earth *through humanity*. Thus this significant medieval understanding was expressed as: the Sun, the unlawful Prince of this world.

And now, my dear friends, let us consider how such views infinitely deepened the feeling in medieval people for the Christ Impulse. For them, the Christ became the Spirit who did not want to find his further task on the Sun, who was not willing to remain among those who directed the Earth unlawfully from without. He wanted to make his way from the Sun to the Earth, to enter into human and earthly destiny, to experience Earth events and follow the path of earthly evolution, sharing the outcome of human beings and the Earth.

Therewith, for medieval humankind, the Christ was the Being, the one Being, who saved for the cosmos humanity's task on Earth. There you have the connection. And now you can see why, in Rosicrucian times, again and again it was impressed upon the pupil: O Human Being, you are not what you are; the Christ had to come to take from you your task so that He might perform it for you.

Much in Goethe's *Faust* has come to us from these medieval views, although Goethe did not understand this. Recall, my dear friends, how Faust conjures up the Earth Spirit. With these medieval views in mind, we can enter with feeling and understanding into the way this Earth Spirit speaks:

> In the tides of Life, in Action's storm,
> A fluctuant wave,
> A shuttle free,
> Birth and the Grave,
> An eternal sea,
> A weaving, flowing
> Life all glowing,
> Thus at Time's humming loom 'tis my hand prepares
> The garment of Life which the Deity wears.[4]

Who is Faust really conjuring up? Goethe himself, when he was writing *Faust,* most assuredly did not fully comprehend who it was. But if we go back from Goethe to the medieval Faust, in whom Rosicrucian wisdom was living, we find that he also wanted to conjure up a spirit. And who did he want to conjure up? He never spoke of the Earth Spirit, he spoke of the *human being.* The longing and striving of medieval humanity was—to be *human.* In the depths of their souls, medieval people felt that, as earthly humankind, human beings were not truly human. How can humanity be found again? The way that Faust is rebuffed—pushed aside by the Earth Spirit— is a picture of how human beings in their earthly form are repelled by their own being. And this is why many accounts of "conversion" to Christianity in the Middle Ages show such extraordinary depth of feeling. They are filled with the sense that human beings have striven to attain their lost humanity and have had to give up in despair—they have rightly despaired of being able to find in them- selves their true and genuine humanity in earthly physical life—and so they have come to the point that they must say: Human striving for true humanity must be abandoned; earthly humanity must leave it to the Christ to fulfill Earth's task.

---

4. *Faust,* I, Act I, Scene 1. Bayard Taylor's translation.

In medieval times, when humankind's relation to true humanity, as well as to the Christ, was still understood in what may be called a suprapersonal-personal way, spirit-knowledge and spirit-vision were still real, were still a matter of experience. This ended with the fifteenth century; and then came that spectacular change, which no one has fully understood. Those who have knowledge of such things, however, are aware of how during the fifteenth to sixteenth centuries, and even later, there was an isolated Rosicrucian school, scarcely known to the world, where again and again a few pupils were educated, and where, above all, care was taken that one thing should be preserved as a holy tradition and not be forgotten. This holy tradition was as follows—I will give it to you in narrative form:

Let's say that a new pupil arrived one day at some such lonely spot to receive preparation. The first thing placed before this pupil was the so-called Ptolemaic system in its true form, as handed down from ancient times—not in the trivial way it is explained today, as something long ago replaced, but in an altogether different way. The pupil was shown how the Earth really and truly bears within herself the forces needed to determine her path through the universe. Thus, to have a correct picture of the world, it has to be drawn in the old Ptolemaic way: the Earth in the center of the universe, and the other stars controlled and directed in their corresponding revolutions by the Earth. And the pupil was told: If one truly studies to discover the best forces in the Earth, then one can arrive at no other view of the world than this. But, it is not so in actuality. It is not so because of humankind's sin. Through human sin, the Earth—in an unauthorized, unjustifiable way—has gone into the kingdom of the Sun; the Sun has become the regent and ruler of earthly activities. And so, in contrast to a world-system given by the gods, with the Earth in the center, another world-system has been determined in which the Sun is in the center with the Earth revolving round the Sun—that is, the system of Copernicus. And then the pupil was taught that here a mistake, a cosmic mistake, has been caused by human sin.

This knowledge was entrusted to the pupils, and they engraved it deeply in their hearts and souls. Human beings have overturned the old world-system, the teacher would say, and put another in its place; and they do not know that this other is the outcome of their own guilt, is really nothing other than the expression, the revelation, of human guilt, but always imagined it to be the proper and correct view of the cosmos. "And what has happened in recent times?" the teacher would go on to say. "Science has suffered a downfall through human guilt. Science has become a science of the demonic."

Around the end of the eighteenth century such communications became impossible; but until that time there were always at least a few pupils here and there who received their spiritual nourishment in some lonely Rosicrucian school, receiving it with "feeling" as a knowledge of the heart.

Even someone such as, for example, the great philosopher Leibniz, was led by his own thought and deliberation to try to find a place of learning where one could arrive at a correct view of the relationship between the Copernican and Ptolemaic systems. He could not discover any such place.

Things like this have to be known to understand properly, in all its shades of meaning, the great change that has taken place in the last centuries in how humankind sees itself and the universe. With this weakening of humankind's living connection with itself, with this estrangement of humanity from itself, came the tendency to cling to the external intellect that rules everything today. Think for a moment: is this external intellect a very *human experience?* Not in any way! If it were a human experience, it would not live in humankind as externally as it does. The intellect really doesn't have any connection with what is individual and personal, with the single individual; we could almost call it a convention. It does not spring from inner human experience, but approaches us as something external.

DURING THE LAST TWO DECADES of the nineteenth century the Austrian-born Rudolf Steiner (1861–1925) became a respected and well-published scientific, literary, and philosophical scholar, particularly known for his work on Goethe's scientific writings. After the turn of the century he began to develop his earlier philosophical principles into an approach to methodical research of psychological and spiritual phenomena.

His multifaceted genius has led to innovative and holistic approaches in medicine, science, education (Waldorf schools), special education, philosophy, religion, economics, agriculture (biodynamic method), architecture, drama, new arts of eurythmy and speech, and other fields. In 1924 he founded the General Anthroposophical Society, which today has branches throughout the world.